WEIRD U.S.
THE ODDyssey CONTINUES

BARBARA SUE MANIRE
APR. 29, 1941
APR. 29, 2005
OUR MOM...
HER HUMOR LIVES ON

STERLING

New York / London
www.sterlingpublishing.com

Weird U.S.

THE ODDYSSEY CONTINUES

Your Travel Guide to America's Local Legends and Best Kept Secrets

MARK SCEURMAN   MARK MORAN

WEIRD U.S. THE ODDYSSEY CONTINUES

STERLING and the distinctive Sterling logo are registered trademarks of Sterling Publishing Co., Inc.

Library of Congress Cataloging-in-Publication Data Available

10   9   8   7   6   5   4   3   2

Published by Sterling Publishing Co., Inc.
387 Park Avenue South, New York, NY 10016

Distributed in Canada by Sterling Publishing
c/o Canadian Manda Group, 165 Dufferin Street
Toronto, Ontario, Canada M6K 3H6

Distributed in the United Kingdom by GMC Distribution Services
Castle Place, 166 High Street, Lewes, East Sussex, England BN7 1XU

Distributed in Australia by Capricorn Link (Australia) Pty. Ltd.
P.O. Box 704, Windsor, NSW 2756, Australia

Sterling ISBN 13: 978-1-4027-4544-7

For information about custom editions, special sales, premium and corporate purchases, please contact Sterling Special Sales Department at 800-805-5489 or specialsales@sterlingpublishing.com.

Design: Richard J. Berenson
Berenson Design & Books, LLC, New York, NY

CONTENTS

Introduction	6
Legendary People and Places	8
Local Heroes and Villains	40
A World of Their Own	62
Roadside Distractions	94
Devoutly Different	134
Strange Societies	168
Curious Collections	196
Far-Out Festivals	240
Local Haunts	264
Puzzles of the Past and Present	290
Grave Matters	314
Index	344
Picture Credits	350
Editorial Credits	351
Acknowledgments	352

Introduction

Greetings once again friends and welcome to the second volume of our grand *Weird U.S.* adventure. It's hard to believe, but it's been four years since the first *Weird U.S.* book was published in 2004. Since then, we've been so busy traveling around the country collecting strange stories to share with you that we've hardly even noticed the time passing by! When we pause now to take a quick glance in the rearview mirror, we can see more than two-dozen *Weird* state books in our wake, and still more coming up just on the horizon.

Our journey has literally taken us to the four corners of this great country of ours—from an unlikely desert in the heart of Maine to the deserts of southern California's Death Valley, from an underground city in Seattle, Washington, to the aboveground cities of the dead in Key West, Florida—and every state in between. We've logged thousands of miles crisscrossing this land in planes, trains, and automobiles—not to mention an occasional ride in a subterranean cave craft. After all these years spent tracking down, investigating, and documenting weirdness in all its myriad forms, it never ceases to amaze us just how much is still out there to be explored and reported on.

Of course, no quest such as ours would be as much fun without some fellow travelers to share the ride with, and we've met some fascinating folks along the way. Not the least weird of these people we've come in contact with are the many authors from various states around the nation with whom it has been our pleasure to collaborate on this *Weird U.S.* project. To call ourselves the authors of this book is really only partly true. Yes, we have written a great many of the stories contained in this particular book, but a number of tales featured here have been contributed by a variety of like-minded writers whom we have befriended along the road. We're sort of like the tour guides driving a bus full of kindred spirits, all wandering the countryside together on a mystical journey searching for the offbeat, the bizarre, and sometimes the downright frightening.

One of the wonderfully weird cohorts we picked up along the trail was Matt Lake. We've been working with Matt since the early days of our book series; he edited *Weird N.J.* and *Weird U.S.*, and was the author of our books on Pennsylvania, Maryland, and England. Aside from being a great storyteller, Matt has an easygoing nature and wicked sense of humor that make him a terrific traveling companion. And his enthusiasm for all things out of the ordinary is nothing short of exuberant, rivaled only by our own passion for this intriguing subject matter. It was for these reasons that we asked Matt to come on board with us as a full-fledged co-author for this book.

So just what is it that we are looking for out there as we traverse this all too often overlooked exotic landscape of the strangest facets of American culture? It is any person, place, thing, or action that is so unique, unusual, and unexpected that it can only be described using one word—weird. For us weirdness is like a breath of fresh air amid the stagnant doldrums of normalcy—a welcome respite from the commonplace, a reprieve from the run-of-the-mill. Sometimes it is just something so absurd and ridiculous that all you can do is laugh about it. Other times, though, it is something so disturbing that it makes you uncomfortable and ill at ease. Weird is often an intangible thing, hard to describe, something that gives you a feeling that you can't quite put your finger on. For us it is the spice of life and something to be savored, admired, and revered.

Weird is the mystery of the unknown and unexplainable. It's that little unanticipated chill that gives you goose bumps, the unfamiliar sound emanating from the shadows that pricks up your ears. It is the tingle that runs up and down your spine when you find yourself in a dark and possibly dangerous situation or place. And believe us when we say that there are plenty of places, people, and things out there to give you these sensations. In fact, it's been our experience that the more weirdness you discover, the more you realize how much more is out there yet to be found. Sometimes it can all be a little overwhelming, and we feel compelled to stand, reflect for a moment, and ask ourselves, Will wonders never cease? The best answer we can offer is this: While we remain alive, open-minded, curious, and inquisitive there is no reason why they ever should.

—Mark Sceurman and Mark Moran

Legendary People and Places

Some legends are based in fact. Others are just stories with a sense of place and purpose. And some legends are people. But whatever kind of legend you're talking about, there are usually a couple of outrageously weird ones thrown into the mixture. These are the ones we at *Weird U.S.* spend our days researching.

Whenever someone calls or writes to tell us about a Revolutionary War hero buried in two different places, we're off to investigate. If someone reports a man who, surrounded by goats, wandered the southern states for most of his adult life, we're on the case. And when we find out that a college cafeteria was once named for a notorious cannibal— we're in line, ready to order the ribs.

Some of the legends we've checked out for this chapter are entirely true and have already been verified by journalists and historians. Some of them have a kernel of truth fleshed out with a whole mess of imagination—
and for our purposes, that's just as good. And some of them have sprung almost entirely from the dark places in people's minds that long to be scared—which can actually be better.

The Green Man

Of all the local legends in western Pennsylvania, the tale of Pittsburgh's Green Man is the best known. This horribly deformed man, also called Charlie No-Face, could be seen at night, blowing cigarette smoke through the holes in his cheek, lurking by the roadside, trying to stay out of sight. It sounds like a classic bogeyman story, except for one detail. It's true. Well, some of it is.

As the story goes, the Green Man had an accident that ruined his face. Some say he was a West Mifflin man working for the power company, struck by lightning or shocked by a downed power line. Others suggest he was a factory worker splashed with acid. Whatever the cause, all agree that the accident turned his skin green and melted his facial features together. Depending on who's telling the tale, the Green Man either died immediately (so all subsequent sightings were of his ghost) or survived and hid out in a boarded-up house.

A variant on the story gives late-night thrill seekers a place to look for the green glow of their hero's skin. The accident took place near one of the many abandoned railroad tunnels in greater Pittsburgh, and that's where the Green Man ran to after his accident. Many different locations are touted as the site of his tunnel, but the most popular is in South Park Township, just off Snowden Road, a site used by the township for storing rock salt for snowy days.

So much for the stories. Here are the facts: For fifty years, right up till the 1980s, Raymond Robinson used to walk a lonely stretch of road between Koppel and New Galilee for exercise. He did this at night because of what happened to him back in the summer of 1919. On a dare, the eight-year-old Raymond had climbed up the pylon that held the power lines for the Harmony Line trolley in Morado. A bird had built a nest there, and his buddies wanted to know if there were any eggs in it. Ray never saw the nest . . . or anything else again.

He lost both eyes in the accident, so he never got to see the Beaver Falls newspaper headline about what happened up that pylon: MORADO LAD, 8, SHOCKED BY LIVE WIRE, WILL DIE. But he proved the headline writer wrong. Two months later the *Daily Times* reported, "In spite of all his affliction, the boy is in good humor." After a lengthy recuperation, Ray Robinson was released, with a prosthetic nose connected to a pair of dark glasses that concealed his empty eye sockets. He passed his days listening to the radio, reading Braille, and making belts and wallets out of leather. He mowed the lawn with a manual mower. And at night, he went for walks along Route 351.

Word soon spread about the disfigured night hiker. Local teenagers began calling him Charlie No-Face; people from farther afield called him the Green Man. And folks began driving to the area just to meet him. Some nights, there was such a flow of traffic to the road that the police had to come to move things along. Generally, Ray would hide when he heard traffic approaching, because of a few disrespectful types. But some curiosity seekers befriended him, and he came to appreciate their company. They'd give him cigarettes and beer, and sometimes snap pictures of him with them.

During the Vietnam War, draftees from the Pittsburgh area took pictures with him, and so the legend of the Green Man spread across the theater of war and back to the United States. And the stories became more exaggerated as they were retold. They are still repeated to this day, even though Ray Robinson died more than twenty years ago, on June 11, 1985. He is buried in Grandview Cemetery, near the site of his accident, but his legend walks on.

Ghost Train of the Green Man Tunnel

August 4, 1969, 9 p.m., just another dog-day of summer in Pittsburgh. As usual, we were at hamburger row near the entrance of Allegheny County's South Park. A new girl was there, and we decided that Green Man's Tunnel was just the ticket to get her interested. In the 20-minute drive to the tunnel, we told her about the Green Man and how he had been electrocuted and turned a shade of green. The tunnel is about 25 feet wide and 30 feet high. The Montour Rail Road constructed it in 1934. You cannot see through the tunnel because of the bend. Next we heard a train noise coming from the tunnel. Not just a normal, diesel train, but a steam locomotive. I watched for the engine's headlight, but saw nothing. The train noise was getting louder and changing pitch, as if coming through the tunnel. The train was getting closer and changing pitch again, coming out of the tunnel. Then all we could hear was the creaking and clickety-clack of the rail cars on the rails. Two days later, Jack and I talked with the South Park Township Police at their station. The police told us that back in the 30s, a man killed his wife and child in that tunnel with a hatchet. Then the man jumped in front of the train. Since then, people have reported seeing a hatchet flying at them and hearing strange crying sounds. They had quite a large file on the incidents.–*Keith W. Klos*

Witch of Pungo

These days, Witchduck Road in Virginia Beach, Virginia, connects Routes 264 and 225. This unusually named thoroughfare causes many who travel on it to scratch their heads, but beyond that, most don't give it too much thought. But to natives this road and its name are reminders of one of the darkest incidents in Virginia's history, an event that didn't meet its final resolution until 2006, three centuries after it occurred.

In 1698, Grace Sherwood lived in Pungo, Virginia. Even today, Pungo, which is now an outlying neighborhood of Virginia Beach, boasts only one hundred residents. It has always been a place where everyone knows everyone, for better, or in Grace Sherwood's case, for worse.

Grace Sherwood must have been a standout in the seventeenth century. She was very beautiful—and also a strident nonconformist. She dressed in men's clothes and refused to meet the traditional standards that were so pronounced in seventeenth-century society. This led to a fierce level of bitterness between Grace and her neighbors. As this discontent grew, the good folk of Pungo began whispering that Grace was a witch and blaming her for any bad luck they experienced. All told, Grace Sherwood appeared in court over a dozen times—sometimes she was being sued by her neighbors for witchcraft-related behavior, and sometimes she was suing them back for slander.

One year many in the area found that their crops weren't growing. Predictably, they blamed Grace. When one local woman suffered a miscarriage and said Grace was responsible, gossip and finger-pointing became all-out hysteria. In 1706, Grace Sherwood was formally charged with witchcraft. This time the charges were taken much more seriously than any of the petty disputes previously brought before the courts in regard to Grace.

Before the courts would commit to calling Grace Sherwood a witch, they took some preliminary measures. They asked a group of local women to check her body for any unusual marks. Not surprisingly, these women, who had spent years fostering a distrust and dislike for Grace, claimed they did indeed find such marks. Still, the courts didn't take this as evidence worth declaring Grace a witch.

Instead, they decided that Grace Sherwood should be tested through the infamous process of "ducking," during which she would have her hands bound, then would be tied to a piece of wood and tossed into a river. If she sank, she would be declared innocent, although she would be dead. If she floated, it would be taken that the water, which had been blessed by religious officials, was rejecting her for being evil and impure and that she was, in fact, a witch.

It was announced that on July 10, Sherwood would undergo the tests at the Lynnhaven River. This is the only incident of witch ducking to ever take place in Virginia. Word spread throughout the state, and thousands came out to witness firsthand the ducking of the infamous Witch of Pungo, as Grace had come to be known—a nickname that stuck and is still used by all in reference to Grace.

The day finally came, and the ducking was undertaken. After initially sinking, Grace, ever the nonconformist, managed to untie her wrist restraints and swim to the surface. The assembled crowds were horrified to see that she was, by their standards, in fact a witch. While for years there had been rumors about her, it was always assumed to be the result of Grace's feuds with her neighbors, simple hearsay. But in 1706, witch ducking was regarded as incontrovertible evidence and taken as seriously as any scientific test. Witchduck Road, as well as the Witchduck Point section of the Lynnhaven River, were quickly named in honor of the occurrence at this site and have since been forever linked with Grace Sherwood and her trial.

At the age of forty-six, Grace was officially branded a witch and thrown into prison. For eight long years she stayed there. Eventually, she was able to pay a large amount of back taxes on her property, and with the help of then governor Alexander Spotswood, she was released from her captivity. She returned to Pungo, where she lived a quiet life, isolated from her neighbors, until passing away in 1740 at the age of eighty.

But the story of Grace Sherwood does not end there. Over the years, Grace's story has grown and has become one of the defining pieces of folklore for the Virginia Beach region. People have come to realize that ducking is not a scientific method of testing anything, and that Grace Sherwood was probably at worst a strong-willed, mildly eccentric woman. As in many localities that made people suffer through such trials, there was a sense of embarrassment in Virginia that such ridiculous actions were taken here so long ago.

In 2006, much of this embarrassment was quelled when Virginia governor Timothy Kaine informally pardoned Grace Sherwood for the crime of witchcraft. On July 10, the three hundredth anniversary of her trial, her name was finally cleared. As Kaine told the Associated Press on that day, "With 300 years of hindsight, we all certainly can agree that trial by water is an injustice."

Each year a reenactment of Grace Sherwood's trial takes place, run by volunteers at the historic Ferry Plantation House. The same volunteers are working to erect a statue of Sherwood to serve as both a reminder of this incident from Virginia's past as well as a public recognition of the wrongs perpetrated against her.

Grace Sherwood will be remembered forever as the Witch of Pungo. However, as time passes she will be known less and less as a sinister, magically powered villain and more as a victim of the hysteria and injustice of a very strange era of American history.

Alferd Packer, Man-Eater

What can you say about Alferd Packer that hasn't already been said? He was a self-styled Colorado mountain guide, universally described as incompetent. He was a man who couldn't spell his first name consistently; he went by Alferd and Alfred without missing a beat. He became the subject of many books, four movies, and a stage musical. He lent his name to the student cafeteria at C.U. Boulder. Oh, and he was widely regarded as an opportunistic murderer and cannibal.

His strange story began in April 1874 when he walked into Los Piños Indian Agency in Colorado Territory without the party of prospectors he had taken into the mountains two months

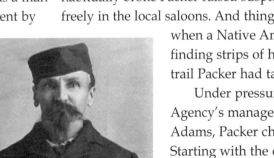

earlier. Packer claimed he had been left behind when he suffered a bout of frostbite or snow blindness. But the habitually broke Packer raised suspicions when he spent freely in the local saloons. And things really came to a head when a Native American guide reported finding strips of human meat along the trail Packer had taken back to town.

Under pressure from the Indian Agency's manager, General Charles Adams, Packer changed his story. Starting with the oldest, Israel Swan, sixty-five, the men succumbed one by one to exhaustion, cold, and starvation and were eaten by the survivors until only Packer remained. He confessed to eating human flesh until the snow melted enough for him to find his way out of the wilderness, and away from the crime scene. And sure, he took the dead men's cash and Swan's Winchester rifle. They didn't need them anymore. Packer was jailed on suspicion of murder for robbery, and an investigation began.

The victims' remains were found with hatchet marks on their heads and the backs of their hands. At least one man appeared to have put up a fight. Another may have been shot in the abdomen. While this evidence was being gathered, Packer escaped the jail. It took nine years for him to resurface, but he was eventually recaptured in a Wyoming saloon. A Colorado grand jury indicted him for the murders and robbery of the five prospectors. (The more heinous act of cannibalism was not actually a crime in cases of dire emergency.)

Packer's story changed again. Now he said the other men were starving but alive, weak, and starting to rave when he left to look for a trail to civilization. He returned to find Shannon Wilson Bell roasting human meat over a fire. Bell grabbed a hatchet and rushed him, Packer said. Packer shot him twice at close range with his pistol. He soon found himself reduced to eating bits of his late clients out of desperation. The hatchet marks on Bell were because he struggled with Packer, who lost his gun in the snow, and Packer finally wrested away the hatchet and used it on Bell to finish him off.

Packer was formally accused only of the premeditated murder and robbery of one of the prospectors, Israel Swan. Swan's relatives claimed that their late kinsman had carried about six thousand dollars plus the expensive Winchester rifle—more than enough motive for his murder—and his body had shown signs of a struggle, not

A plaque marks the site of the murders.

privation, as Packer had originally claimed. One murder charge, it was reasoned, would hang Packer. There were enough witnesses to piece together the story, despite testimony that changed at times.

Packer was grilled on his contradictory stories and became tangled in lies about his mountain guide experience, age, military service, and even his epilepsy. He made his case worse with bluff and bluster, and to no one's surprise was convicted on Friday, the thirteenth of April, 1882, of premeditated murder. Packer was quietly removed to a Gunnison jail to thwart a possible lynching. A new gallows was planned, and printed invitations to the hanging were sent out, however lengthy legal appeals won Packer the right to a new trial in 1885. The Colorado Supreme Court set aside the murder conviction because there had been no state murder statute in 1874, when Colorado was still a territory. And the crimes took place on what was then an Indian reservation.

So Packer was retried on the charge of voluntary

How the C.U. Boulder Student Cafeteria Came to Be Named for a Cannibal: A True Story

It's sometime toward the end of April, 1968, and student unrest is sweeping the United States. Protests swarm against the escalating war in Vietnam, racial discrimination and violations of civil rights. And at Colorado's flagship school, the University of Colorado at Boulder, two graduate students are deep in conversation. The President of the Student Assembly, Paul Talmey, turned to his VP, Paul Danish, and vented about a matter closer to home—the school cafeteria.

"The food's so awful there they should rename the place for Alferd Packer."

Danish thought that this would bring a note of refreshing frivolity, so they teamed up with Bob Ewegen, a former editor of the student newspaper, the *Colorado Daily,* to make it happen. Such a resolution was sure to win overwhelming approval at the upcoming Student Assembly, but how would they ensure it would survive the real power on campus, the Colorado University Board of Regents? The Regents, after all, were a conservative lot. Ewegen, then on hiatus from graduate school, had a plan to bring Walter Cronkite into the picture.

"I was working for UPI (United Press International),"

says Ewegen. "I knew Walter Cronkite was an old UPI man. I said I'd write the story and I'd send it over the wires as the students having approved the name change on the cafeteria."

"I knew if Cronkite reported it on the evening news, well, it had to be true. The regents could tell him he was wrong, and they'd might as well commit ritual hari-kari if that happened. Or they could get right with Jesus, the UPI and Cronkite and go along with it."

And so it happened. Shortly after the dedication, CU Boulder began holding Alferd Packer Days every spring. The Big Day featured a piano-and-song rendition of "The Ballad of Alferd Packer" as rendered by Pete Smyth, CU Boulder grad, local radio personality and mayor of his own fictional creation of East Tincup, Colorado. Rib-Eating Contests. Raw Meat Tossing Contests. Rock bands performing. Dancing. And a gigantic version of the Packer Grill's by-now famed Packer Smacker foot-long sandwich.

The beginning of the end for Alferd Packer Days started in the late 1980s. The guilt of an awakened social conscience sounded the death knell for the Packer fest, with protests against the blatant waste of food and downright gluttony. This led to the celebration's demise by 1999—but not until it had made its impact on one Trey Parker, a CU Boulder student who was inspired to make a student film called *Cannibal! The Musical* in the early '90s. Parker and fellow student Matt Stone went on to create the equally irreverent animated series *South Park* for television.

—*Charmaine Ortega Getz*

manslaughter of all five men. He was convicted again and on June 8, sentenced to forty years in the state penitentiary in Canon City. He was then forty-three years old.

After sixteen years of incarceration, Packer's bid for parole was rejected. But the *Denver Post* began a long campaign to free him, and in 1901, based on his deteriorating health and a long petition signed by notables, Packer won conditional parole. He worked for a while as a security guard for the *Denver Post* and later as a ranch hand in Jefferson County. An unfounded rumor persists that he turned vegetarian. Neighbors knew him as a kindly man who was popular with children, generous with candy and tall tales of the Old West. He never won the official pardon he hoped for.

He eventually died quite peacefully, at age sixty-four, on April 24, 1907. He is buried—at least most of him—in Littleton Cemetery, Littleton, Colorado, under a modest military grave marker with the spelling Packer himself sometimes used: ALFERD PACKER, CO. F. 16 U.S. INF.

But he was not allowed to rest in peace. Packer's gravestone has been stolen and replaced at least once, and the Littleton Cemetery Association was forced in 1973 to have the grave covered in cement to discourage ghouls. It may have been too late. As far as anyone knows, Packer's body is intact, but some claim that his head was separated from his body before the burial and sold to a traveling sideshow. It wound up in the hands of an oddities collector who sold it to the famous curiosity exhibitor Ripley's Believe It or Not! Ripley's confirms it has Packer's purported head, but it's not currently on display.

Packer's notoriety has been a source of much entertainment. In addition to serious books on his case (including Ervan F. Kushner's 1980 volume *Alferd G. Packer: Cannibal! Victim?*, which called for a posthumous pardon), there have been four movies: *The Legend of Alfred Packer* (1980), *Ravenous* (1999), *Devoured: The Legend of Alferd Packer* (2005), and *Alfred Packer: The Musical*, also known as *Cannibal! The Musical*. That last one has also been shown on stage.

And a cigar-smoking self-styled bishop of the Liberal Church even tried to absolve Alferd of his sins. "Bishop" Frank H. Rice led six men dressed in black and a goat named Angelica to Packer's grave site in the dead of night in September 1940. They performed a ritual for the transference of Packer's sins to the goat. Rice died in 1945. There is no word on the fate of the goat.

Floyd Collins, the Greatest Cave Explorer Ever Known

For most of us, six feet under is as deep in the earth as we'll ever know. For one cemetery resident in Kentucky's Mammoth Cave National Park, that's closer to the surface than he's been for most of the last eight decades. He's William Floyd Collins, the nearly forgotten folk hero of song, stage, and film, regarded by many as the Greatest Cave Explorer Ever Known.

Collins was a central figure in what came to be known as Kentucky's great Cave Wars of the early twentieth century. His family owned Crystal Cave, one of several local show caves that competed for tourist dollars with the popular Mammoth Cave. Unfortunately for the Collins family, theirs was too far off the beaten path to meet with any great success. So Floyd Collins spent much of his time delving into the ground, hoping to discover better caves closer to visitor traffic.

In January 1925, his explorations were focused on one of his more hopeful finds, a sink that would later come to be known as Sand Cave. Rumor has it that Collins discovered a large chamber, but sadly, he would never

have the chance to explore it: He became hopelessly stranded in the chasm while trying to make his way to the surface. With very little fuel left in his lantern, the daring caver had shimmied into a narrow channel and gotten himself wedged in.

There he was, alone, without food, crammed in a dark, damp, narrow space with only cave crickets to hear his cries for help. And he had failed to tell anyone where he was going. Luckily for him, the sons of the cave's landowner came looking for him the very next day. They found him with his left leg pinned by a boulder, about one hundred and fifty feet from the cave's entrance.

The locals tried everything they could to get him out, but with no luck. Potential rescuers began arriving in swarms. Miners, firemen, geologists, military personnel, stonemasons, a basketball team, and, of course, reporters, all showed up. By the ninth day, as many as ten thousand looky-loos had come together, all to get a peek. The National Guard was called in to establish crowd control, and some people began to suspect that the whole thing was a publicity stunt to help Floyd win the Cave Wars.

But despite the attention, Floyd got no closer to rescue. Someone strung a lightbulb into the passage to help keep him warm. Others brought milk, coffee, and soup in Mason jars to feed him and to raise his spirits. Three hundred men worked on a vertical shaft round the clock for twelve days to finally reach the stranded caver. For fear that steam shovels would hasten collapse, the whole thing was dug by hand. Unfortunately, miscalculations brought them in at the wrong end and they still couldn't get to his pinned leg. But it didn't matter, anyway. By the time they reached him, Floyd was dead. Everybody dispersed, and diggers filled the shaft back in and left Collins where he was. Later, though, the family did manage to dig its way to their fallen member, having to cut off his trapped leg in the process, and bring him home for a proper burial.

Now, you'd think that would be the end of the story, but it only got stranger from there. When Crystal Cave was sold two years later, the new owner disinterred Floyd's body, transferred it to a glass-topped casket, and put it on display inside the cave like an odd spelunker aquarium. Finally, in 1961, the National Park Service purchased Crystal Cave and closed it down for good, but Floyd Collins remained there till 1989, when his family buried him in Flint Ridge Cemetery. Of course, that hasn't stopped reports of Floyd's ghost roaming the area.

Be Prepared Throughout the Week To Do Your Share To Fill The Community Chest To Overflowing

A National Newspaper
20 Pages Today

The Courier-Journal.

Largest Morning Circulation Of Any Kentucky Newspaper

VOL. CXLI. NEW SERIES—NO. 20,362 *** LOUISVILLE, TUESDAY MORNING, FEBRUARY 17, 1925. THREE CENTS

COLLINS' LEG TO BE CUT OFF IN CAVE TO FREE DEAD BODY

OUTSTANDING FIGURES IN DISCOVERY OF FLOYD COLLINS' BODY

FUTILE ENDING OF LONG WORK SADDENS MEN | QUIN, BARNES OPEN CHESTAS DRIVE STARTS | James Duffin Heard In Disbarment Case QUIN PROCLAIMS | KELLOGG IS O.K.'D FOR U.S. CABINET | FATHER GIVES CONSENT TO AMPUTATION

The Two Graves of Mad Anthony Wayne

Of all the heroes of the Revolutionary War, Major General Anthony Wayne is the only one we know of who's buried in two different places. The fiery-tempered soldier was universally known as Mad Anthony during his life, but he was so widely respected that after his death, people across the states named forts, counties, and towns after him. But his own family treated him with somewhat less respect.

The strange tale of his two graves begins with his death in Presque Isle on the shores of Lake Erie in northwestern Pennsylvania. Wayne was buried where he died, however, his family wanted his bones in the family plot in southeastern Pennsylvania. So thirteen years after his death, his son Isaac traveled in a small horse-drawn cart along what is now U.S. Route 322. His mission: to return his father's bones to Chester County.

Isaac paid to have his father's remains dug up, but he got more than he bargained for. When they opened the coffin, Mad Anthony Wayne was practically intact. One leg was partially decayed, but the rest of him looked as though he'd been buried yesterday, not thirteen years earlier. This posed a transportation problem. Isaac had brought only a small cart for the four-hundred-mile trek home. He didn't have room for a whole passenger. Clearly, a radical solution was needed; it came in the form of Dr. James Wallace, who for a large fee agreed to separate Mad Anthony's bones from the rest of his remains. Butchering takes you only so far in such an operation, so he ended up boiling the bones in a large cauldron to remove those clingy bits of tendon and meat. The raw filet of Wayne, his organ meat, and uniform were placed back in the original grave, along with several quarts of General Wayne stew. Isaac stuck the warm bones in the box and drove back home with them. Along the rough road, as the story goes, the box fell off the wagon a few times, spilling bones by the roadside. The rumor has it that every year on the general's birthday, New Year's Day, he rises from his Pennsylvania grave and rides all the way across the state, looking this way and that for his missing parts.

In a masterstroke of strange taste, the Erie County Historical Society now proudly displays the iron kettle in which the Revolutionary War hero was boiled up—with a cellophane fire beneath it and hollow plastic bones inside. On the outskirts of town, behind the retired soldiers' and sailors' home at Third and Ash, stands a restored blockhouse on the spot where Wayne was buried more than two hundred years ago. Whatever's left of Mad Anthony's bones rests at St. David's Episcopal Church on Valley Forge Road in Radnor.

Tom Quick and the 99 Indians

One of the most violent tales to come out of the Pennsylvania-New Jersey borderlands is the story of Tom Quick—a man whose bloodlust against Native Americans reached legendary proportions. Just how much of Quick's story is fact and how much has been embellished over the years has long been a point of debate. But it all began peacefully enough in the mid-1700s along the Delaware River. Young Quick, who roamed the hills along the Delaware rather than working at his old man's gristmill, got on with the Indians, with whom he often shared the catch of the day along the river.

When the French and Indian Wars began, things changed. Fearing European encroachment on native territory, Indians turned against settlers. Dressed in full war paint, they attacked the Quick family as they fished, mortally shooting Tom's father and wounding Tom in the leg. The others escaped injury and managed to drag Tom to safety, but they witnessed the Indians scalping the elder Quick and cutting off his head. Tom became frantic and swore that he would never be at peace so long as Indians could be found on the banks of the Delaware.

Two years after the wars, Tom was drinking at a local tavern on the Neversink when he met an intoxicated Indian named Muskwink, who boasted of killing a white man along the Delaware and produced the silver buttons that were on the jacket Tom's father had been wearing when he was scalped. The drunken Quick marched him

MONUMENT TO TOM QUICK, THE INDIAN SLAYER, MILFORD, PA.

outside the tavern and shot him right in the head. He then went back inside, finished his rum, and left town.

Shortly thereafter, Quick openly killed an entire family of Indians he encountered canoeing along the Delaware. He shot the man and finished off the woman and two children with a tomahawk. After that, he started killing in secret. He would stalk Indians while they were hunting deer, kill them, and take their catch—and their weapons. In some cases, he would pretend to befriend an Indian and invite him out to hunt. In his lifetime, he hoped to kill one hundred Indians, but as legend goes, he was one short of his goal as he lay dying of smallpox. So he reached out from beyond the grave to continue his insane revenge; he donated the blankets he used during his illness to Indians.

For some reason, the town of Milford, Pennsylvania, chose to commemorate this man's life almost a century after his death. They erected a monument in 1889 with an inscription that reads:

TOM QUICK

"THE INDIAN SLAYER" OR "AVENGER OF THE DELAWARE"

1734–1796

MADDENED BY THE DEATH OF HIS FATHER AT THE HANDS OF THE SAVAGES, TOM QUICK NEVER ABATED HIS HOSTILITY TO THEM UNTIL THE DAY OF HIS DEATH, A PERIOD OF OVER FORTY YEARS.

Not surprisingly, many folk are none too fond of the monument or of the man that it commemorates.

Goat Man

If you grew up in the South between 1930 and the mid-1960s, you will have heard of—and maybe even met—Charles "Ches" McCartney. But you probably knew him by his nickname, the Goat Man. Ches was a wanderer with an iron-wheeled cart and a herd of goats, who spent thirty-five years going from town to town, meeting people, telling tales, and creating cherished memories among those he met.

Ches grew up in Iowa at the beginning of the twentieth century, and at the age of fourteen he ran away to New York City. There he hooked up with and eventually married a professional sword thrower. They were an unlikely pair: She was more than a decade older than he was and threw cutlery at him for a living. They

had a child together, but eventually his wife left him. Ches worked for the WPA, although that didn't work out well either: A tree fell on him one day, and he didn't wake up until the mortician pricked him with a needle to inject him with embalming fluid.

After all these misadventures, Ches had had just about enough. He decided to do things his own way. He bought himself a large cart, trained goats to pull it, and just started traveling. Thousands upon thousands of people would see the Goat Man during his time out on the road. For most these would be random encounters, usually from the vantage point of a passing car. In the days before Interstates, anyone heading south by automobile would have to use small, dusty two-lane roads. The Goat Man would often slow down traffic by taking up precious room on these roads. Travelers new to the experience would stare, slack-jawed, at the bearded drifter and a herd that sometimes consisted of thirty goats. Those who traveled often knew that a honk of their horn would get a wave and a smile from the generally good-natured Ches.

Each night he'd stop to feed himself and his goats. In some areas, he had regular spots that he'd inhabit while passing through; there townspeople, and especially kids, would flock to the Goat Man's campsites. He was known as a master storyteller, and he took pride in relating the tales of his many adventures out on the road. He would sell postcards featuring images of himself. This is by and large how he made money on his travels. Ches also accepted food for himself and his goats, and had regular stops where he knew he could rely on such charity. On nights when he found himself alone, he would subsist on a diet of goat milk.

Ches's goats were celebrities in their own right. Children loved the baby goats (kids love kids!), and he had a favorite with no front legs that would ride in the driver's seat of his wagon and could even hop around like a kangaroo. In his travels, Ches is estimated to have covered over one hundred thousand miles. While most associated with southern states, particularly Georgia, he claimed to have visited every state except Hawaii.

But, like all good things, the Goat Man's journey eventually came to an end. By the 1970s, he had settled down in a shack in Jeffersonville, Georgia, with his son, Albert. When the shack burned down, they moved into a broken-down yellow school bus that sat in the woods outside town. He stayed put in Georgia for the rest of his life, except for one brief fling with the road: In 1984, he hiked to Los Angeles to try and meet the actress Morgan Fairchild. He failed and got mugged on the streets of the city. After that, he moved into assisted living in Macon. In

1998, Ches learned his son had been shot and killed, and he lost the will to live. Within a few months, the Goat Man died.

In the ten years since his passing, the legend of the Goat Man has flourished. While whole generations haven't grown up seeing him traveling America's roads, those who did encounter him remembered him in songs, in a series of documentaries, and in books and magazine articles. His memory hikes on.

This Land Was His Land

How many other statues have you seen that include on their inscription the number of acres of land once owned by the honoree? The giant folk art statue of Lucien Bonaparte Maxwell in Cimarron, New Mexico, does, and for good reason: Maxwell was once the sole owner of the largest area of land ever controlled by one person. One would expect his statue to be equally grand. Instead, it looks like the result of a couple cans of paint and a giant mess of paper mache. It's endearing—and hey, I couldn't do any better.—*David Pike*

Celebrity Mummies of America

The Outlaw Who Wouldn't Give Up

1973–1978: Steve Austin, astronaut—a man barely alive.
1911: Elmer J. McCurdy, an outlaw—very, very dead!

Who would have thought that these two show biz personalities would ever meet up in sunny California? Well, they did in 1976, during the filming of an episode of the TV show *The Six Million Dollar Man*. When the film crew was setting up for a shoot in the defunct Long Beach funhouse called Laugh in the Dark, a stagehand accidentally broke off a wax dummy's left arm, revealing a human bone sticking out from the shoulder.

Forensic investigators determined that it was a human mummified body, and it had been shot by a .32-caliber bullet manufactured between 1830 and 1920. Inside the mouth of the mummy was found a 1924 penny and a ticket from the Museum of Crime in Los Angeles. That ticket helped identify the body as outlaw Elmer McCurdy. After a career of murder and train robbery, McCurdy was shot dead by a posse in an Oklahoma barn and brought to a funeral home in Pawhuska. There he was embalmed with a massive dose of arsenic. The unclaimed body became an attraction at the funeral home. The mortician even named him the Bandit That Wouldn't Give Up and charged a nickel fee, which the citizens of Pawhuska had to drop into the mummy's mouth. Eventually, two men showed up at the funeral home claiming to be cousins of the mummy. The undertaker had no choice but to give up the stiff to its next of kin, but it turned out they were sideshow promoters who took Elmer throughout Texas with the same billing: The Bandit That Wouldn't Give Up.

Elmer was shuffled as collateral from one sideshow to another and eventually faded into obscurity. No one knows exactly how he ended

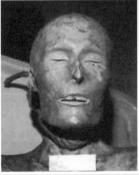

up at the Laugh in the Dark funhouse in Long Beach, but when *The Six Million Dollar Man* crew found him, his final journey to the grave was almost over. McCurdy was given a proper funeral in Summit View Cemetery in Guthrie, Oklahoma, in 1977 and was buried in the same place as such notorious figures as Wild Bill Doolin (of the Doolin–Dalton Wild Bunch) and Tom Capers, in Oklahoma's only Boot Hill.

Skeleton in the Funeral Home's Closet

One of the greatest characters in the history of Alton, Illinois, was a weird figure known as "Deaf Bill" Lee, a mummified man who spent the great part of eight decades in a closet at the local funeral home.

Deaf Bill made his living fishing the Mississippi River, but made his name as a legendary drinker and brawler and drunken riverbank preacher. He died at the Madison County poor farm in November 1915 and was embalmed using an experimental process until relatives could come to claim the body. As the years passed, Bill remained unclaimed, and in time the Alton morticians became aware of the publicity that their morbid conversation piece provided. And so Deaf Bill was put on display.

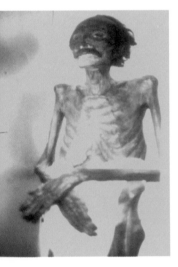

The mustachioed mummy was around five feet three inches tall and weighed about sixty pounds. His legs were crossed, and his arms were folded across his waist. Thanks to the embalming fluid, the skin had turned dark and leathery and felt like wood to the touch. He was clad only in a loincloth during the entire time he was left on display.

In 1996, Dallas Burke and Brian Fine, co-owners of the Burke-Fine Funeral Home, decided at last that it was time to put Bill to rest. For his final viewing, Bill wore a turn of the century tuxedo coat, trousers, and shirt with a black string tie. His face was made up to look lifelike, his dark hair and thick mustache were nicely trimmed, and his hands were crossed over a spread of red and white carnations. Hundreds of Alton residents came to see Deaf Bill one last time, and members of the Knights of Columbus served as his pallbearers at the St. Francis of Assisi Cemetery in Portage des Sioux. While there was no proof that Bill was related to him, a plot was obtained next to an Edward Lee, who was buried in West Alton, and Bill was buried a few feet away on June 25, 1996. Deaf Bill Lee could finally rest in peace—more than eighty years after he died.

Most Famous Dead Guy

On June 9, 1929, the body of a middle-aged man was discovered in a ditch along the Wilmington Pike in Sabina, Oregon. He seemed to have died of natural causes, but nobody could identify him. The police gave the body a name—Eugene—and turned him over for embalming at the Littleton Funeral Home. He stayed there for over thirty years, with occasional outings as a Halloween prop on people's porches or as a "guest" at frat parties. In 1963, the Littleton funeral home decided it was time to lay Eugene to rest and buried him in the Sabina Cemetery.

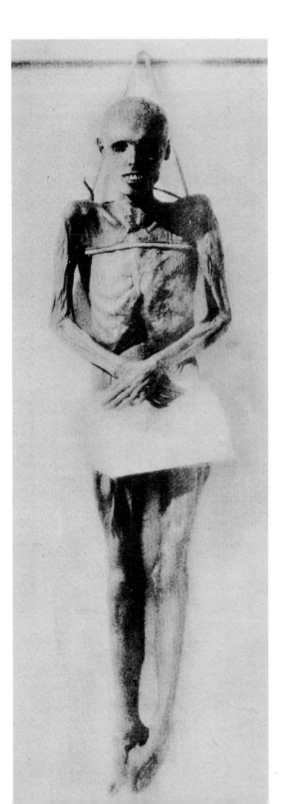

Spaghetti, the Mummy of Laurinburg

The oldest funeral home in North Carolina once had a long-term visitor who just kept hanging around, waiting for his father to show up. Literally. He hung for years on the wall of the embalming room, dead as a doornail. Local wags nicknamed him Spaghetti, but his real name was Cancetto Farmica. To most folks, he was known as the Laurinburg Mummy.

Farmica blew into town in 1911 as a roustabout with a traveling "mud show," but his fiery temper landed him in a fight with a fellow worker. Farmica came off badly in the argument: His colleague hit him in the head with a tent peg, delivering a fatal injury. He never regained consciousness, and no one came to claim the body, so it was prepared for burial at the nearby McDougald Funeral Home. A few days later Farmica's father arrived to identify his son's body, but he didn't have enough money with him to cover the embalming, let alone the funeral. He would have to go back home to get the rest of the cash needed for the services. He never returned.

For the next twenty-eight years, Cancetto Farmica's dried corpse hung on the wall of the third-floor embalming room, attracting visitors with each passing mummy craze—from the 1923 discovery of King Tut's tomb to Boris Karloff's 1932 performance as *The Mummy*. Eventually, protests from the Italian-American community about disrespect to their paisano got results. In 1972, McDougald made arrangements to have him laid to rest. Several hundred people were on hand for the Catholic funeral as Farmica's casket was lowered into a grave at Laurinburg's Hillside Cemetery.

Queho's Quorpse

The "Mad Indian" Queho was southern Nevada's own bogeyman. To most, he was a mad killer. To some, he was a kind of folk antihero, fighting back against the white man's oppression. All agree, though, that he was responsible for twenty-one murders. From his first killing (either the 1910 bludgeoning of J. W. Woodworth with a length of timber or the fatal maiming of his half-brother Avote, whose severed hand he kept as a souvenir), Queho went on a spree that would last for almost thirty years. Every time a dead body was found in the region, fingers pointed at Queho. In one instance, he even got blamed for the murder of a man who turned up very much alive, surprised to hear about his gruesome demise at Queho's hand.

But by 1940, it became clear that Queho's reign of terror was over. That February three prospectors found a mummified body in a cave overlooking the Colorado River. A tripwire attached to a bell had served as an alarm. Loaded rifles were near the cave entrance, ready to defend against an ambush. The desiccated corpse inside was Queho's.

The coroner's jury declared that he had died from "sickness and starvation." The corpse was hauled down the mountain—and straight into a controversy. A fight broke out over who owned the remains. The prospectors who found the body, the sheriff, the chief of police, the coroner, and the Elks Lodge wanted the corpse. Even two people claiming to be the Mad Indian's heirs came out of the woodwork.

After a while on display at the courthouse, Queho's

Face to Face with the "Stone Man"

Back in 1951 I heard of the "Stone Man" in Lafayette, Indiana. A young mortician said, "Come to the fourth floor and see for yourself!" To my surprise, there was the Stone Man. He was in an old coffin: a wood frame with leather pulled around the frame. You could see him through a small window that was located by his face. The Stone Man's face had turned into a prune surface; his nails and hair had grown. There was a death certificate from 1880 or 1890.

The story is that when he died, the funeral home embalmed him and wrote to his European family. They received no reply. Every time they sold the funeral home, the new owner got him along with the business. Little children used to be let in to see him in the 1940s for Halloween. They stopped it because he was too frightening to look at! He would be easy to find if you ask around. Beware: he isn't nice to look at, but I swear I'm telling you a true story.–*Richard Gray*

body was moved to Park's Palm Funeral Home in Las Vegas, where it was stored in a glass-topped coffin for three years, until Frank Wait, the police chief who had hunted Queho, paid the storage bill and turned the body over to the Elks Lodge. The Elks used it as an exhibit in their Helldorado Days Carnival; some reports state that the corpse rode in a car in the carnival's parade.

In the mid-'50s, someone broke into Helldorado Village, stole Queho's body, and dumped his bones into the Bonanza wash. They were retrieved and passed around among private collectors until 1974, when it was announced that his bones were going to be part of a display at the Museum of Natural History at the University of Nevada, Las Vegas. Protests from local Indian groups put an end to this idea. Eventually, an ex-lawyer named Roland Wiley procured the remains for one hundred dollars and interred them in a spiritual theme park called Cathedral Canyon. Since Wiley's death in 1994, Cathedral Canyon has fallen into disrepair, but Queho's grave is intact at the side of the parking area overlooking the canyon. The slab of concrete that covers his grave reads QUEHOE 1889-1919 NEVADA'S LAST RENEGADE INDIAN, HE SURVIVED ALONE. The handprints in the concrete at the base are of the witnesses to the burial.

A Tale of Mystery and Imagination

The tiny burial square attached to Westminster Presbyterian Church at the corner of Fayette and Greene streets in Baltimore, Maryland, is home to one of the most beloved characters in weird-dom, Edgar Allan Poe. His body was buried in back of the Westminster Burial Grounds after his mysterious death in 1849 at the age of forty. In 1875, it was moved to

lie under an impressive monument near the front gate.

That would be pretty much the end of the story, except for a strange visitor who began appearing at Poe's grave on the centennial of his death. On Poe's hundred and fortieth birthday, January 19, 1949, a cloaked man in black appeared at the grave in the early hours of the morning. He raised a glass, murmured a tribute to his hero, and made his way off as quietly as he had come. He became known as the Poe Toaster, and he appears at the site almost every year at the same time. His appearance has certainly been witnessed every year since 1977, when the curator of the Poe House and Museum, Jeff Jerome, began keeping an annual vigil with a group of whoever is willing to join him. On some years, the Poe Toaster leaves a tribute of red roses, a half-full bottle of cognac, and a letter at the monument. His note in 1993 said, "The torch would be passed." In 1998, a note announced that the originator of the tradition had died.

Over the years, many people have claimed they or someone they know was the real Poe Toaster, but only one of them has the stamp of authenticity. Shortly before Poe's hundred and ninety-ninth birthday, a ninety-two-year-old man named Sam Porpora stepped forward to claim credit. He was a historian who had worked for years to promote the Westminster Church, and he claimed that he and his fellow heritage workers dreamed it up as a fun stunt. They had performed the annual ritual ever since. "We made it up, never dreaming it would go worldwide," he told CNN reporters, with a twinkle in his eye and a mischievous smile. In the *Washington Post,* however, Jeff Jerome, said, "There are holes so big in Sam's story, you could drive a Mack truck through them."

So on the approach to Poe's bicentennial, one mystery may be solved. But another remains: Is Poe actually buried in Poe's grave? When they moved his bones in 1875, there appears to have been some confusion about his precise location: He was buried to the right of his grandfather, but the headstones had been reversed to face the West Gate a decade earlier. So it's entirely possible that all these years the Poe Toaster—whoever he is—may have been toasting the bones of a soldier named Private Mosher.

House of Blue Lights

When Charles and Mary Test named their newborn Skiles, it's a safe bet to assume they wanted him to do something extraordinary with his life. And he did. He gave the state of Indiana one of its most enduring legends: the House of Blue Lights.

By the early 1900s, Skiles Test was a self-made millionaire in the realty, motel, and transit businesses. He also bought eighty acres to set up a farm. Of course, his farm had a forty- by eighty-foot pool, a power plant, and a multistory bathhouse. Every Christmas it was decorated with distinctive blue lights. One year the lights stayed up, and they were never taken down again. Stories began to spread about the reason for this year-round celebration, and most of them were dark stories. They say that Test's wife died in a tragic accident in the house, and Test had placed her in the living room in a glass coffin with blue lights all around it—to commemorate her favorite color. Others believed the color blue attracted spirits.

For years, visiting the House of Blue Lights was something of a rite of passage for Indianapolis area teens. Beginning in the 1950s, on an almost regular basis, carloads of kids would drive to the Test property and then dare each other to go up to the house and ring the doorbell. Most never made it to the front door. But a few who did swore that as they approached the house, they could see the body of a woman encased in a glass coffin surrounded by dozens of blue lights.

Test tolerated the trespassers for a while, but eventually built a huge fence that only served to intensify the legend. After his death in 1964, people flooded the estate auction at the property and found that, while there was no glass coffin, there were plenty of other souvenirs. Test was a packrat with means, so souvenir hunters spent three days collecting memories of the place they had visited by night. And it's a good job they did: By 1978, the House of Blue Lights and all its outbuildings had been bulldozed. In their place you can now visit the Skiles Test Nature Park.

You would think that would be where the story ends . . . but it's not. Even now, people report seeing strange blue lights among the trees at the Skiles Test Nature Park. And the park is expanding its trail system closer to the spot where the House of Blue Lights once stood. So there's no telling exactly what a late-night hiker might encounter.

Black-eyed Kids

All across the country, people have seen them and been scared. They carry a sinister aura that's impossible to shake, despite their young age. And it all comes from their eyes. These youngsters have no pupils, no irises, and no whites. Between their eyelids is nothing but blackness, and so they're universally known as the Black-eyed Kids.

The first report of these creepy kids came in 1998 from Texas resident Brian Bethel, who posted his account to the alt.folklore.ghost-stories Internet newsgroup and to the Web site ghosts.org. In a parking lot outside a movie theater, Bethel encountered two kids demanding entry into his car. Here is how Bethel described the encounter:

"'C'mon, mister,' he said. 'We won't hurt you. You have to LET US IN. We don't have a gun. . . .'

"That last statement scared the living hell out of me, because at that point by his tone he was plainly saying, 'We don't NEED a gun.'

"He noticed my hand shooting down toward the gear shift. The spokesman's final words contained an anger that was complete and whole, and yet contained in some respects a tone of panic: 'WE CAN'T COME IN UNLESS YOU TELL US IT'S OKAY. LET . . . US . . . IN!'"

Since Bethel's posting, there have been many other reports, along with many theories about the kids. Some are convinced they are aliens or demons. Some assume the black eyes are contact lenses, a trick of the light, or out of control imaginations. Others insist that the stories are a hoax. Is there a race of black-eyed creatures posing as earthling children and terrorizing America? This growing local legend may fizzle away and die, or it may continue to grow in notoriety. Either way the question of the truth regarding these creatures may never be fully known.

Cold Voice on a Warm Night

I have to tell you about one of the scariest things I've ever encountered—and I don't scare easily.

I live in Union, New Jersey. I was leaving a supermarket close to closing time, and loading my bags into my car by myself. I heard a voice call out.

"Hey lady," it said, "need any help?"

Before I even turned around, I knew that the owner of the voice was bad news. The words were sort of devoid of emotion, of any sort of accent, of any sort of life. The voice itself cut right through me. I felt cold, even though it was a warm night. I turned around.

There was a kid there. Just one. He looked totally normal.

"Let me help," he said. "I'll load all that stuff up for you. You just have to give me a ride home."

He grinned at me, and I honestly felt sick to my stomach. In a heartbeat, I realized why—his eyes were black. Not just the pupils, not just the irises, the whole eye. There wasn't a piece of it that wasn't dark black. There was something almost hypnotizing about them, but in a way that was very aggressive and just plain old bad.

"No!" I yelled. I threw the last bag of groceries into the trunk, spilling a bunch of items all over the floor. I turned around and ran to the driver's seat. As I got in, I heard the same voice giggling, laughing at me.

I drove away, and tried to just forget about it. But I can't.
—*Kathy Woods*

Black Eyes at the Door

One spring morning a few years back, my doorbell rang. I answered it. Standing in front of me was a boy, I'd say about the age of 15, and a girl who looked to be roughly the same age.

"Can I help you?" I asked.

"Can we use your phone?" the girl asked in response.

"No," I answered, and shut the door.

I slammed the door on these kids because, although they seemed pleasant enough, they had black eyes. And I'm sorry, but that's just way too much for me. I figured you guys may have heard something about this. Am I going completely insane, or what?—*David Casey*

Dark Curse of the Congelier House

North of Pittsburgh stands a site that once contained the most haunted house in America. The house stood at what is now the intersection of Routes 65 and 279, a stone's throw from PNC Park, the home of the Pittsburgh Pirates. It was called the Congelier Mansion, and its sordid history of gruesome murders came to an abrupt end in 1927 when an explosion annihilated the building and left a trail of destruction across a twenty-mile radius.

At least, that's how the story goes. As it turns out, almost every element of this tale, which has been circulating for at least twenty-five years, can be disproved. Just enough tantalizing details are accurate to lend the story an air of authenticity— for example, a gas explosion did destroy part of the neighborhood. Still, the tale's just too good to miss. Read it as a local legend and take it with a grain of salt. But don't let it put you off going to see the next Pirates game.

The story goes that in the 1870s, carpetbagger Charles Wright Congelier built a house for himself and his Mexican wife, Lyda, at 1129 Ridge Avenue in Manchester, the North Side neighborhood of Pittsburgh. Unfortunately for Congelier, the household also included a young servant named Essie, for whom he developed a fatal attraction. When his wife discovered their liaison, she stabbed her husband to death and decapitated his girlfriend. Lyda was found the next day, cradling the head of her rival in love and sobbing her apologies. She would spend the rest of her days in an asylum, and the house would remain empty for twenty years.

The next residents of the Congelier place were migrant railroad workers who moved out as soon as they could, telling tales of a woman's late-night screaming and sobbing. Then, around the turn of the twentieth century, a scientific researcher named Dr. Adolph C. Brunrichter bought the place and moved in.

Although the doctor kept to himself, his neighbors thought he was a nice enough chap. That changed on August 12, 1901, when they heard a scream and experienced a shattering explosion that rocked the floors, split the walls, and sent a red flash through the house. Every window shattered. When the mansion was searched, there was no sign of the doctor, but there were six dead women in the building. One had been strapped to a bed for a long time, and five of them were buried in the basement. In a chilling echo of the Congelier murder, the women were headless. The doctor was nowhere to be found, but his papers revealed the nature of his experiments: He was trying to keep the women's heads alive after they had been removed from their bodies. And he was so deranged, he believed that the experiments had been successful.

When the mansion was searched, there was no sign of the doctor, but there were six dead women in the building. One had been strapped to a bed for a long time, and five of them were buried in the basement.

Once again, the house lay empty, until the nearby Equitable Gas Company put up some immigrant laborers there. Two of the men left their rooms one night and were discovered dead shortly afterward in the basement, one hanging from a rafter, the other impaled by a plank of wood. The house became so notorious by 1920 that Thomas Edison came to explore it and began to hatch one of his more extraordinary schemes: to create a machine that would record the voices of the dead.

Seven years later, shortly before the house was destroyed, a police report surfaced from New York that shed a little more light on the evil goings-on there. A drunkard was picked up in the Big Apple, full of wild stories concerning sex orgies, demonic possession, torture, and murder. The man was held for some time, until his ravings subsided, but he was then released. He had given his name as Adolph Brunrichter.

A month later a freak accident completely destroyed the house and spread devastation around the area. A gas tank exploded with such force that windows shattered across the river in downtown Pittsburgh. Shards of metal and brick fragments scattered everywhere, and when the dust settled, nothing at all was left of the most haunted house in America.

But that's not the end of the story—nor is it the beginning. Locals claim that the area where the house stood had never been settled by the local Indian tribes. They called it the Dark Place and feared it. They would hold their enemies captive there, and according to some stories, would torture, kill, and bury them in the area. But they'd never live there.

And even now some claim a pall of evil hangs over the place. They mutter darkly about frequent traffic accidents at the intersection of Routes 65 and 279. While we won't make light of such claims, State Farm Insurance doesn't agree; its annual Dangerous Intersections reports have never listed Pittsburgh in the top ten. But statistics won't silence the tales of the Dark Place. We can only hope that they make drivers take more care at that busy intersection. If they do, perhaps the Dark Place that once played host to the Congelier mansion may act against type and finally do something good for the world.

Villisca Ax Murder House

The small Iowa town of Villisca is a quiet place with only thirteen hundred residents, so it's small wonder that it's still buzzing with tales of a gruesome incident that happened nearly a century ago. A whole family and two visiting children were murdered in one night; the murders remain unsolved after all this time. And of course, the house where it happened is abuzz with reports of ghostly activity.

On June 10, 1912, Josiah B. Moore, five members of his family, and two children staying as guests lay down to bed. They never saw the light of day again. Sometime between midnight and five in the morning, an intruder entered the house, closed the curtains, and bludgeoned all eight in the head with an ax. Men, women, children—the killer was indiscriminate. At some point, he prepared a plate of food for himself, but it remained uneaten. And curiously, he removed a few slabs of bacon from the home's freezer and placed them on the floor.

In a small town like Villisca in 1912, this was a life-changing event. Residents bought new locks and new guns. They spread wild rumors about a shirtless man canoeing around in a local river. As a result, hoboes were arrested across all of Iowa and throughout neighboring states. A business competitor of Mr. Moore's and a local priest were under suspicion, but never charged. A private detective agency investigated a man named William Mansfield so zealously that he sued and won more than two thousand dollars.

At this point, the likelihood of the Villisca ax murderer ever being identified range from extraordinarily slim to none. But the memories of what happened here will never go away. And the spirits of those who were so brutally wronged, it seems, will never rest. In the years since the murders, dozens of people have reported having terrifying experiences there. The house is now a historic sight, and tours and overnight stays are offered, so these haunting reports will most likely continue well into the next century.

A Stay at the Ax Murder House

A few years ago, my girlfriend and I were watching some TV show about haunted places. A certain episode was dedicated to a little town in Iowa called Villisca. This past summer we were roaming online and saw that this same house was also available for overnight stays. A few weeks later there we were there. During the night, we heard a few noises and bumps. One of us felt a little tug, and there were cold spots and hot spots throughout the house. At one point, something unseen pushed

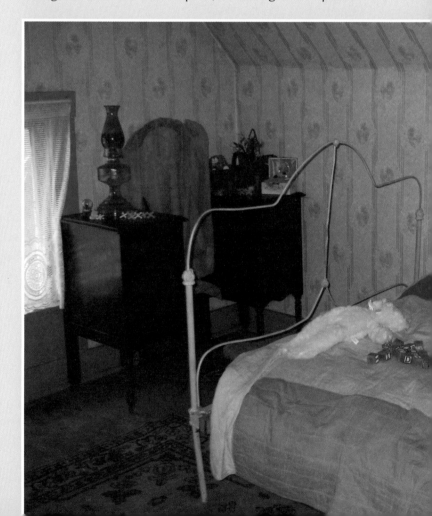

a ball across the room. We watched it spin in a complete circle and roll back. Even stranger was when we were packing up to leave the next morning, at about the time the family's bodies were found. The front door was held shut with an old solid iron. Suddenly, it was as if someone had kicked the door open and in came a big gust of wind. It was quite an experience. I most definitely will do it again.—*Manda*

What Do You Expect in the Ax Murder House?

If you look in the windows, you can see some of the people who were murdered. Right after it happened, my boyfriend's grandparents moved into the house, and were visited nightly by the spirits. They moved out right after this started happening.—*Kylie*

Face in the Courthouse Window

In November 1876, the Pickens County Courthouse in Alabama burned to the ground. Suspecting arson, residents wanted to punish the person responsible. After more than a year, a former slave named Henry Wells was arrested in connection with a string of burglaries and taken to the newly rebuilt courthouse. Thinking Wells was also responsible for the arson, a mob gathered outside, ready to hang him.

From a garret room upstairs, Wells was reportedly peering down at the angry crowd when a bolt of lightning struck near the courthouse and somehow etched the anguished expression on Wells' face into the glass of a window pane.

Since that time, people have seen the impression of a face in the lower right-hand pane of the upstairs window of the courthouse. Over the decades, people have tried to clean the image from the window, some scrubbing it with soap or rubbing with gasoline, but the face remains unchanged. Hundreds of people visit Carrollton each year to see it. The courthouse stands at the intersection of Alabama highways 17 and 86 in downtown Carrollton.

—*Kelly Kazek*

Lady of the Lake

Lake Ronkonkoma is the largest freshwater lake in Long Island, New York, and a popular summer destination. According to legend, it is also cursed. Men beware—this body of water is said to be the home of a vengeful spirit that claims one male life per year.

Supposedly, Ronkonkoma was the name of an Indian princess of the Setauket tribe who fell in love with a white settler named Hugh Birdsall who lived near the lake. Upon their meeting, the princess and Birdsall immediately fell in love, but this union was forbidden by her father. Every night for seven years, they would sneak out to send messages of love to one another. Ronkonkoma would paddle her canoe out to the middle of the lake, where she would then float a message the rest of the way to her lover, who waited on the opposite shore. This continued until one day the princess was unable to deal with this arrangement and snapped. She sent a final farewell note to her lover. He received it on the shore, and minutes later the canoe washed up in front of him as well. Inside it was the princess's body—she had plunged a knife deep into her heart. Heartbroken and distraught over the death of his one true love, Birdsall too committed suicide on the spot.

Since that day, Ronkonkoma has haunted the lake, becoming known to many as the Lady of the Lake. Angered because she wasn't allowed to love in life, she now drags one man into the lake each year. It is said that at least one person has drowned each year in Lake Ronkonkoma for the past two hundred years, the large majority of them male. Many people have reported being drawn by some unseen force out to the center of the lake, as if something was trying to drag them in. These

> **It is said that at least one person has drowned each year in Lake Ronkonkoma for the past two hundred years, the large majority of them male.**

souls have been lucky to be able to resist the pull of the Lady of the Lake and to live to report the existence of this strange phenomenon. There hasn't been a drowning at Lake Ronkonkoma since the year 2000, causing many superstitious locals to wonder, is the Lady of the Lake gone forever or just lying in wait, taking her time in choosing her next unlucky victim?

Besides the stories of the Princess's vengeful spirit, there are other stories of Lake Ronkonkoma regarding its water's physical properties. One legend says that a number of powerful whirlpools can be found at the center of the otherwise tranquil lake. Others purport that the lake is bottomless and that its depths are dotted with many caverns and subterranean passageways. Many of the bodies lost to Ronkonkoma never surface on the lake, but are sucked into these underground tunnels and later turn up in Long Island Sound, on the shores of the East River in New York City, and even as far away as Connecticut. In some cases, bodies have disappeared for as long as three months before washing ashore miles away from where the unfortunate victims vanished.

To at least a certain degree, the legends of Lake Ronkonkoma have more validity than your average tall tale. There is some factual evidence that backs up the fears of local residents. For example, statistics show that three quarters of drowning incidents in the United States claim the lives of males. Yet, since 1963, there have been thirty-two drowning deaths at Lake Ronkonkoma, all of them claiming male lives.

Those who have firsthand expert knowledge of the lake also lend credence to the stories. For example, we had a chance to meet David Igneri, who served as the head lifeguard at Lake Ronkonkoma for thirty-two straight summers. His accounts of the lake and its dangers help support the idea that supernatural or not, this lake seems to have a sinister side to it.

"From 1877 to 1977, there was something like a hundred and forty-seven drownings," Igneri told us. "At least thirty in my thirty-two years here."

We asked Igneri about some of the rumors regarding the lake's physical properties.

"I've swam across [the lake] hundreds of times. I've never seen a whirlpool. But this is what I do know," Igneri said. "Once you get deeper than about twenty or so feet in this lake, it's totally black. You cannot see a thing. You'll think you're swimming up when actually, you're swimming down." As can be imagined, this made the lives of Igneri and his fellow lifeguards very difficult at times. "Once they get to ten feet, if you don't get them, you can't find them."

We asked Mr. Igneri his opinions on the validity of the Lady of the Lake legends.

"I have never actually seen her," Igneri said. "That doesn't mean she's not there. I was one who just believed in the concrete, something I could see, something that I could understand. I didn't believe in the supernatural at all."

For Igneri, that began to change in 1965, when he was twenty-one years old. During February of that year, he had the same bone-chilling nightmare seven nights in a row. In his dream, David was attempting a rescue. "I was diving in the very deep water," he recalled. "I was going down a ledge into the darkness, and as I got down to about twenty-five, thirty feet, I was out of air. I had lost orientation and I couldn't figure out which way was up or down."

Igneri, in his dream, began to panic. He eventually realized that by following the direction of air bubbles he blew, he could make his way back to the lake's surface. His anguish at the failed rescue was always punctuated by the same occurrence as he emerged from the water, an image of fireworks exploding high in the sky above him. Igneri feared the coming of July that year, as he took his series of dreams to be a premonition warning him that a disaster was going to occur at Lake Ronkonkoma on Independence Day.

"In the dream, I came up saving myself. I didn't save the person," said Igneri. "But I dismissed that and said, 'Well this time, we are going to figure out a way, and are going to stop the legend. This time, we are going to stop the curse.'"

When the holiday finally came, Igneri, as well as the crew he had warned about his dreams, realized that they had their hands full. "We had about two thousand people on the water, and about another four or five thousand on the beach," Igneri

recalled. "I had told all my guards what was going to happen, and that we were going to stop it."

Throughout the entire day, Igneri and his skittish crew remained completely on guard. Before the day was out, they were called into action. "At four thirty, four thirty-five, an epileptic boy, six feet tall, fifteen years old, had a seizure in the water," Igneri recounted, fear and determination still in his voice. "We dove for forty-five minutes. We did the human chain. We did everything we could."

As time went on, most were giving up hope. But Igneri soldiered on, remembering his dreams and his resolve to avoid their outcome becoming a reality. "Finally I said to the guys, 'I'm gonna take one more dive myself,'" he said. "I went down a ledge. It was so dark and murky that I couldn't see where I was going, lost concentration, got disoriented. . . ."

At that point, Igneri's experience took a terrifying turn, eerily matching up with his nightmares. "I followed my bubbles to the surface," Igneri quietly told us, "and firecrackers went off. A beautiful boy of fifteen had just died."

This powerful experience convinced the previously skeptical David Igneri that there might just be something truly sinister and strange taking place at Lake Ronkonkoma. While he has never seen the Lady of the Lake personally, and in fact has never met anyone who claims to have seen her ghostly image, he still believes that it's better to be safe than sorry.

"If you're a girl in the summer, go swimming in Lake Ronkonkoma," Igneri advises. "Go have all the fun you'd like. But if you are a boy, lock yourself in your mother's car. Tie yourself to a tree, but don't go in the water."

Lake Ronkonkoma is a site of anguish, lost love, and vengeance. Be mindful while walking its shores—the Lady of the Lake is forever looking for a new lover to keep her company.

Every town has its local characters. They might be the group of old guys who spend all day yakking in the barber shop. They could include the feisty waitress at the diner where everyone wants to have breakfast or a civic figure like the mayor. All these folks are fixtures in neighborhoods across the nation, but they're not the only notable locals. There's another kind too . . . and you can spot them coming from a mile away.

These are a special breed of people, fiercely individualistic, who possess the courage it takes to stand up in public and proclaim, "I am embracing my inner pixie." The people who routinely dress up as superheroes and roam the streets looking for ways to make the world a better place. Or the guy who charms you with his conversation, even when it turns to the subject of alien abduction, which of course happens to him on a regular basis. And don't even get us started on vampires stumping for votes in elections and sports heroes frozen in liquid nitrogen.

Local Heroes and Villains

These are our kind of local characters—a kind that's just as close to our hearts as the people who serve us our daily dose of morning coffee and conversation. You don't even need the Weird Eye to see them coming. In fact . . . look out! Here they come now!

Randy Constan—A Pixie in Never-Never Land

When our *Weird* Web master first called to inform us that our Web site had been nominated for a Webby Award, our initial reaction was, "Cool . . . what's a Webby?"

"You don't understand," he said, "the Webbys are like the Oscars of the Internet. Only about a hundred nominees are chosen from millions of Web sites."

"What category are we nominated in?" we asked.

"Well . . . WEIRD!" he exclaimed.

"Who are we up against?"

"The Bigfoot Research Society, Disinformation, Fortean Times, and some guy that dresses like Peter Pan."

"Peter Pan? Hmmm . . . that sounds like trouble!"

After much discussion about the possibilities of winning such a coveted award, we decided to trek on out to San Francisco to see what all this Webby fuss was about. When the night of the gala award ceremony arrived, we were ready. With our official *Weird* tasseled fezzes firmly in place, we gathered with the other nominees and reporters on the red carpet outside the opulent San Francisco Memorial Opera House. We walked into the theater calm and collected, prepared to accept our well-deserved trophy.

About an hour into the program, actor Alan Cumming, the MC, announced that the next category, was his "favorite,"

Weird. The nominees were announced. As emissaries from the mystical East (Coast), we were quite surprised at the volume of applause our Web site received from those in attendance. That's it, we thought—it's in the bag! We've got it!

Then the auditorium fell silent in anticipation of the announcement of the winner. With bated breath, we listened as the host opened the envelope and read the words "and the award goes to . . . Peter Pan's homepage!"

With that, a waiflike middle-aged man in kelly-green tights bounded down the aisle of the darkened auditorium. The spotlight found him as he pranced onto the stage and leaped gazellelike toward the podium, throwing handfuls of glittering pixie dust in his wake. The Webby Awards require all winners to keep their acceptance speech to only five words, so each must choose his or her words very carefully. The Peter Pan look-alike approached the mike, doe-eyed and tanned, wearing a broad, exuberant smile. He sported a Dorothy Hamill hairdo circa 1976 beneath a forest-green felt Robin Hood–style cap complete with feather plume, and uttered the five words, "Weird? God loves us all!"

Later that night at the after party, as we bellied up to the bar in an effort to recoup the cost of our plane fare in complimentary cocktails, we wondered just who this character was

and according to the Web site, he began putting them on in an effort to remain in touch with his youthful side, even at the age of fifty-four. Many may ask, Why does a grown man find it so important to publicly dress as a famous fairy-tale character? We recently had a chance to interview Randy, and he gave us his answer to that seemingly complex question.

"I'm sure the answer is too simple and obvious to satisfy anyone," he told us. "I do these things simply because I like to . . . and because it makes me happy and feel wonderful. Why do I enjoy it so much? How do I know? Some tell me I should seek some psychological counseling to figure it all out and keep all this hidden away until I can explain them acceptably. But I think not! Perhaps that's the life lesson in all this. Why do we always have to know 'why' or feel compelled to answer 'why'? Why do you like (or dislike) vanilla ice cream? It's a silly question, right? You just do or don't."

As Randy went on to explain, those who insist on hassling him about his motivations are probably the types who won't understand the answer anyway. "Perhaps a 'higher power' intentionally brings about people like me to serve as a blaspheme and offense against many of the unwarranted 'standards' people dream up as being 'acceptable.' In truth, the real question on the minds of the people you mention is more like, 'Okay, even if you do like and enjoy this stuff, why do you insist on doing it in spite of the fact that I (and by extension 'everyone' else) thinks you're crazy?' For myself, I seldom answer those that are so out of touch that they don't understand that being happy and making others happy is more important than fitting into their small world."

And why did Mr. Constan go on to build a Web site about his endeavors? "A central theme of my Internet presence has been to encourage others to embrace their own 'inner pixie,' or whatever inner manifestation they

who had robbed us of our award. Just then, what to our wondering eyes should appear—it was Peter Pan himself partaking of a little pixie potion! Always on the lookout for a story, we decided to sidle up to Mr. Pan and introduce ourselves. The man in tights seemed to be a very pleasant and surprisingly, dare we say it, "normal guy," who seemed to enjoy a free drink just as much as we did.

Beginning with that conversation, we've been fascinated with Peter Pan. Our research into his past, his lifestyle, and his unique worldview have proved to us that he is truly one of the most unusual individuals in the entire country, with no exaggeration. A visit to www. pixyland.org shows everything that is great about the man born Randy Constan. Randy's costumes are all homemade, have always wished to express," he said. "The Internet has been a wonderful vehicle for self-expression, making friends, and meeting kindred spirits. But I also believe God made us all unique, and that embracing the uniqueness in ourselves and others is a major key to personal happiness and our success as a civilization. So my willingness to 'put myself' out there, on-line, has given weight to that encouraging message. If you have anything positive to share, the Internet certainly provides one of the most powerful tools for doing so."

On his site, Constan constantly refers to himself as boyish and goes to great lengths to explain his views on the importance of staying in touch with a childlike sense of wonder. He further explained to us that he has never agreed with the traditional gender roles defined by American society. "I usually have to flip two coins just to pick a gender," Randy told us. "Yes, two coins. There are at least three possibilities there."

With these views on gender, the closed-minded of the world might think Randy would have a hard time finding love. And yet, perhaps most touching about the Peter Pan homepage are Randy's numerous references to how he hoped that, by his creating such a public space, his own personal Tinkerbell might find him. In recent years, Randy reported to the loyal fans of his homepage that indeed she had. A fellow pixie enthusiast met Randy, and he began dedicating a large portion of his Web site to accounts of their travels together and photos of them dressed in incredible, elaborate costumes. The fairy dust finally hit the fan in October 2007, when Mr.

Pan announced on his site that he and his Tinkerbell were engaged. To the longtime fans of the Peter Pan homepage, it was a thrilling and heartwarming development.

Many other pixies throughout the world have contacted Constan, and their photos are featured prominently on his site's "Pixie Friends" section, which has become one of the most popular parts of the site. Constan's Web presence also serves as a sort of on-line runway for the many outfits he has designed and made. There are Little Boy Blue outfits, rabbit costumes, fairy garb of various hues, as well as holiday-themed pixie costumes. We asked Randy which of his outfits was his most beloved, which he would take to a desert island if he had to. Not surprisingly, he was hard-pressed to choose just one.

"Well I don't know. I guess I'd take the Peter Pan outfit or maybe Blue Boy or maybe the Fairy princess. . . . I have no idea." Eventually, he stopped trying to pick favorites and instead went with practicality. "Maybe the Little Lord Fauntleroy one, the one made of black velvet and white lace, in case it gets cold."

Peter Pan's homepage was one of the early Internet sensations. Even after all these years, the site is still going strong; Randy's annual holiday charity drives still bring in thousands of dollars. Like the Lost Boys of the tale upon which Mr. Constan has based his life, the site isn't feeling the effects of passing time. Instead, Peter Pan's legacy, mission, and work have continued to spread farther and wider, as if they are flying high on a magical concoction of fairy dust.

Terrifica: Caped Crusader Thwarting Cupid

Superman may be faster than a speeding bullet, but he's got nothing on Terrifica. She burst upon New York City in the mid-1990s, wearing red spandex tights, red boots, cape and headband, and a glittering golden mask. But she wasn't there to look cool on the club scene. She has a mission: to protect the city's female population from the advances of lecherous men.

Like every good superhero, Terrifica has an origin story and secret identity. Under her given name of Sarah, she left Pittsburgh for New York City in her early twenties. Her longtime boyfriend broke up with her just before the move, and her romantic encounters in the big city ended in confusion and heartbreak. So she vowed to empower herself and all women: In her superhero guise, she began to patrol bars and parties in search of predatory men with tipsy women. Her primary goal was to prevent the women from doing something they would regret, but if the women felt they were unlikely to regret anything, she would offer condoms to make sure that they were safe on at least one level.

Terrifica doesn't have extraordinary powers. She's never demonstrated super strength, telepathy, invulnerability, or any of the standard comic-book fare. (She told a reporter for *New York* magazine, "I don't have any superpowers. I'm not crazy, you know.") The only weapons in her utility belt, cunningly disguised as a fanny pack, are a cell phone, lipstick, candy, a camera to photograph male predators, a journal, Terrifica fortune cards to hand out, and pepper spray to use on any man who might fly into a rage. And she has an automobile that she refers to as "Carrific."

After nearly a decade of superheroics, Terrifica appeared in a 2002 ABC News article that offered a glimpse into the psyche of one of the world's most active superheroes.

"I protect the single girl living in the big city," says Terrifica, sporting a blond Brunhilda wig with a golden mask and a matching Valkyrie bra. "I do this because women are weak. They are easily manipulated, and they need to be protected from themselves and most certainly from men."

Terrifica also has an archnemesis—the velvet-clad lothario known as Fantastico. Terrifica's objections to Fantastico's womanizing ways aren't just moral ones. In this case, it's personal. Fantastico was one of the men who broke her heart in her early days in New York. Naturally, Fantastico has a different take on Terrifica's motivation. As he told ABC reporters, "She seems to have an obsession with me. She seems to have it in for men. I'm convinced she is loveless and would love to have the rest of the city as loveless and miserable as she is."

Then, just as Terrifica's popularity was exploding, she disappeared. She had often told reporters that she would leave the superhero scene once she found true love. Could this have been her motivation? Not according to a blog reply she posted later on the Web site songdog.net.

"Since the ABC article came out (but not because of it), I've decided to hang up my cape. No regrets, no hard feelings. I just can't continue because people at work are

close to unmasking me and I could deal with that except that I couldn't bear for one co-worker in particular to laugh at me. Thanks for caring. I still love Metropolis and will fight predators."

Terrifica is occasionally still heard from. In 2006, she was interviewed by Kevlex, another superhero, who manages the Web site worldsuperheroregistry.com. Terrifica offered her views on being a superhero. In her opinion, not everyone has the potential to be one.

"There is no 'starting out.' You know your mission or you don't. You are born a super human or you're not. You have power or you don't. No one can choose to be a super human. You can't just make up a power or a purpose. But if you are a super human, you have a choice about being a hero. You can choose to be a villain too. Villains make more money."

It seems that the world needs Terrifica now more than ever. Perhaps someday she will take up her mantle once more and protect us all from the dangers of fleeting, regrettable hookups.

Looking for Action with Captain Jackson

He's caped, and he's a crusader. And technically, says Captain Jackson, he "fits the definition of a superhero." In his purple cape, his Batman-style helmet mask, custom trunks, and spandex leggings, Captain Jackson looks the part. And he has a superhero's tag line too: Champion of All that is Civil and True in the city of Jackson, Michigan. Sure, he's wearing running shoes instead of boots, and he can't fly or melt steel with a blast from his eyeballs. But when darkness falls in downtown Jackson, the captain prowls its back alleys and bars to let the criminal minded know they had better think twice.

"I like fighting crime here" is his motto, emblazoned at the top of his Web site, captainjackson.org. *Weird U.S.*

couldn't resist the chance to talk to a real-life superhero, so we called and asked him if he started out by reading action comics.

"No!" yelled the Man of Purple. "I think superhero comics are dumb! I never read comic books or dressed up as Superman!"

His beginnings as a masked crime fighter are much simpler than the back-stories of your average comic book hero too. "One day I called into a local talk show," said the captain, "and introduced myself as Captain Jackson. I said I just got here from Detroit, and I'm here to save this city. I had the idea of being a bridge between the police and the people."

arts, specializes in working against domestic violence. "She just showed up on the street one night in her own uniform," said the captain. "I was like, oh, Baby! She was hot, and I was newly single, and before long we'd gone out on three dates." A superhero romance was born.

At first, people thought the Terrific Trio was a joke. "By the time they realized we were serious about the Neighborhood Watch Program, it was too late to stop us," he told *Weird U.S.* "Today, the downtown Loop is the safest and most crime-free part of the city."

Captain Jackson doesn't make arrests, but he calls police if anything unusual is going on. He compares his role to that of Curtis Sliwa's Guardian Angels, the New York-based group that began safety patrols in a crime-ridden area of the Bronx over two decades ago. The Jackson authorities apparently appreciate his presence: They appear with him at civic events and have made him an honorary deputy fire chief. So far, he hasn't had to fight anyone, but he did get sucker-punched in a downtown bar one night. Within seconds, four patrons were holding the offender down, so he wasn't forced to unleash his full powers upon the attacker.

The captain has loftier goals than mere safety patrols, however. His ultimate hope is to find backers for a foundation to promote residents' taking back their neighborhoods and to provide scholarships for future law-enforcement officers.

Of course, every hero has his kryptonite, the inevitable

The captain admits his first uniform (don't call it a costume!) was a bit on the lame side, with its homemade felt cape. His original sidekick, his daughter Crimefighter Girl, then nine, wore a flowered bathing suit with a towel pinned around her shoulders. Today the Debonair Duo (Crimefighter Girl is now seventeen) sport uniforms with custom components, including plastic logos that attach with Velcro. "A lot of the uniform is handmade," said the captain. "I mean, it's not like you can walk into Wal-Mart and ask for the superhero clothing department."

They've also added a third member to the Crimefighter Corps, the lovely blond Queen of Hearts who, besides displaying a considerable talent for martial

Achilles' heel. The captain admits he doesn't like heights, so you won't see him dangling from any rooftop parapets. He also had the misfortune, while out of uniform, of being arrested for driving while visibly intoxicated. The captain regrets the incident, of course, but the worst part in his view was that the local newspaper, the *Jackson Citizen Patriot*, seized upon the chance to expose the captain's legal name. At first, he thought he might have to move to a different city. But then, using his Super-Thinking Power, he realized there was a simpler solution . . . changing his legal name.

All the publicity has inspired a league of superhero wannabes. "Kids are always wanting to do this," he said. "This is a one in a million thing. It's not like I could go anywhere and try it again, it just happened. People's reactions have always been one hundred percent respectful. This is about good-deed doing."

There is, by the way, one thing Captain Jackson truly wishes he could change about Jackson, but it's unlikely to happen. "There's no phone booths!"

he exclaimed. "Where's a superhero supposed to change these days?"

Henry's Heroes

Lay minister and marine veteran Henry C. Cowan has erected a collection of homemade monuments to local and personal heroes in the town of Bear Grass, North Carolina, southwest of Williamston in Martin County. Some of the figures are in front of the Bear Grass consolidated school, one of the smallest one-unit schools in the state, with elementary, middle, and high schools all joined together. The majority of the figures, though, are scattered around his own property, several blocks away on the corner of Green and Ayers streets. Cowan began building the monuments in the 1980s, teaching himself how to shape concrete over wire armatures to make the near life-size freestanding figures. The base pedestals of some include stone tablets with the names and dates of local military veterans.

Back on the Chain Gang with Sheriff Joe Arpaio

One of the most controversial figures in the state of Arizona today is Maricopa County's sheriff, Joe Arpaio. Some see him as a tough crime fighter. Others view him as a cruel, self-promoting windbag. Both camps just might be right.

What sets Joe apart from other elected law officials is not his strong opinions. It's the fact that he puts them into practice. He makes extensive use of chain gang labor crews for men, women, and children. He maintains the Tent City jail, where fifteen hundred convicts while away their days and nights in Korean war–era army surplus tents in the brutal Arizona desert, surrounded by an electrified razor wire fence. And inmates are allowed no luxuries: That means no cigarettes, no cable television except for educational channels, no movies beyond a G rating, and no weights to lift. They don't even get coffee.

"Under my watch, prisoners are treated like criminals and not like guests at the country club," Joe states on his Web site, reelectjoe.com.

Born in 1932, the son of Italian immigrant parents, this Korean War veteran began his career as a cop in the '50s and spent twenty years working with the Drug Enforcement Agency. He successfully ran for the office of sheriff of Maricopa County in 1992 and has been reelected four times since—in 2004, by a landslide.

"I do have the support of the people," he told us. "So, when I do things, I get away with it. I've been investigated by the Justice Department, Amnesty International, the Civil Liberties Union—but I'm still here."

Perhaps that's because some of his ideas seem radically reasonable. For example, he started what he calls Hard Knocks High, an accredited high school program that gives young offenders a high school

education behind bars. He has instituted various drug rehabilitation programs. And he runs a Web site that posts pictures of deadbeat parents along with their last known addresses.

We were fortunate enough to meet Sheriff Arpaio for an interview one summer day. Well, it was fortunate except for the time and temperature: We had to report to the Maricopa County Jail at five thirty a.m., when the temperature was already 114 degrees. We hitched a ride with a female chain gang to a blazing hot stretch of Arizona asphalt, where the inmates began picking up litter from the sides of the highway. Soon afterward, a car pulled up and a stout man jumped out. Dressed in full suit and tie despite the heat, the sheriff obviously meant business—and Joe's business is to promote Joe. He clearly loves his work.

Weird U.S.: Sheriff Arpaio, we've heard that you're the toughest sheriff in America.

Sheriff Joe Arpaio: In the world.

Weird U.S.: You actually wrote the book on being tough (*America's Toughest Sheriff: How We Can Win the War Against Crime,* published in 1996). So what makes you so tough?

Hello from Sunny Arizona!

SJA: Well, I just use common sense. I have a philosophy, when you're convicted and doing time, you should be punished . . . PUNISHED. I take away your privileges, take away your nice things.

To this sheriff, nice things include weekends and meals. He works his inmates seven days a week and feeds them two meals a day without condiments or coffee. Joe says pulling coffee from the menu saves him $150,000 dollars a year, and serving bologna sandwiches instead of a cooked meal slashes another half million from the budget. He walked us over to the prisoner transport bus to show us the chain gang's lunch: A plastic baggy containing a slice of bologna between two pieces of white bread and an orange. Oh, and he charges for lunch too. One CNN report stated, "Arpaio makes inmates pay for their meals, which some say are worse than those for the guard dogs. Canines eat a dollar ten worth of food a day, the inmate ninety cents."

Joe denies this. He feeds his inmates for thirty cents a day, not ninety, and he is very proud of that. In fact, he boasts about how much better he treats animals. He is an animal rescue advocate who campaigned for Proposition 204, which makes cruelty to animals in farming illegal. And Arpaio tells us with pride that his chain gangs contribute thousands of dollars of free labor to taxpayers each month. But for all his cost-cutting measures, his methods have cost the county millions. A variety of lawsuits include a wrongful death suit settled for $8.5 million and $1.5 million for an inmate who died because he was denied medical treatment.

Still, this sort of thing doesn't seem to deter the chain gang's march—or rather shuffle—in Maricopa County. In fact, as Arpaio shouted to the women cleaning up roadway litter during our interview, "You have made history. There has never been a female chain gang in history, around the world. You are part of history. Eight years ago I put the women on a chain gang. You know why I did it? Because we should never discriminate against women. We put men on the chain gang, why should you not have the opportunity? I am an equal opportunity incarcerator."

So how does Sheriff Joe get away with using a punishment that much of the rest of the country considers barbaric? Believe it or not, he gets his inmates to volunteer.

"When they violate our policies . . . we put them in a lockdown with three others, four others. The only way they're going to get out is volunteer for the chain gang. They all volunteer."

After our visit with the chain gang, Sheriff Joe escorted us to Tent City. On a tower above the tents is a blinking neon vacancy sign, just to let everyone know that this jail always has room for one more guest.

We held a smuggled digital thermometer up to the level of the upper bunk of one of the prisoners' beds to gauge how hot it was.

Weird U.S.: It's a hundred and thirty-seven degrees in here!

SJA: Well, you're in front of the fan. That's cooling it off.

Weird U.S.: Cooling it off? It's one thirty-seven.

SJA: It's a hundred and twenty degrees in Iraq, and our soldiers are living in tents too, and they have to wear full battle gear, but they didn't commit any crimes!

Here's an odd thing: Wherever he goes in Tent City, Sheriff Joe is surrounded by a group of inmates clamoring for his autograph! While we were there, Arpaio joked casually with the men and signed his name on prison-issue postcards, each bearing different images of Joe with a funny slogan about just how tough he is and how miserable he makes life for his prisoners. So there he stood, in the center of about twenty-five prisoners wearing traditional black and white–striped prison pants. In an age of orange jumpsuited inmates, Joe's choice of black and white horizontal stripes on prisoners is another throwback to the penal practices of yesteryear. But it's what's

underneath those stripes that's really shocking . . .

Weird U.S.: Sheriff, we've heard that you force the inmates, both men and women, to wear pink underwear. Why is that?

SJA: Because they don't like it! That's the reason I did it, because if they liked it, I probably would not do it. But they don't like it. That's why I do it. [Addressing the crowd of inmates]: So, how do you criminals like life here in my Tent City?"

Anonymous Inmate: "It's like camping—except without the fun, Joe!"

The sheriff pretends not to hear the jab, but watching his face closely, we notice the quick flash of a smile cross his lips and a twinkle light in his eye.

Weird U.S.: Sheriff, you seem to have a good rapport with the prisoners here—almost like a father figure. We can almost see you putting them to bed and reading them a story at night.

SJA: I do.

Weird U.S.: You do? How do you do that?

SJA: I film myself in a beautiful room with a fireplace and the 'Mr. Rogers' sweater on. I have a German shepherd at my side and I make a videotape to show on the jail's TVs. "Hi, inmates, it's the Bedtime Story Hour with me, your host, Sheriff Joe. For the next thirty to forty-five minutes you will be treated to a literary treasure. . . . Good night, see you tomorrow."

Hmm, maybe Sheriff Joe ain't so tough after all.

Sending a Message to THE MAN

In Perry, Oklahoma, there is a rancher who apparently has a beef with the local government. David Nemechek's home has been turned into an ever-growing statement against the government of Noble County and its law enforcement officers. It's sometimes referred to as the X-Files ranch, or, sometimes the conspiracy house.

The story seems to go like this: David Nemechek moved to Noble County with his family. After a period of time, something happened, either to get him on the bad side of the law, or to get the law on the bad side of him. That is when strange things started to occur in his life: cattle mutilated and murdered, harassing phone calls, strange drum beats in the middle of the night, and threats on his family's lives. David did not appreciate this, so he fought back the only way he knew how: by posting signs in his front yard.

Some are small, short lines, saying simple things such as WE ARE WHISTLEBLOWERS and STOP YOUR LIES. Some are long, telling the complete story of what seems to be going on. Some are on wood, hand painted and painstakingly crafted. Some are on steel, with stick on letters forming the message. The signs form what looks like a giant ransom note, pieced together from various sources, all lined up along his property.

The first time I came across this place was on my way out to one of the Indian Hospitals in the state to work on their computers. It was just random luck that I happened to take the road I did, and came by Mr. Nemechek's home. It felt creepy, but I was so curious that I slowed down to read them all. Taking the time to read them is a dangerous sport, however. The road is highly traveled, with signs warning against stopping on the side of the road. When I got the pictures you see here, I was taking them at 35 mph (the speed limit is 60, I believe) with a county sheriff tailing me the whole time. Needless to say, I was only able to get a few good shots.

Everything I have read about this place tells me that Mr. Nemechek is a nice man; however, I was quite creeped out by the place. Of course, it didn't help that I was being followed by a police officer at the time. I do, however, plan on going back for more pictures.—*Colby Weaver*

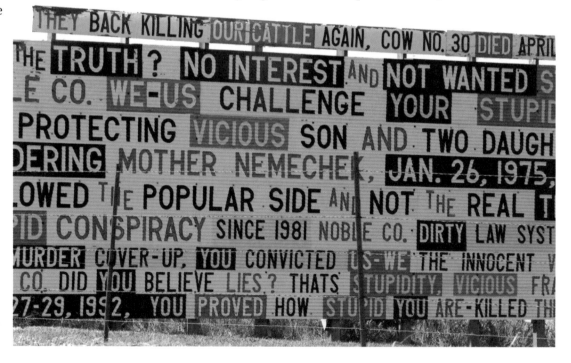

Riley Martin, Intergalactic Ambassador

UFO enthusiasts have known of Riley Martin for years. And even nonbelievers may know him from his many appearances on the Howard Stern radio show, as well as his own radio programs on the Artist First World Radio and Sirius Satellite Network. Martin has achieved this level of exposure due to his detailed accounts of being abducted by alien beings every eleven years since his childhood. His dealings with seven different alien races are the basis of his fame. Even his book, *The Coming of Tan,* was co-authored by an alien being.

We recently visited Martin at his (earthly) home and found a man who had some incredible tales to tell, and had an equally incredible amount of charisma. We're not here to say his words are true, nor are we here to present him for any sort of mockery. Instead, we present to you Riley Martin, in his own words.

Weird U.S.: Maybe you could give us a brief history of how your encounters began.

Riley Martin: I was born in the state of Mississippi in 1946, month of May. My family moved across the river, into northeastern Arkansas, that year. It was there, near the banks of the St. Francis River, in 1953, that I saw lights above the river three nights in a row, in the wee hours of the morning. I would wake up and observe the lights.

On the third night, I heard something distinctly saying, "Friend Martin, come out. We have need to speak with you." So I got dressed and went down to the river to investigate these lights. I could feel static electricity in my hair, the leaves were shaking, the dog's hair was standing up. And as I stepped into a clearing near the river, I saw the ship. It was standing about three to four meters above the ground. And it was moored by three flexible legs, not

standing gear. And it danced kind of like a cork on water. It was silver in color, and it had two rows of light, one on the outer edge, one on the inner edge. And they seemed to revolve against each other. I decided to run for it. But the moment I had the thought, bam, I was hit with a blue-white light. I could not move. My dog, Brown Boy, a very noble dog, would fight anything, but he cut out and left me! Anyway, there was a bright light at the bottom of the ship, and I saw two beings walk out of that light. The taller one was wearing a green, seamless jumpsuit and a bubble-head helmet. The shorter one was wearing a sky-blue jumpsuit, bubble helmet, covered all over, gloves. On his left breast was a seven-pointed star, in the middle of which was kind of like a fat H. On her left breast was the

sign of the fish. Inside the fish was a little small H.

They held me by each arm, and said, "Friend Martin, come and go with us." They took me out to the great Mothership. It is located between Saturn and one of its great moons. These same extraterrestrials visited me roughly every eleven years and took me up. I have spent time ranging from three to nine days on that great Mothership. They gave me inroads into their technologies, their food, their robotics, their thought processes. Their sociology, their reproduction manners, their physiology, and all of these things.

On December 28, 1987, in the Ozark Mountains, was my last visit. This was the time they told me, "Friend Martin, it is now time for you to remember all of the information that we have given you. The earth is in a lot of trouble." I tried to beg off. I said, "Look, I got no education, I'm a minority, I haven't always stayed within the law. They're not going to listen to me!" He said, "Friend Martin, the truth must be felt, as well as heard. Those who have hearts will feel."

Weird U.S.: You seem to have more of a recollection of your time spent with them. A lot of people have like a memory loss scenario. They have vague recollections or it needs to be brought out through hypnosis or something like that.

RM: I did undergo several hypnosis sessions, but after then I needed no more. Now all of these things I tell you, and I tell you truly, I did not go to Harvard or MIT, nor have I studied physics or math to any great extent. Is what I say feasible? Or is it obviously plagiarized or stupid or fake? If you decide that it is feasible, and you want to pursue it further, then we shall.

Weird U.S.: You've mentioned several different alien groups. Targzyssians, and what not. Are these people coming from different planets? Different galaxies?

RM: They are coming from different solar systems in the Milky Way galaxy.

Weird U.S.: Now, these aliens that are visiting us, do they have our best interests in mind?

RM: Aliens, they're flesh and blood. I find the Biaviians to be the most lovable among them. To some of the others, we're no more than items of study. To others, like the Targzyssians, the necessity of manipulation or of using certain materials from this planet, such as the blood of animals, is a done deal for them. As far as literally harming us on a massive scale or controlling us on a massive scale or altering our destiny on a massive scale, this is not allowed. Or the whole galaxy would deteriorate down to wars and massacres, you see what I mean.

Weird U.S.: Can you recognize the difference in the description of the ship from one alien group to another? Because we hear usually very similar descriptions—either there's a cigar-shaped craft or a saucer-shaped craft. Some are triangular, almost like a boomerang.

RM: The triangular ones are Nyptonians. These are the water people. Their bases and everything else are under the ocean. The V wings, especially the larger V wings, are reptilians, especially the Targzyssians and what have you. Biaviians have the classical saucer shape. The Dorians have also a saucer-shaped ship but of a different kind of configuration. Targzyssians also have saucers, but they're soft-edged. And the ether burn on them can be detrimental to human instrumentations. If you got too close, you could suffer radiation burns and things like this.

Weird U.S.: How do they get along with each other?

RM: Thirty-five thousand years ago, in the Taryian constellation, wherein lay the planet of the Biaviians, a new group of extraterrestrials, warlike, came into that vector. These were the Targzyssians—or the smart reptiles—wreaking havoc across that part of the galaxy. Biaviians, Dorians, Nyptonians, Stazyians, and even the Insectillian Screed teamed up to fight them. And took them down. Since that time there has been kind of a grudging peace.

Now, skirmishes were happening as far out as the planet earth up until about thirty-two thousand years ago, when some of the ships were injured and downed on an island in the Mediterranean. I put it about one hundred nautical miles north of what we call Tripoli and Libya, off the coast of North Africa. You have come to call it Atlantis and what have you. And because they were injured, these ships, and they could not get home, ultimately they decided to more or less domesticate through hunter-gatherer sapien biped erectors. You call them man.

Weird U.S.: Having stayed with the aliens for days at a time, could you tell us what their daily routines are like—what they eat, where they sleep? The sorts of things we take for granted.

RM: Human beings need to sleep something in the range of seven to eight hours a night. Human beings need three meals. But them, apparently they don't need much sleep or anything else. There is a short span of time, in the

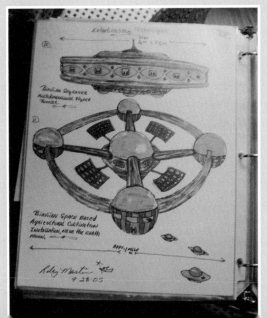

wee hours of the night, when things slow down a bit. I have seen Biaviians step into rest chambers. I passed by them on my way to the Hall of Suspension. I come back five minutes later, he's no longer in there, boom, he slept. So there is a difference.

Weird U.S.: What about food and what not? Can they forego that as well?

RM: I've never seen them eat solids. All their food is made from vegetable matter. But if you want chicken, if you want a steak medium rare, you want eggs over easy, they'll make that for you. They want a human to stay human. They don't partake themselves to any great extent. Once Tan did get loaded with me, drinking a universal-thought liquid. This liquid can mimic anything you can think of that you have done. Whether it be orange juice, sipping whiskey, or whatever, it will become that for that glass. And have the same effects upon you.

Weird U.S.: And you said Tan himself partook?

RM: Yeah, he wanted to know what it really felt like. I was making drinks from this thought liquid. Start off with beer. And then I ended up with like tequila and ripple, and called it Tequipple. He whipped out his straw, said, "Urgh." And I looked back at him, and saw his eyes woozy. His head went back and his feet went up. I caught his head. Laid him down.

Weird U.S.: Does their choosing you put pressure on you in any way?

RM: It would put pressure on me if I had to lie my way through. But I'm simply passing along information that has been given to me. Perhaps it is better that they would consider this information that I am giving them. Because I am tired of this. I could be laying with the beach bunnies on Mars!

Local Hero with a Cross to Bear

Chuck Johnson is a local hero who's not exactly "local." Or you might say he's local everywhere he goes. Either way, he is a man on a mission, and that mission is to tell you about Jesus. You would probably have figured that out, though, if you happened to catch a glimpse of Johnson. He'd be carrying a giant cross as he walked along the shoulder of your hometown highway.

Johnson, who was born in California in 1961 and grew up there, has been traversing the nation's highways and byways nonstop since 2000, carrying his cross and strapping it to the occasional car, truck, or even motorcycle whose driver offers to give him a ride. We happened by Johnson on I-95 in North Carolina one spring day in 2007. After we introduced ourselves, Chuck asked if we could take him about fifteen miles up the road to the next town, Roanoke Rapids, where he could get a motel room for the night for just $28. Of course we were more than happy to oblige the weary traveler, and Chuck set about lashing his eight-foot white cross to the roof rack of our car. As we motored on up the highway, he was kind enough to share his tale with us.

According to Johnson (who's become known as Cross-Carrier Chuck), he started walking in Alamitas, California, in 1987, after being baptized by the Crossroads Bible Study in San Jose. It was then that he had his first cross made, in Tijuana, Mexico—a four-by-four-inch-thick, solid oak version that weighed an unwieldy eighty-six pounds. Johnson was undeterred, however, by its heft—or by the fact that he had only $1.50 to his name. As he tells it, he had sold off all his worldly possessions, keeping only $55, and the cross cost $53 and change to construct. He began carrying it around Alamitas on weekends while he worked during the week. But Johnson eventually decided that reminding people of Jesus' presence was his calling, so he took his cross carrying on the road—literally. Now that's all he does.

Johnson has made at least ten trips across the States and has been through every state except Alaska and Hawaii. He sticks primarily to major highways, where cars come along and offer him rides and friendly passersby support his cause with donations. Depending on the kindness of strangers, Johnson manages to eat often and almost always sleeps inside at motels, where he can rest. The pursuit of his ambulatory ministry is a serious workout. When we came upon Johnson, for example, he'd already walked twenty-two miles that day. And he told us he does it seven days a week, 365 days a year.

Of course, as Johnson got older, it became clear that carting around an eighty-six-pound wood cross on his mission was unrealistic, so he commissioned an eight-by five-foot, eight-pound "traveling cross" made from hollow PVC beams, with a wheel on the end to make the load lighter and to keep the cross from disintegrating as it drags across the miles of asphalt. Aside from a backpack filled with water, rope for securing the cross to vehicles that give him a ride, and other odds and ends, the cross is all Johnson carries. He points out, "The Lord said take nothing with you. The whole message is to keep people thinking of Jesus, and you can rely on what the Lord brings by, you know."

Johnson has started to dictate journals of his travels (he calls his uncle in California periodically and has him transcribe the notes), which he plans to turn into a book that will use his life as an example of the way in which he believes God always provides for people. "It's basically stories of the homeless guy who carries the cross, and if he can make it, anybody can," he says.

Johnson walks rain or shine, covering the northern states in the summertime and the south during colder parts of the year. When asked, he said he'd be willing to

make the trip to Alaska or Hawaii if someone provided the means, but the timing would be important.

In the meantime, he just keeps walking. "I don't know how many miles I've logged," he says. "I've gotten thousands and thousands of rides. I never hitchhike, but if somebody pulls over or offers to give me a ride to the next town, I'll take them up on it. Because I get out in the middle of nowhere all the time. I'm just trying to get from one town to the next. It's been a journey."

Whether or not people heed Johnson's call to keep Jesus in mind isn't his utmost concern. He says he's not a preacher, but simply a man telling people about Jesus and praying for the troubles they relate. But lucky for those of us who cherish this world's weirdest people— the ones who opted to live out their life's dreams in whatever unique and offbeat way they choose. It's hard to miss a man carrying a giant cross as he paces around the country's interstate system. So keep your eyes peeled for Cross-Carrier Chuck and be kind enough to give him a lift if you see him.

A Presidential Candidate Who Really Sucks (Blood, That Is)

It was an early June day on the boardwalk at Seaside Heights, New Jersey, and there was a small crowd of people walking around, playing arcade games and heading to the beach. The smell of food competed for attention with the smells of the ocean and sunscreen. Summer was almost upon us, and so was a Vampyre. *Weird U.S.* was asked to meet this particular vampire—Jonathon "The Impaler" Sharkey—in front of Lucky Leo's, and that's where we first saw him. He was easy to identify among the beachwear-clad tourists: tall, with long black hair, wearing all black and dark sunglasses, and carrying a small bag and a long, thin cardboard box. He greeted us and agreed to talk at a table that got us out of the wind.

Jonathon described himself as an ordained Satanic Dark Priest, Sanguinarian Vampyre, Hecate Witch, and Pagan. He's also been a professional wrestler, boxer, racecar driver, and politician. As the latter, he's run for different offices in New Jersey and other states, most notably for governor of Minnesota in 2006, under the Vampyres, Witches and Pagans (VWP) Party (his experiences in this race have been chronicled in the documentary *Impaler*).

So why was Jonathon out during the day on the boardwalk, instead of being safely entombed in a coffin or other dark place? It's a common misconception about vampires, he explained. "We can go out during the daytime under the sun. It's just that we're not as powerful as we are at night." They compensate during the day by wearing sunglasses and sunscreen with a high SPF and covering up with clothing.

Before we met, Jonathon had asked us to read Revelations 13, which describes the beachside encounter of a dragon and a horrible ten-headed beast that arises from the sea. With the ocean in the background, it was only natural to ask if he considered himself the dragon. He pointed out his dragon-themed jewelry and said, "Wait 'til you see the back of my cloak." He later mentioned that the year he was born, 1964, is the year of the dragon in the Chinese zodiac.

If Jonathon is the dragon, who is this beast arising from the Jersey shore? "No comment," he said. But keeping in theme, living by water is important to him. "I draw my biggest strength from water and wind," he said. He's getting a house in Bay Head and will split his time between there and Indianapolis, which is where he's pursuing a racing career.

For a vampire, Jonathon had a pretty normal childhood. He and his friends hung around his grandmother's house, playing sports. But people "always knew something was different about me." His parents were divorced, which he said is partly due to his "father's bloodlines being vampire, and my mother being a straight-out witch. Witches and vampires don't mix. Their offspring is great, but they don't mix."

Vampires generally have an awakening—the moment they realize they are vampires—sometime in their teens. In Jonathon's case, he was five, and it happened after a drunken uncle pushed him and he attacked back. "That's when my mother enlightened me about the witchcraft side," he said. "I was doing hexes and curses at the age of five."

Despite his early vampire-witch experiences, he was raised a Catholic, going to a parochial grammar school and serving as an altar boy. His experiences in the Catholic Church enabled him "to totally infiltrate my enemies. In reality, a true satanist or somebody in service of Lucifer knows the Christian Bible better than most Christians do."

Jonathon's coven, Kat's UnderWorld Coven, has seventy "continuously active" members and more who aren't full-time, and includes Wiccan, Pagan, Satanic, Vampyre, and Lycan (werewolf) members. He's also established a 1st VWP Militia Regiment, including a Special Forces division he calls his Death Dealers, who go after threats to the VWP Party, such as vampire and witch hunters and the Ku Klux Klan. For example, a conflict with the K.K.K. in Atlantic County escalated into death threats from Daniel Carver, Imperial Wizard and Grand Dragon of the K.K.K. and member of radio host Howard Stern's Whack Pack. Carver revealed the Georgia county in which Jonathon lived, so Jonathon "sent the southern version of the Death Dealers to pay a few people a visit." As a result, the whole K.K.K. is looking for him.

"When I Become President . . ."

Various authorities have become interested in the Death Dealers, especially after Jonathon started to speak publicly about the people he was going to impale after he became President. Among those on his list are rapists, child molesters, and drunk drivers. For thieves, impalement is the third strike. "Think about it," he said. "You're a criminal, and you know I'm sitting in the White House. You look at the White House front lawn and there are

these impaling stakes with the heads of the impaled victims on them. Are you really going to try your luck?"

He also plans on paying a visit to the Supreme Court with his Death Dealers. "I'm going to tell (Samuel) Alito, 'You're a homeboy from Jersey, stand over there, just watch.' I'll say to the rest, 'Your tenure is terminated.'" Executing justices will send a message: "Don't violate somebody's rights." He'll then appoint his own judges: among them a federal judge and a federal attorney in Indianapolis, and a law professor whom he said, "got me vindicated for being wrongfully incarcerated [in Indiana] for 150 days back in 2000." Not surprisingly, federal marshals interrogated Jonathon in June 2007 over these plans.

With talk of impaling and Death Dealers, it's hard to believe that Jonathon has been called a "compassionate satanist," but he has. As he said, "Instead of attacking innocent people, I prefer to use my powers and abilities to attack those who prey upon the innocent. So I'm still satisfying my need for tearing people up, being cruel and vicious, but I'm doing it to the people who are doing it to the innocent people."

When we finished the interview, we took photos on a stage on the boardwalk. Jonathon put on his cloak with its dragon motif and took the impaling stake out of its cardboard carrier, posing for us and looking appropriately evil. A few people noticed what we were doing, but left us alone. Photos done, Jonathon put his stake back in its box, took off the cloak, and made a final comment. "What is weirder [for President]? Me, or someone 'normal' who wants to destroy the world?" While we may not agree with all of "The Impaler's" agenda, it was something to think about later as we ate boardwalk pizza.

You can read Jonathon's thirteen-point agenda, as well as his current impaling list, on his campaign Web site: jonathontheimpalerforpresident2008.us.

Marta Becket—Death Valley Diva

The population of Death Valley Junction needs about seven more people to reach double digits, but eighty-four-year-old dancer-actress-musician-painter Marta Becket has conquered the naysayers and brought civilization to this very small desert community.

As the legend goes, in the spring of 1967 an already seasoned and jaded Marta, who'd been dancing since she was three, had tired of the grind of Broadway, Radio City, and the entire New York scene, so she and her husband at the time traveled out to California for a one-week camping vacation in the antidote to the Big Apple: Death Valley. On the morning their vacation was to come to an end, they awoke to find a flat tire on their rental car and were directed by the park ranger to the nearest gas station, thirty miles away. As the local mechanic took to repairing the problem, Marta used the opportunity to wander about.

Strolling around the lonely buildings in the middle of seemingly nowhere, she was stunned by the tallest structure on the strip. It was a theater. She pulled on the front door, only to discover it was locked, so she ran to the back and was able to peek inside.

It was obvious the stage hadn't been used for years. The floorboards were warped, the once colorful playhouse curtains had faded, and debris spotted the entire room, but in that instant, Marta Becket understood her fate. "Peering through the tiny hole," she says, "I had the distinct feeling that I was looking at the other half of myself. The building seemed to be saying. . . . Take me . . . do something with me. . . . I offer you life."

Immediately the Renaissance woman located the town manager and negotiated a $45-a-month rental contract, with the stipulation that she also assume responsibility for the repairs. Marta not only restored the dilapidated old theater, she ensured a sold-out show every night by taking the next six years to completely cover the bare walls and ceiling with a mural of an audience straight out of the sixteenth century.

Upon these fortifications kings and queens sit pleasantly beside hookers and gypsies. Toreadors dance with the bulls, and mystics from the Orient amuse and delight nearby monks and nuns. The paintings are truly impressive, reason enough alone to visit the Amargosa Opera House. But whether the crowd is human or gouache, Marta Becket still feels the pull of the spotlight, and she has kept to her twice a week schedule religiously since the curtain first came up over four decades ago. She creates her own costumes, choreographs her own dance moves, designs all of her own stage props, has written her own plays, and wouldn't have it any other way.

Now in the twilight of her years, Marta still moves with the grace of a woman who was born to walk the boards, and she is still slaying the critics. At a recent function in her honor, the ever spry performer mused, "I'm so grateful that after thirty-five years, I don't have to worry about a full house: It's just there. I only wish I were twenty years old again."

The Amargosa Opera House is located somewhere in Death Valley Junction, California. You can't miss it. It's the tallest structure on the strip.

Ted Williams—A Hero on Ice

Most scientists agree: Dying is the leading cause of death. So far, there is no known cure, but that doesn't mean we're not trying. If only we had more time. . . . Well, if you have enough liquid nitrogen, maybe you can preserve your parts until there IS a cure. At least that's what John Henry Williams was hoping for his dad, Ted.

In the annals of Red Sox history, few names are as revered as Ted Williams. It wasn't until 1939, at the age of twenty, that Williams went pro. The Boston Red Sox signed the young slugger and were immediately impressed. Under nicknames like "The Kid," "Splendid Splinter," and "Teddy Ballgame," he led the league in R.B.I.'s and had his name tossed around the MVP ballot. In 1941, on the last day of the baseball season Williams played in two double-header games, where the Splendid Splinter hit 6 out of 8 in the two games to raise his season average to .406. No player has matched that record since.

On September 28, 1960, Ted Williams was playing his final professional baseball game. The Sox were home at Fenway facing the Baltimore Orioles. Williams was at his very last at-bat in the eighth inning. Teddy Ballgame hit a home run for a storybook ending to a colorful career. In his final years, Williams suffered a series of strokes, congestive heart failure and, on July 5, 2002, died of cardiac arrest in his Crystal River, Florida home.

Ted was a legend, but somehow that wasn't enough for his son, John Henry Williams. Reportedly within hours of his death, the body of Ted Williams was shipped to the Alcor Life Extension Foundation in Scottsdale, Arizona, where the head was removed in a process

called "neuroseparation" surgery. Holes were drilled in the slugger's head in order to preserve the brain tissue and to implant sensors that could detect cracks in the head, which was then placed in cryonic suspension at a c-c-c-cold –196°C. The head resides in a metal can the size of a lobster pot while the rest of Williams's body sits in its own frozen suspension in a large cylinder in the same room. According to the FAQs section on Alcor's Web site, no human has ever yet been revived from cryonic freezing; the company is counting on that technology's existing in the future, perhaps in "a century or more."

What makes the story of Ted Williams's frozen head and body even worse is that apparently Ted may not have wanted to be frozen. In most cases, Alcor has a lengthy legal document signed by their clients while they're still of sound mind and body. In Ted's case, all that turned up was a scrap of paper that said he, his son, and his daughter wanted to be frozen so they could potentially live together in the future. There are more problems. Verducci reported that John Henry paid only $25,000 of the $136,000 bill that Alcor submitted ($120,000 for the procedure and $16,000 for transporting the body).

It's been said that John Henry was looking at the potential of selling his famous father's DNA, and others contend that Ted Williams's will stated that he was to be cremated. The financial matters between the Williams family and Alcor were eventually cleared up, and John Henry Williams died from leukemia in March 2004 at age thirty-five; his will stipulated that he was to join his frozen father in Scottsdale. Now the father-and-son team waits for science to figure out two big issues: How to thaw frozen people, and how to cure them of death.

A World of Their Own

When most people think about turning a house into a home, they hire contractors, make trips to Home Depot, and pore over paint samples until they find exactly the right shade to paint the walls. After taking a couple of trips to a garden center and setting up a schedule for tree trimming and lawn mowing, they're done.

These are not our kind of people. Our kind of people have bigger, grander, and much less conventional plans for their property. Instead of installing vinyl siding and double-glazed casement windows, they haul boulders around to build castle walls two feet thick. Forget about lawn jockeys and garden gnomes—they adorn their gardens with concrete reproductions of Mount Rushmore and tin sculptures welded to the tops of poles. And instead of having a durable welcome mat at a paneled front door, the entranceways to their houses are tunnels you have to crawl through.

You may not choose to live in a place like this yourself, but let's not deny it: Properties like these are great to visit. It's like entering a world that sprang straight from the imagination of its creator, without a visit to the typical lumberyards you and I go to for our picket fences. And that makes these places well worth a visit.

Eliphante

There is an alternate world in Cornville, Arizona, and the portal into it is a tunnel of driftwood arches. It opens onto a meadow full of sculptures made from flotsam, tree limbs, and discarded metal. Through a stucco and chicken wire cave, you are funneled into a man-size duct formed by what appear to be stiffened bedsheets.

Before you know it, you're crawling on your belly through near darkness, with only a small cherry-colored window to guide you. At the other end, you emerge into an isolation chamber, a very sparse and very calming room that offers only one way out: a squeeze-through doorway atop a five-foot ladder. Back in the sunlight, you suddenly recall what birth was like.

Welcome to Eliphante.

And that's only the beginning of this three-and-a-half-acre abstract universe. You still have Pipedreams, the Hipodome, Birdland, and myriad mixed-media sculptures ahead of you. It's a world that has to be experienced firsthand rather than merely seen. In fact, interaction is a requirement. It's as if all the pieces in a gallery fused with the walls, were devoured by the earth and the trees, continued to grow, and want you to be part of it. It's like being in a collaborative reality conceived by Lewis Carroll, Andy Goldsworthy, and Tim Burton after a few too many trips to the bar.

But it was Leda Livant and Michael Kahn who actually designed and built the place. And their landlord who came up with the name: The first improvised structure they built in 1979 developed a long, igloo-like entryway that resembled an elephant's trunk. The landlord jokingly hailed, "Eliphante!" and the name stuck.

Though Michael and Leda make their home in this grove of surrealism, they're surprisingly down-to-earth people. The average suburbanite might throw around the word hippy at first sight, but the term doesn't stick. True, not a corner of their environment escapes some kind of artistic alteration; but they do have a phone, they do use electricity, and they do run a business. They love to talk about their art and their visions, but not in a really esoteric and pretentious kind of way. Some of what they do may seem unconventional—like the fact that they've covered the entire ground outside with artificial turf—but they usually have a sensible motive. The plastic grass cuts down on mud and snakes, that's all. In short, they're practical people, just a little more lenient on where they draw the line at eccentricity.

Is Eliphante a sculpture park? A playground? A museum alfresco? You'll have to figure that out for yourself. To learn more and to schedule a visit, you can visit Michael and Leda's Web site at www.eliphante.org.

One Man's Castle

While traveling down State Highway 165 west of Colorado City, Colorado, motorists are often shocked to lay their eyes upon an ornate castle. It's the kind of building that belongs in the forests of Bavaria, not on a roadside in the American West. They are even more shocked to learn that this huge castle is the handiwork of one man, Mr. Jim Bishop.

Bishop Castle is the largest one-man construction project in the United States, and possibly in the entire world. It also proclaims itself as the place "where dreams happen!" Jim Bishop began building the castle in 1969 at the age of twenty-five, aiming only to build a one-room cottage

for himself and his new wife. But he has slowly added to the structure ever since. He can still be seen working there every weekend and for six weeks during the summer while he takes a vacation from his day job in the family ironworking shop. Whether it's adding new stained glass, touching up the tower or ballroom within the castle, or tinkering with the fire-breathing dragon perched eighty feet in the air atop the edifice, Bishop has consistently managed to find new features to add onto his creation. It now reaches a height of 160 feet.

Bishop has gathered most of his materials by collecting rocks from lands in the San Isabel National Forest, owned and operated by the National Forest Service. He has a permit with the government allowing him to gather as much rock as he can without the use of heavy machinery.

Perhaps the most miraculous thing about Bishop Castle is that for all these years of construction it has been open to the public and free for admission. Bishop does ask for donations, which go toward buying new supplies to augment the castle proper, as well as the adjoining grounds, gatehouse, and walls.

Even in his sixties, Jim Bishop hasn't slowed down the building process one bit. Battles with local government never stopped him, and it seems that at this point, nothing will. In fact, Bishop says that the day he stops working on his castle will be the day he dies. It appears that for the foreseeable future, Bishop Castle will continue to be the place where dreams happen.

Bishop Castle is open May through October seven days a week during daylight hours, and weekends from November through April. The easiest way to get there is from I-25. Take exit 74 at Colorado City and head toward the mountains (right off the exit ramp from the north and left off the exit ramp from the south). This puts you on Colorado state highway 165 and it's twenty-four miles without a turn to the castle.

Millennium Manor— the House That Faith Built

Some new homes come with a ten-year warranty from the builder. That wasn't nearly enough for a mason and carpenter named William Andrew Nicholson back in the 1940s. When he and his wife had finished their home in Alcoa, Tennessee, he confidently stated to an Associated Press reporter that "if nothing wrecks it, there is no reason why it shouldn't last a million years." And he confidently expected to live in it himself for at least a thousand of them.

It's easy to see why he was so confident. The two-story home is built like a small castle on an acre of land. The whole thing—walls and roof and floors alike—is built of rocks, cement, and Tennessee pink marble. The walls are two to three feet thick, and the arched windows are built like bridges with a keystone to keep them structurally solid. A massive feat of engineering, it was hand-built over the course of eight years entirely by Nicholson and his wife, who were in their sixties at the time. Nicholson built a wooden-framed house, covered it with a rubber tarp, and then he and his wife, Fair, hauled and placed 432 tons of stone and marble on top of it, and poured 4,000 bags of cement over the whole thing to seal the cracks. When it was completed in 1946, the interior wooden form was removed, and the house was finished.

To begin with, their castle attracted a lot of good attention. It was a haven for local children, who were allowed to play around the place (the couple had ten children of their own, who had grown and moved on).

But things changed after Fair Nicholson died of cancer in the early 1950s. The couple had been together since their teens, and when she was gone, the place began to acquire a darker reputation that was only heightened in 1957 when an Associated Press reporter ran a widely reprinted article on the house and its builder. Hal Boyle's article called the Nicholson place "the Millennium Manor" and "the house that faith built," and though he portrayed the eighty-year-old widower as a devout man and a dedicated husband, Nicholson also comes across as a bit odd. He criticized his wife for dying ("My wife believed in me, but her faith in eternal life was weak.") and stated that when the apocalypse came (which would probably happen in 1959), he would be among the select 144,000 who would survive it. Afterward, he would live in his house for a thousand years.

Around town after the article came out, unfair rumors circulated that he had worked his wife to death building his strange house. When Nicholson finally died in 1965, none of his ten children chose to come back to the house their parents built. It lay derelict for a while, except for a brief stint as a meeting place for the local chapter of the Odd Fellows. It even gained a new name when a photograph of it appeared on a 1978 Knoxville Grass album called *Darby's Castle*. The song (which was written in 1973 by Kris Kristofferson) had nothing to do with the place, but many people started calling it Darby's Castle from then on. It remained an empty curiosity for decades and was on the verge of being condemned and demolished in the mid-1990s, when a local firefighter named Dean Fontaine bought the place and began renovating it. Fontaine moved into a white kit house on the property that the Nicholsons lived in when they were building the castle. He's still there, restoring the place to its former glory—and for everybody's sake, we hope that it'll remain glorious for the next million years.

A Pleasantville Surprise

Nestled in a quiet neighborhood just outside Atlantic City, New Jersey, is an amazing architectural marvel dreamed up and created in an ever-evolving fashion by a gentleman named Mr. Wilberforce Sylvester. He has painted a mural that completely surrounds his home and depicts scenes that, according to him, "reflect passages of everyday life."

The mural includes renditions of local highways complete with a traffic stop and police issuing a ticket to a motorist, trains passing by, musicians, boxers, a bullfight, soldiers in desert conflicts, the sinking of the *Titanic*, and the incident when Steve Irwin held his baby while a hungry crocodile snapped its jaws below. Soon to come are more multidimensional renditions that will be "open to interpretation."

This meticulously decorated masterpiece in Pleasantville has been Mr. Sylvester's home for over thirty years.

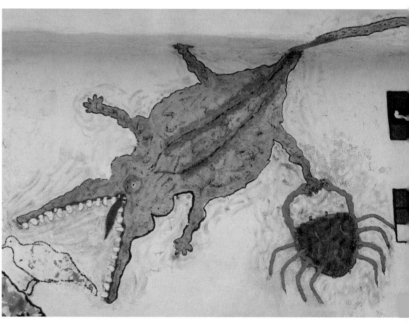

The home was much smaller when he first began to build upon it his textured designs, but he's added to the house over the years, and will not be running out of room for his designs soon. And as a union bricklayer for over three decades, he knows what he's doing. Working through improvisation, he etches and paints the cement as the ideas come to him. In addition to the murals, he's also created symmetrical arrangements of brickwork in brilliant colors that highlight and balance the structural components bordering each window and door, which in turn separate the murals.

He has also expanded his creation by sculpting a giraffe in the backyard on a smaller structure. And in keeping with the proximity of the property to the shore, he created a functional lighthouse in his driveway that serves as a beacon during the darker hours.

A handy artisan with a trowel, Mr. Sylvester is not planning on concluding his decorative efforts anytime soon. When he feels the time is right, he will use more bricks and pick which vision to "build and create."

In addition to his brilliant talent for painting scenes from real life, he also crafts melodies that are rather catchy, and I found myself humming one of them a few days after hearing it. His songs are about the local political scene in Atlantic City. He minces no words, and in a bluesy, island style of songwriting, gets the point across as in, "Let's Say a Prayer for Atlantic City."

Every once in a rare while, I meet someone who is a positive and impressive personality, and Mr. Sylvester is one of those people. Coming to New Jersey from his homeland in Jamaica, he has a gentle, easygoing style that was readily apparent as soon as I began to talk to him. Despite being quiet in person, he is outspoken with both his visual and musical work.

Mr. Sylvester is very proud of his work. People have come from several states away to see his amazing creations, and his art has been featured in several publications. As I sat and spoke with him, I was grateful to have been let into his private world to find out the story behind the man and his works. When you pull up a chair with someone like him, it is not a moment you will soon forget: a priceless moment with one of New Jersey's unique artisans.—*Wizard343*

Enoch Tanner Wickham's Strange Statuary

Most hardworking men in the last century retired in their sixties. Especially for those who lived through the Great Depression, it was generally accepted that a lifetime of hard work earns the right to relax during one's twilight years.

Enoch Tanner Wickham did not subscribe to this philosophy. When he reached sixty-nine years of age and moved from his tobacco farm to a log cabin on Buck Smith Road in Palmyra, Tennessee, it wasn't to relax. It was to begin a second life as a visionary sculptor.

E. T., as he was generally known, hand-sculpted over fifty cement statues between 1952 and his death in 1971. Each one took six long weeks to complete, and he did it all by hand, with only minor assistance from family members. Even the concrete bases upon which he placed his larger-than-life creations were hand-built Wickham originals. His statues generally depicted people he admired, including Andrew Jackson, a World War II soldier, Patrick Henry, and John F. Kennedy.

Before passing away, E. T. made sure that his legacy was set in stone—literally. He built a statue depicting himself riding a wild bull, dressed in a cowboy outfit, and brandishing a lasso. The bull was wired so that its eyes glowed red at night. And inscribed in the base of this statue is what seems to be a eulogy Wickham wrote for himself: E. T. WICKHAM, HEADED FOR THE WILD AND WOLEY WEST. REMEMBER ME BOYS WHEN I AM GONE.

The world has remembered Wickham, as his pieces still stand. Unfortunately, a combination of weather and vandalism has taken

its toll, and most of the statues have not fared well since Wickham's passing. Thankfully, some have been placed in local museums. Others have been moved to a more secure property nearby with fencing to keep vandals at bay. For more information on visiting Wickham's statues, see www.wickhamstonepark.com.

Sunnyslope Rock Garden

Ever dropped a dinner plate and cursed the process of scavenging for the pieces, which now seem good for nothing? If you have—and most of us have— you may have been overlooking a prime opportunity to create a magical piece of art. At least, Grover Cleveland Thompson would have seen it that way.

Thompson, an Oregon native who retired to Arizona, saw more in broken pottery than just a mess to be cleaned up. In fact, he saw more in rocks, old bottles, marbles, and refrigerator magnets than most of us do too. When he moved to the Sunnyslope section of Phoenix with his wife at age sixty-five, he took all these things and transformed them into Sunnyslope Rock Garden, a fantastical folk-art world. Of course, that's what we call it. Thompson just called it his front yard.

In a process that lasted more than twenty years, Thompson created more than a hundred structures and figures by recycling junkyard finds and breaking brightly colored Fiestaware into shards to be fashioned into mosaics. Gathering inspiration from Peterson's Rock Garden, a fixture near his childhood home in Bend, Oregon, as well as from places to which he had traveled, Thompson went about replicating Dutch windmills, Inca villages, and even the Seattle Space Needle (although his version was only nine feet tall!). Shrines, fountains, animal characters, human faces, and towers were spread over the three sections of his 60-by-250-foot property.

One might wonder why a mechanic without any artistic training spent so much time on such an imaginative postretirement hobby. When asked, he simply said, "Beauty continues the will to live."

It seems that Thompson, like many other creators of spectacular personalized properties, was just trying to make his little corner of the world a bit more beautiful. While he was alive, he encouraged visitors—especially children, whom he asked to bring trinkets that he might later put to use— to stop by and marvel at his garden. When he died in 1978, this cause was taken up by Marion Blake, who cared for the property from 1979 until recently. Sunnyslope Rock Garden is now closed to the public (though the outside can still be seen from the road). There has been some talk that the property might soon be managed by Arizona State University or perhaps the Kohler Foundation. However, at the time of this writing, the future of Grover Cleveland Thompson's masterwork is still uncertain.

Thompson's creative process was painstaking, so it's no wonder that it took him so long to fill up his entire garden. *Raw Vision* (issue 52), a magazine dedicated to outsider and contemporary folk art, describes the way in which Thompson created his fantasyland:

Working in a method called Pique Assiette (stolen from plates), Thompson formed armatures of salvaged metal, then applied concrete to produce the desired shapes. While the concrete was still wet, he pressed bits of pottery, shells, tile, glass, or brightly colored stones into the surface, creating a mosaic effect. Small structures and buildings were made of scavenged sheet metal covered with layers of small stones, glass, or tile bonded with polyester resin. In an interesting use of found objects, Thompson created anthropomorphic figures by filling children's Halloween masks with concrete. After the concrete cured, the mask was stripped away and the molded face was painted.

Florence's Rock Garden

When Florence Deeble's mother asked her daughter to fill in the fishpond in their backyard, she could hardly have imagined the results. The old lady's fear that children might fall into the water led to a rock garden whose fame has spread beyond Lucas, Kansas, and across the nation.

Miss Deeble showed an early fascination with concrete sculptures, but displayed no signs of creating anything herself until she started pouring the concrete into the pond—and kept going. Before long, the fifty-year-old woman's concrete creations included stone-inlaid bridges, columns, and towers, altars, and cactus plants. In the first five decades of her life she had traveled to garden showcases—including Utah's Capitol Reef National Park and Lucas Lake—and she incorporated

rocks she had brought home from her travels. The garden's centerpiece is definitely a reproduction of Mount Rushmore with all four of the original's Presidents peeking out of a sheer face of concrete (with Roosevelt looking out through twisted-wire spectacles).

Florence continued to work on her garden for the last half of her life, almost fifty years, until her death at the age of ninety-nine in 1999. Her home on Fairview Avenue in Lucas is now open to the public as part of the town's Grassroots Art Center tour, and makes a great side trip from a visit to nearby Dinsmoor's Garden of Eden, another rock masterpiece. Check them both out together.

Magic Garden of Philly's South Street

Philadelphia is home to hundreds of house-size urban murals, thanks to a long-standing civic movement called the Mural Arts Project. Originally welcomed because it stemmed the creeping blight of graffiti in the 1980s, the Mural Arts Project has turned many once bleak brick walls into colorful representations of hope and nature. And local heroes are also celebrated. Whether it's Mario Lanza (who was born here) or Frank Sinatra (who wasn't), Philadelphia has found a wall to cover with his image.

But even in this profusion of colorful walls, one property really stands out. On South Street a few blocks over from Broad Street, you can find walls covered with tons of mirrors, ceramics, statues, bottles, bicycle wheels, and colored grout. The mosaics stretch to cover entire three-story houses between South and Kater streets, and surround a house-size lot that's filled with odd statuary, a tiled floor, and all kinds of junk held together with cement. It's called the Magic Garden, and it's the vision of one tireless artist named Isaiah Zagar, who has lived and worked in the neighborhood since the 1960s.

It doesn't take much effort to appreciate the Magic Garden. It's huge and impressive in its scope, but if you turn your attention to any given square yard, you're rewarded with an absorbing level of detail. You could be staring at a statue of a man with three right arms (and wondering what on earth it means), looking at a cartoon painted on a tile, or puzzling over what a broken piece of Mexican ceramic art used to be. You might be reading a piece of poetry or taking in Zagar's slogan, repeated often enough in his work to qualify as a mantra: "Art is the center of the real world." Some of the elements in the garden look like slapped-together outsider art, but the scope and scale of the thing look like the work of a professional. And the steady stream of people who file past daily, snapping pictures through the locked gates or up the enormous walls, often have no idea of what's behind this spectacle.

But if you happen by at just the right time, you may catch sight of a gray-bearded man with a puckish smile and messy clothes who can explain what it's all about. And if you look as though you're really appreciating it, that's exactly what Isaiah Zagar will do. If he's not in the middle of a project (which is rare), or if he feels like taking a break, he may step out of his studio and welcome strangers into his house just down the street. He draws people into his cellar, which is covered from floor to ceiling in the same mosaic style, and

describes his work. He'll show his paintings and those of his friends. He'll describe the ceramic works by other people, which were broken in transit on the way to his wife's gallery, that he incorporates into his work. He may mention his time in the Peace Corps in Peru and describe how he moved to South Street on his return, when it was a run-down slum about to be cut off from Philadelphia's civic center by a bypass. He may describe how the community banded together to stop the plan, but he will usually stop short of saying what most people say about his part in that movement, namely that he's largely responsible for reviving what was once a run-down rat hole of a street and making it the cool place it is today.

Not everyone is a fan of Zagar's work. In early 2004, the owner of the Magic Garden lot, an absentee landlord in Boston who had turned a blind eye while it was just a rat-infested dump, gave Zagar notice to clear the lot for sale. The holding company that held the title to the lot, GS Realty Trust, intended to sell the gap between two buildings for $300,000, a price the newly gentrified South Street market could probably bear.

Zagar and others mounted a legal and fund-raising campaign to save the garden. Using a collection bucket at the site, they raised several thousand dollars. Fund-raising events and "Save the Garden" specials at Zagarís Web site (www.isaiahzagar.com) raised some more. But it wasn't until Zagar formed a nonprofit organization called Philadelphia's Magic Garden and secured a promise of $100,000 from an anonymous donor that the Magic Garden was saved from a bulldozer.

Zagar still needs to pay a hefty mortgage on the lot, however, so heís opened it to the public for a small admission fee and sells photographs and bits of his art in the foyer. We suggest you get over to the garden and drop a few bucks in the collection bucket because this is one of the few times in which fans of the weird can make a concrete contribution to keep the weird alive. Go ahead. Be part of the magic.

Somewhere Over the Rainbow

Somewhere Over the Rainbow in Phoenix, Arizona, has everything under the sun. To its creator and curator, Gus Brethauer, there's nothing that isn't worth saving. He's got rocks of every kind, some on prominent display, some in piles. He's got artifacts salvaged from ill-fated buildings. He has what he claims to be the world's largest collection of petrified wood. There are also dinosaurs, UFOs, tuberculosis shacks, and hieroglyphs. And it's all lined up for thorough perusal.

Basically, it's a theme park without a theme. It's the manifestation of Gus's knowledge, interests, and imagination, coarsely blended and sunbaked for half a century. A tour of it all, afforded by a disorienting pathway half a mile long, can take as much as two hours. And mother, if every yard isn't mind-bogglingly fascinating! As the sign says, the exhibit stands "without equal or parallel on the face of the earth."

"I suffer illusions," Gus begins his tour, "all kind of illusions and fantasies here. I'm under the impression that I'm a maintenance man at a flying-saucer rest stop. And the stonework—the stonework is awesome." It's part of the patter he's repeated countless times along this path, a routine that mixes history, science, and hallucination to the point that you can never be sure if he's being genuine or if he's putting you on. But it reflects the nature of the exhibit. In one spot, you learn about Phoenix's long-gone underground sidewalks and the rarity of the crested saguaro, then just around the corner you're introduced to Art, one of two resident aliens on hand to serve as your "psychological" guides.

In all honesty, it's impossible to quantify what Gus has assembled here. What should a person make of the Temple of Doom and the triceratops who dwells inside? The alley of claustrophobia and radiators, the solar system in reverse, or the haunted house centered around a killer pack rat? The occasional sign attempts to interject some sort of guidance, but the words they offer rarely help: "Classic Castle: A Popular Floor Plan." "Fake Rattle Snake Hole." "Herbs Make Good Sense."

Sometimes it's a well-orchestrated museum; other times it's a scattered junkyard. Every item, though, no matter how useless it looks, has a history that Gus could recount if you asked. Everything that's here is here on purpose. The historian-showman has spent decades expanding and developing his world of wonders, bit by deliberate bit. "In fifty years," Gus loves to say, "you'd be surprised what you can do."

Still, he could use more time. Gus states apologetically that, even now, Somewhere Over the Rainbow is simply a "gathering," that nothing is yet as he envisions it. One wonders what treasures are hidden in the piles he has yet to organize. He's still working on things, but unfortunately Gus has slowed down a bit these days. For the most part, he is now discouraging visitors. Perhaps if the world proves its worth, someone with as large a vision as Gus has will step in and take up the slack.

Chief Rolling Mountain Thunder's Monument

Speeding east on Interstate 80 in Nevada one day, we caught a glimpse of something so odd that it was enough to make us do two U-turns to get back to see what we had missed. Curious travelers who pull off the highway, as we did that day, will find themselves wandering a deserted area filled with houses and shacks made of all manner of salvage, plus statues of Indians and others, screeds criticizing the U.S. government and its treatment of Native Americans, and some piles of plain old junk. You can't help but wonder who built it and why.

Thunder Mountain Monument is the creation of a man who was born under the name Frank Van Zant on "the 11th day of the 11th month" of 1921 in Okmulgee, Oklahoma. When he transformed himself into Chief Rolling Mountain Thunder, he also changed his birth year to ten years earlier; apparently he wanted to keep those elevens up.

Van Zant was a man who loved telling stories, and often the fiction blended with the fact. One thing is certain, though. Even before he became Chief Thunder, he was a multitalented man capable of reinventing himself. He had joined the military in World War II and claimed to have been injured when "a German bazooka" hit a tank he was in. Later in life, he would fight an unsuccessful battle with the U.S. government for veteran's compensation.

After the war, he studied to become a Methodist minister, but decided it was not for him. He moved to Yuba City, California, and went into law enforcement. He ran for sheriff and coroner and was a private investigator. In the fall of 1968, after a divorce, he took his ex-stepchild and new wife on a trip across Nevada. For some reason they stopped, and stayed, at a desolate site just east of the Imlay exit on I-80.

The most commonly told version of the story is that their 1946 pickup truck broke down or became stranded there. They spent the night and built a makeshift shelter. Legend has it that Van Zant's car wouldn't let him leave. When he got it out on the road it started running worse; then he turned it back around and it started running better. "I was just going to drive away and leave it. Only I couldn't get away. I got forced back with a full load, and there was a car sittin' there on the prairie. It was the guy who owned the property. And he offered me such terms

that I couldn't turn it down," Van Zant-Chief Thunder told a reporter in 1975.

However it was he came to stay there, it does seem to be true that from 1968 on, Thunder didn't leave the spot for the rest of his life. He built a unique environment in which to spend his days. Everything used in its construction came from junk that was found lying around. The materials included stones from the area as well as typewriters, car parts, farm equipment, bottles, TVs, windshields, and just about anything else. The only time Thunder left was to get bags of cement to hold it all together.

The first building was constructed around a travel trailer, which slowly became a concrete and bric-a-brac igloo. He added two stories to it and started working on other buildings. A roundhouse, a storage shed, a hostel house, and an underground room and guest cabin joined the budding village.

Somewhere along the way, Van Zant had become Chief Rolling Mountain Thunder. Like everything in his life, he told different versions of how it happened. He claimed to be at least a quarter Oklahoma Creek Indian, although some have disputed that he had any native blood at all. At one point, he claimed that he had visions of Thunder Mountain as early as 1947, when the Great Spirit entered his head and said, "The Big Eagle will return to his nest," and transformed him into an eagle, flying over desert mountains. Sometimes he told people that an old medicine woman had told him that "in the final days, there shall rise a place called Thunder Mountain," and that only the people who lived there would survive the coming end-times.

When he moved in, sometime in 1968, he totally transformed himself into an Indian shaman persona. In the beginning, he attracted nomadic hippie types, who might pull off the road and stay for months. They would help with the construction of buildings and sculptures. Thunder Mountain had become a hippy commune. Thunder raised his family on the grounds, giving his offspring the Indian-style names Obsidian Lightning Thunder, Thunder Mountain Thunder, True Brave Eagle Thunder. (To make matters more confusing, there was another Rolling Thunder in northern Nevada at the time. This Rolling Thunder, also know as John Pope, was a Cherokee medicine man who had a commune in Carlin.)

The years rolled on, and things changed at Thunder Mountain. The hippies faded away. Van Zant's wife left him, taking the children with her. Some of the houses had burned or collapsed. For these, and reasons known only to himself, in early January 1989, Chief Rolling Mountain Thunder committed suicide in the roundhouse, using a gun to send himself to the spirit world.

After his death, the encampment fell into further disrepair, with curious travelers, and some vandals, still pulling over for a look—and perhaps a souvenir. In his suicide note, Chief Thunder willed the property to Daniel Van Zant, his son from his first marriage. Daniel got the place fixed up a bit and attracted the interest of the state of Nevada in preserving it. Eventually, it was declared a State Historic Site and a National Monument. In the 1990s, there was a caretaker who lived on the grounds and maintained a gift shop. Groups could get guided tours, and people donated money to keep the place running.

These days there is no one there, and many of the buildings are fenced off, but it is still viewable and still a very weird place. There are statues of Indian icons like Sitting Bull and Sarah

Winnemucca, but also odder sculptures—like one devoted to Lyman Gilmore, an aviation pioneer who made the dubious claim that he had beat the Wright brothers at heavier-than-air flight. Perhaps Thunder identified with Gilmore's outsider personality, or maybe it reminded him of that time he turned into an eagle and flew to his desolate destiny in the middle of the rolling mountains of Nevada.

Too Liggett to Quit

You can't expect a retired military man who grew up in a sharecropping family to keep his opinions to himself. But even among his peers, M. T. Liggett comes across as a bit of a curmudgeon. And he's chosen a very striking way to get his outspoken opinions across. As you drive west from Mullinville, Kansas, along Highway 54 and Route 400 toward Dodge City, you can hardly fail to get the message. You'll see a forest of metal sprouting up along a half-mile stretch of roadside next to Liggett's farm, and you'll hardly believe your eyes.

Welded to the top of an iron pole stands a cartoon rendered in sheet metal. It portrays an angry-looking man running toward the

right, his body made out of a swastika, clutching a Soviet hammer and sickle in one hand. Beneath it is the caption HILLARY CLINTON, SIEG HEIL, OUR JACK-BOOTED EVA BRAUN. On the pole next to it is an iron-clad knight with a swastika on his helmet labeled RENO, QUEEN OF WACO. And just to prove he's an equal-opportunity critic, another cartoon is labeled DUBYA—BRING BACK SLICK WILLIE.

These are just three examples out of literally hundreds of sculptures M. T. has put up since he retired from the air force in 1989. And he shows no signs of slowing up. He sets seventeen-foot poles into the ground and welds any scrap bits of metal he can find onto them. Not all of them are metal cartoon heads, either. Sometimes he sticks old

plowshares on the poles, or other bits of farm equipment that his neighbors donate to the cause.

And just in case you feel like dismissing M. T. as a crotchety old man, let us set your mind at rest. Not all of his sculptures come with heavy-handed political commentary. Some of them are more personal comments that only the locals—or perhaps only M. T. himself—could understand. We don't know who Skaggs and Cliff Bone might be, but the cartoon of the angry cow with a human body is fun to look at anyway. And some of the sculptures don't seem to be attacking anyone. They're just sitting on top of metal cart wheels and other ersatz fence material around the Liggett property, looking as though they fell on Kansas out of the Beatles cartoon movie *Yellow Submarine*. And frankly, that's good enough for us.

Tiny Town of the Bone Zone

Outside the small town of Madrid, New Mexico (once a coal mining town, then a ghost town, then revitalized as an art colony), we spied a dilapidated trailer with a lot of weird junk in the front yard. This funky, not-so-mobile home sits alongside Route 14 and is surrounded by the most eclectic collection of junk we've ever seen . . . miniature buildings, bird cages, iron bedsteads, farm implements, bicycles, baskets, old appliances. . . . You can't be sure if it's a weird antiques place or just someone's idea of lawn decor.

Well, not long ago, we found out what it is: the Bone Zone! In a recent issue of the local paper, there was a feature article that explained it all. Evidently a woman known as Tattoo Tammy (for obvious reasons) is the folk-art genius behind this odd display. Originally from Arizona, she moved to New Mexico and settled down in the artist town of Madrid. She had a talent for creating folk art out of old scraps of junk, and her favorite medium to work with? Bones!

A friend donated an old trailer for her to live in, and she began work on her extensive masterpiece, Tiny Town. At the time we first saw it, she had only begun some of the buildings and was in the process of collecting the necessary junk to continue. She had one of her most famous pieces, the Boney Rider motorcycle perched atop the roof of her trailer. She has since greatly expanded her scrap kingdom.

Welcome to Tiny Town!

As you enter Tiny Town, you can see it is a collection of broken bits of furniture, scrap metal, and bits of junk put together to loosely resemble buildings, some more successfully than others. After seeing a newspaper article, I decided to revisit the expanded site and take a few more photos. Tammy herself came out and took me on a tour of her domain. The building to the left is the saloon, then comes a converted potbellied stove for the jail, and next door is the brothel.

Many of the buildings are "furnished" and even have "residents," such as the G.I. Joe visiting the lovely Barbie in the brothel. Tammy has put down Astroturf walkways with holes cut out so the whole town doubles as a mini golf putting course. She keeps a supply of bent golf clubs and beat-up golf balls on hand for visitors to her attraction. She has also created a bowling alley with glass bottles as pins. She loves the sound of breaking glass and uses the shards in her artwork as well.

One of the more recognizable and best-done buildings is the church. To the left is a smaller building she hasn't figured out a use for yet and next to that is the Wells Fargo Bank. Another building to the left of that is the Better Bones and Gardens shop. She likes puns using the word bone in them, as bones are her favorite art medium. "Nature's pearly little jewels" is what she calls them.

Across the way from the church in the central town square is the gallows, which Tammy refers to as the "entertainment center." There is also a mini working guillotine nearby.

Tammy's latest creation is the mansion, which is made from corrugated metal sheeting, an upturned cut-glass bowl for the central window's awning, and assorted bits of metal trim. It's really quite nicely done, and I asked her to pose for me by it.

Some of Tammy's work, including her buildings and the Boney Rider sculpture, has been on display at the American Visionary Art Museum in Baltimore, an institution that specializes in folk art and the bizarre. Tammy plans to keep on working on her Tiny Town and continues to collect unwanted junk from locals with which to build. "If it ain't busted, rusted, or dead, I can't work with it!" she laughingly told me.

Tammy is a real character and she loves to talk to visitors about her creations. She has a guest book for all to sign and leave their comments, as well as a "Bonations" box for any cash they might want to contribute. It was quite a visit and I plan to keep an eye out for further developments. I guess she's creating her own scrappy version of Tinkertown.
—*Debora L. Carr, Albu-Quirky*

Leading Lights of the Albany Bulb

The San Francisco Bay Area has a history of doing interesting things with trash dumps. In the 1960s, a litter-filled vacant lot in Berkeley became the People's Park. In the 1980s, a city dump in Mountain View became the Shoreline Amphitheater. And more recently, a mile-long spit of overgrown landfill on the shores of the East Bay has become an anarchic art zone called the Albany Bulb.

In the counterculture tradition of the Bay Area, the Albany Bulb put down its artistic roots without any permission from "The Man." By the early 1970s, its trash was loosely covered with dirt and it had begun to grow vegetation. Then it began to attract visitors, drawn by its splendid isolation and fantastic view of the Pacific through the Golden Gate Bridge. It's an urban hiker's and dog-walker's paradise, but it also attracted a motley assortment of freewheeling creative types who found the dump to be a rich mine of materials for creative self-expression. Here, trash dug out of the landfill becomes the canvas for all kinds of outsider art. Psychedelic

art adorns planks of rotten wood, and sculptures of mangled metal lie everywhere. Well-known artists Osha Neumann and Jason De Antonis have created huge driftwood sculptures on the Bulb's north side. There's an amphitheater dug out of the landfill, surrounded by a wall of concrete, sheet metal, and compacted trash, surrounding a concrete plinth topped with a welded sculpture of the tragic Greek hero Icarus. And here and there you'll see shacks made of sheets of old wood panels, daubed with paintings by a group of Oakland artists called Sniff, who used to come up here almost every Saturday for a painting party.

At the southwestern tip of the landfill, a plaque hangs on a rough-and-ready two-story castle, announcing to the

Bay: TO CALIFORNIA, HEART OF GOLD, LIVE UP TO IT, LET GOOD TIME ROLL.

The creator of this particular message, a man universally known as Mad Mark, actually lives behind the parapets of the castle, safe behind walls of old concrete and broken shopping carts. He's not very welcoming if you don't know him—which makes sense when you reflect that he built his own castle—but he clearly believes that this area reflects what's best about California, its heart of gold.

But although the Bulb has been allowed to grow without interference from The Man, that won't be going on for much longer. In the late 1990s, some counterculture types, squeezed out of legitimate housing by the dot-com boom, squatted on the site, which drew the attention of the authorities. Many of them were ousted in 1999, and since then, a noble plan to make a public park along the Bay's eastern shore threatens to consume this haven of outsiders and turn it into a more sanitized form of public place. Just in case The Man wins out, we suggest you get on over to the Albany Bulb with all haste. The Weird may be wearing off soon.

Missile Silo House

"*My name* is Edward Peden, and I live in a decommissioned missile base."

This is how Ed greeted us as we entered his home in Dover, Kansas. At first glance, it's obvious that Ed is no warmonger. His long haircut and personal style speak to a more relaxed attitude in life. And yet he lives in the cold war—and when we say in, we mean it literally!

Ed isn't looking to cling to a life of military aggression by living in a missile base. Instead, he's converted what was once a piece of the military-industrial complex into one of the nicest homes in America. He purchased the thirty-seven-acre Atlas E Missile Base of Dover in 1982, and spent the next twelve years converting its silo into 6,000 square feet of luxury living space for his family. One of the first places we stopped on Ed's tour of the premises was his garage. The average American garage is approximately 400 square feet. Ed's is nearly 3,000.

"There was an Atlas missile here," he told us. "Every home should have one, right? This forty-seven-ton door would open and they could back a large semi truck in here with a missile, and then the missile that was lying horizontal here would be drawn upward, erected, and then it would be fueled, ready for launch."

The missile that was once housed in Ed's garage was over seven stories tall and ten times as powerful as the atomic bombs dropped on Japan.

"The taxpayers spent twenty-five million dollars here," Ed told us, about the cost to the government of building his eventual home. "And twenty-five million dollars in 1960 dollars is a little different than we think of today. I bought the thing for forty thousand."

Now that's buying at the right time!

Ed continued his tour. "There's probably ten, fifteen feet of earth over us here," he said as we entered another room. "So we're really in the ground. This was the launch control room. It's now our living room. We pretend to have windows."

Ed continued, although he became less lighthearted as he spoke of his living room being the former site of a room that could have literally triggered Armageddon. "This was a very serious room. There were three air force personnel in this room around the clock, twenty-four/seven, for the four years the site was active. And these people were prepared

and capable of launching that rocket to go halfway around the earth and kill a million people."

Ed paused. "So, the energy of this room is pretty serious."

There are many differences between silo living and regular life. "We take the garbage up, and we mow the roof," Ed joked. But there are also more serious variables one must take into account before moving into a giant bunker. "Down here we are managing the air. We have a large dehumidification system that air-conditions and filters the air and does a very nice job of air quality down here."

There are issues with the water, as well. "There are some chemicals in the groundwater around the property. The U.S. government is taking complete responsibility for that and doing some remediation." He paused, and then smiled. "It's still costing them money."

Ed Peden's success at living in the silo has led to him co-founding the Web site www.missilebases.com. Here he sells similar properties throughout the country. So if you're looking to excavate, remodel, and eventually live in a subterranean remnant of our nuclear past, Ed can help.

At the end of the day, while it's quite strange, Ed's missile base is a perfect place to raise a family. It's huge, spread out, and most of all, safe. Even in an environmentally volatile area of the country such as Kansas.

"This was rated to withstand a single megaton airburst about a mile from the structure," Ed told us. "We don't feel very worried about tornadoes."

Roadside Distractions

The great American highway has been the focus of many a novel, movie, and daydream. That open expanse of road leads to a future that nobody can predict, but it may just carry you to the greatest adventure you ever had. For us here at *Weird U.S.*, it's not the highway itself that counts; it's not even the destination. Instead, our focus is on the stuff by the side of the road that makes you apply the brakes, pull over, and exclaim, "What in the world is THAT?"

The continent is littered with eye-catching oddness in all shapes and forms. In fact, there's simply too much of it to chronicle completely in one chapter. There are enough fiberglass giants alone to fill several books. (But don't worry—we've included one place that has five of them in one front yard, just to give you a taste.)

So instead of being all-inclusive, we've touched on the cream of the crop. Here you'll find a sixty-foot-high bull's head and a whale at a roadside pond. You'll see replicas of Stonehenge made out of all kinds of unlikely materials. You'll wonder at the strange trees that have more shoes on their branches than leaves. And you'll visit places where the laws of physics have been revoked.

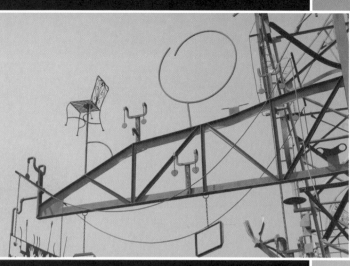

Creative Constructions

When homeowners think of decorating their front yards, they usually go no further than a fancy mailbox and lawn jockey or two. And even in the most liberal townships, the same goes for art in public places. Oh, people certainly cut loose a bit more at Halloween and other holidays, but for most of the year, most roadside sights are largely predictable.

That's not how things are in the weird world, though. When people with the Weird Eye start construction projects, the going gets REALLY strange. If you need proof, look no farther than the next few pages. We've got your proof right here.

The Mindfield

Billy Tripp doesn't concern himself with other people's opinions much, and, truth is, he doesn't get around enough to really hear them. He spends most of his time dozens of feet in the air. When we pulled up to his property in downtown Brownsville, Tennessee, Billy was dangling at the end of an extension ladder, suspended from the top of a ten-story water tower. He was painting the shaft in stripes, covering as much as he could reach before scrambling back up, repositioning, and starting again.

So it goes, day to day, as he steadily expands his life's work, a vast steel structure he calls the Mindfield. This scrap metal cathedral of industrial art towers eighty feet high and covers about an acre. In its battleship gray livery, it's often mistaken for a power substation, but the Mindfield is much more personal, a testament to Billy and his family. The names of his parents and brothers are fashioned into the main structure, along with words and symbols that commemorate events from Billy's own past. A succession of handprints that reach toward heaven honor his late father, a minister. A heart pays remembrance to his mother. And we can only guess what significance the bathtub, giant footprint, and skull and crossbones hold in Billy Tripp's personal narrative. But he did explain where the latest additions to the

Mindfield came from: He found the tower by an abandoned lamp factory while on vacation in Kentucky. He calls the watersphere Deena after the daughter of the man who owned it before him.

The Mindfield is in a prime location for attracting public criticism—it stands just three blocks from the county courthouse—but it is widely supported, even by local officials. When a building inspector tacked a violation letter to the structure, the planning board enthusiastically declared the construction site a work of art, immune to regular zoning regulations, and dismissed the notice. When Billy explained that the Mindfield is a conversation with himself about his life, the board's official response was, "Ramble on."

The board's ruling had an artistic as well as a practical result. It allowed the Mindfield to stay in its powerfully symbolic location—between a motel and a drainage ditch. As Billy explains it, our residency in this life is only temporary and then we wash away like the water and dirt we're made of. It's a sentiment that will take on even more meaning in the years to come, as Billy has chosen the site as his final resting place. In death, he'll reside amid the story of his life, buried at the foot of the tallest beam, the Mindfield serving as both his private cemetery and headstone. The mayor himself signed the permit.

Porter Sculpture Park

It's hard to miss the Porter Sculpture Park along I-90 in Montrose, South Dakota. Where else can you find a bright red, sixty-foot-tall bull's head and fifty other metal sculptures? Once you enter the place, you realize that this is very much a family affair. The sculptor himself, a self-taught artist and expert welder named Wayne Porter, often guides tours. If he isn't around, his parents heed the call. Often Wayne's mother will escort you partway around the site, at which point, Wayne will emerge from one of his latest pieces to finish up the tour. Wayne's brother Ron also helps run the place.

Wayne Porter's work is diverse, but he loves to depict animals. A series of goldfish seem to be fleeing the huge bull's head, and dinosaur skeletons stand around mounted in attack positions. A butterfly sits on a giant steel hand. And among the other oddball works on display is a hand sprouting from a head with a scowling silver face.

Visitors are invited to walk around inside his most famous creation, the bull's head, which, like many of his pieces, contains other sculptures hidden within. This makes the park a dynamic place to visit. Along with hidden treasure troves of sculpture and the

chance to meet the artist himself, this park offers the visitor plenty of surprises.

The Porter Sculpture Park is open from Memorial Day through Labor Day, rain or shine, from eight in the morning until six at night. Kids under the age of twelve are admitted free. There is a $4 charge for teenagers and a $6 charge for adults. If you'd like to visit, just head down I-90. You can't miss it — it's the one with the giant metal bull's head.

Musica: Busts of Bronze

In 1999, private art patrons raised $1.1 million and commissioned sculptor Alan LeQuire to conceive and construct a work to stand as the new icon for Nashville, Tennessee. It would be placed at the entrance to Music Row, the center of the South's music industry, and was intended to embody the city's deep-rooted musical heritage. And what better way to exemplify the widely recognized heart of both country and Christian music than with giant naked hippies?

Conceived as a fountain that was to be known as the *Spirit of Music,* the work was originally intended to feature semi-clad figures frolicking amid sprays of water. But somewhere along the line, the water was scrapped and so were the clothes. The end result, unveiled in 2003, was *Musica,* a statue comprising nine larger-than-life nudes springing forth from limestone boulders like a volcanic eruption of undress.

Conservative Nashville was shocked. While the sculpture did have its supporters, a large number of people reacted with disdain. They called it lewd and inappropriate, and feared that the work made it too easy for the city's children to get an eyeful.

In typically amusing retrospect, a 1999 newspaper article quotes the chairwoman for the Metro Nashville Arts Council predicting that the attraction would become a place "where every visitor will want his or her picture taken." Instead, citizens quickly labeled it "the nekkid statue" and accused it of violating obscenity laws.

A local Baptist pastor publicly complained, saying it was hypocritical of our nation to allow the display of naked statues on a public land while copies of the Ten Commandments are prohibited.

In a letter to the editor of Nashville's newspaper *The Tennessean* one man rejected the relevance of *Musica*'s "effeminate males with Neanderthal heads" and insisted that government would probably have less of a problem with displays of the Ten Commandments if they included "a totally nude Moses holding them while looking longingly at a nude Aaron."

"[*Musica*] isn't about music. . . . I cannot recall one instance of people celebrating the sounds of music AND displaying their most private parts at the same time," commented one detractor, apparently oblivious to Woodstock. He added, "Did this design come from the Sodom and Gomorrah scrapbook?"

The sculpture also inspired a parody song that swiftly made its way onto local radio stations and the Internet. The chorus goes:

> *And they're dancin' in circles and*
> *   flittin' around.*
> *The women look chilly, the men sure*
> *   look proud.*
> *If it makes you think dirty, go ahead,*
> *   honk your horn.*
> *Oh, the mayor done bought us some*
> *   hillbilly porn.*

In the critics' defense, the only obvious correlation to music is the statue's lone, golden tambourine. According to the work's creator, however, *Musica* isn't about a single, narrow view of music. The figures are meant to represent the nine Greek muses, the inspirational spirits of the arts, as well as the city's cultural diversity, signified by the figures' varied ethnicities. As for the full frontal nudity, he remarks, the genitalia "don't really grab your attention."

The Awakening

For the past three decades, Washington, D. C., has been under attack—not by a foreign power, but by a mysterious giant emerging from the very core of the earth. Directly across the Potomac River from Ronald Reagan National Airport the bearded face of a screaming giant breaks through the earth. One of his arms and one of his legs barely break the surface, but his right arm extends a full seventeen feet into the air.

The invading creature is actually a series of five statues called *The Awakening,* created by sculptor J. Seward Johnson in 1980. But suddenly, after its slow and rather unsuccessful twenty-eight-year-long attempt to break out of the earth, *The Awakening* may be moving to Maryland. The sculptor himself has final say over this move, which was announced in 2007, but we're in favor of keeping it where it is. D. C. has many a monument, for sure. The Lincoln Memorial may evoke the most civic pride. The Vietnam Memorial may be the most solemn. And the Washington Monument may be the most majestic. But we like *The Awakening* best, because it is, hands down and by a very wide margin, the weirdest piece of public art in the District.

Update! It was reported in the *Washington Post* in February 2008 that the National Park Service would be moving *The Awakening* from its home for the past twenty-eight years in East Potomac Park, in Hains Point, to Prince Georges County, Maryland. *The Awakening* had been on loan to the Park Service, but the owner, California-based Sculpture Foundation, sold the piece (or more accurately, five pieces) to the developer of the National Harbor project in Prince Georges County.

Monument to Strong Women

She's known formally as *The Winds of Change,* but most people just call her *The Lady*. She is twenty-one feet of glistening metal, standing against an imaginary wind in homage to the strength of woman.

For more than twenty years, she's been in Jeffersonville, Indiana, although her history and her meaning have been almost entirely forgotten even by those who work near her every day. Admittedly, she wasn't granted the best location, deep within an industrial area situated between a railroad line and a shipping-pallet manufacturer, both just across the road from a sewage-treatment plant. But she remains protected and admired, even if no one here knows where she came from.

As it turns out, *The Lady* was built by a metal-working business that previously occupied the site along Champion Road. The owner, Larry Myers, wanted to find a way to honor the women who worked for him. "At the time I employed many women and was inspired by how they balanced work and family," he was quoted as saying in 2003. "I wanted the sculpture to represent the strength I saw in women." So Myers hired Denise Freville, a high school student and the daughter of one of his employees, to design the sculpture. He paid her $5 an hour. Others from the firm volunteered after work to help put it all together—a group of hard-nosed metal workers welding a tribute to womanhood.

The finished piece, which is oddly reminiscent of a Tim Burton claymation character, was joined by another work, a more straightforward installation featuring a giant scale. On one side is a boulder labeled LOVE, on the other a boulder labeled EVERYTHING ELSE.

The final touch, carved into a fading wooden plaque and beautifully misspelled, is a poem written by those who helped build it all:

I am your mother
yet
I am
standing into the "winds of change."
Expected to be strong
yet gentle.
Expected to be better
then good.
Yet not reflect
that I know
I am good.
The winds force me
to change.
Yet I do not want
to be anymore than I am.
A woman - - - your mother.
Take my hand.
We will stand together
into the "winds of change."
The Lady

Unger, Land of the Giants

Most people who buy collectibles on-line limit themselves to Department 56 miniature villages or Hummel figurines. Pam and George Farnham see things on a different scale. They collect twenty-foot-tall fiberglass people and fairground rides and set them up in front of their farm near Unger, West Virginia. From the street, it's impossible to miss their two enormous Santas (who spread good cheer year-round), Big John the grocery bag boy, a lantern-jawed Muffler Man, and a twenty-six-foot-tall beach bum with his California smile, cool shades, and can of cola.

The Farnhams' farm is one big valentine to lovers of roadside oddities and fun fairs. It's dotted with novelty trash cans from closed-down theme parks, fiberglass replicas of cartoon characters, and vintage signs. Even the name of their alpaca farm—Fantasy Farm—was taken straight from a theme park sign they bought at auction a few years ago. And in a country where zoning regulations make it hard to add anything out of the ordinary to your property, they neatly sidestep the issue—"The muffler man and twenty-foot Santa are just lawn ornaments," George told us.

The Farnham collection began less than a decade ago, but it quickly transformed the front of their property and the look of their neighborhood. They had just finished arranging dozens of unusual concrete statues when George told his wife that what he really wanted was one of those giant fiberglass statues that used to advertise muffler shops. Pam went on-line and found one going very cheap in California. Of course, the cost of trucking a twenty-something-foot statue across the country boosted the price, but in a matter of weeks, they were the proud owners of a Muffler Man. Shortly afterward (and from places much nearer to home), Brian the surfer dude and Big John the bag boy joined him.

A couple of Santas and a collection of smaller, sub-ten-foot-tall cartoon characters later, the collection was really beginning to take shape. And the drive-by visits started in earnest. Their collection is not a formal attraction, but the Farnhams are used to people pulling up and gawping from their cars. "You don't put something like this in your front yard and expect people not to notice," George told us.

The Farnhams' Fantasy Farm is only a hundred miles from D.C. and Baltimore, from which fans of fiberglass giants regularly make the trek out to see them. People will drive miles out of their way to see just one Muffler Man—and Pam and George have five different ones, with another lying at their feet awaiting a concrete foundation. One of them is so tall that a full-grown man stands barely higher than his knee.

What's next for the Farnham farm? Well, they are hoping to get a girl in to keep these big boys company. "Miss Uniroyal is the gold standard," George told us. "But there are only about a dozen of her, and nobody's selling." Even without a giantess, the Farnham Farm continues to attract visitors from far-flung places prepared to drive along the Winchester Grade Road in Unger in search of giants. And although the road is long and winding, rest assured it's impossible to drive past five fiberglass giants without noticing something out of the ordinary.

Boll Weevil Monument

Boll weevils are vicious critters that destroy crops by the acre. At one point, the beetles, which are only a quarter of an inch long, nearly ruined the nation's economy. They found their way into Texas around 1895 and by the early 1920s had devastated cotton production, one of the country's largest industries.

You would think that farmers in a farming town would want nothing to do with the critters, but at the height of the epidemic in 1919, Enterprise, Alabama, erected a thirteen-foot-high sculpture celebrating this pest, right in the middle of the town's business district.

Why would farmers salute their hated enemy in this way? Well, the emergence of the boll weevil actually forced farmers to diversify. Rather than fight off the weevils, many farmers turned to peanuts, which they quickly found even more profitable. Others began to rotate crops, which increased the productivity of their land. All of Coffey County, Alabama, was blessed with an economic resurgence following the boll weevil disaster. And that's the story behind one of the nation's most unusual monuments.

Forced Bug Tourism

All elementary students in Alabama are forced to take a field trip to Enterprise to see the statue of the Boll Weevil. The teacher spouts off how in 18-something the beetle destroyed Alabama's economy and in 1919 they built this big ugly statue to honor it. Then the big yellow buses take the kids to McDonalds and they all go home.—*Teresa Davis*

A Whale's Tale

The sad fate of many roadside attractions is that they are designed to attract flocks of people but end up seldom visited and falling apart along lonely roads. But there's another type of roadside oddity that's exactly the opposite—the landmark that was meant to be private but somehow became a public stamping ground. One of the most famous of these is the Blue Whale of Catoosa, Oklahoma.

In 1974, Hugh Davis, of Catoosa, decided that he was going to do something special for his wife, Zelta, upon their anniversary. He was going to get her a huge present—literally. Davis and a friend, Harold Thomas, built an eighty-foot-long blue whale and placed it in a pond on the Davises' property. His mouth was open. His massive belly housed a deck for people to sunbathe. And his tail contained a diving board. Hugh had figured that his wife and kids would enjoy his whimsical creation more than a normal deck.

But a curious thing began happening. Local teenagers would show up, sneak into the whale, and go swimming. Hugh spent more time than he would have liked chasing these kids off his property. Most landowners would chalk it up to experience and dismantle the whale, but Hugh Davis went in the completely opposite direction. He hired lifeguards, built a concession stand and restrooms, and installed a series of picnic tables along the pond's banks. He also built a large wooden rendition of Noah's Ark and housed animals inside. For

many years, he ran his strange roadside playland. The Blue Whale and its companion attractions thrived for many years, but as Hugh and Zelta got older, it became impossible for them to manage the site. They closed it down in 1988. After Hugh's death in 1990, the area fell into complete disrepair.

At the turn of the millennium, the Blue Whale made an improbable return to life. Town officials repainted the whale and reopened it to the public. While swimming is now prohibited, visitors are encouraged to have picnic lunches in the shadow of this odd beast.

The blue whale is the biggest mammal in nature. And with the many twists and turns it has taken during its lifetime, Oklahoma's roadside Blue Whale rises to the stature of its real-life counterpart.

Forbidden Gardens

You would think Texas has enough eccentric millionaires, but sometimes you need a little foreign competition to keep the roadside weirdness thriving. In 1996, a real estate magnate from Hong Kong raised the bar a notch when he opened a forty-acre park that remains one of the most wonderfully odd attractions to hit the state. Ira P. H. Poon spent millions of his own money to open Forbidden Gardens, a sort of Chinese historical theme park in Katy, just west of Houston.

The park's centerpiece is an enormous one-twentieth-scale model of Beijing's Forbidden City, a restricted-access imperial complex built in the fifteenth century using traditional materials and construction techniques. The two hundred amazingly detailed buildings are populated by between 10,000 and 20,000 tiny, hand-painted royalty figures and their servants. There's even a one-third-scale version of the 6,000-strong terra-cotta army that guards the tomb of the Emperor Qin (pronounced chin), the monarch who first unified China.

What's most surprising about Forbidden Gardens, though, is the fact that hardly anyone knows it exists. Advertising for the attraction is almost nonexistent, for reasons that are hard to come by. Perhaps it's because the blazing sun and humid Gulf air have ramped up maintenance so much that the miniature Great Wall has not yet been built. Perhaps it's because Mr. Poon is rather reserved and shies away from publicity.

Maybe one day, though, Mr. Poon's staff will outpace the weather, enabling him to complete his ambitious masterpiece so he can reveal it to a wider audience. Otherwise, it may just have to be unearthed over time, like Qin's clay cavalry.

The Tennis Ball *Tree of Utah*

When traveling on Route 80 through the Great Salt Lake Desert, there's not much to see. The terrain, while beautiful, is endless, and many travelers find it to be a tough drive. So when a giant tree covered with multicolored tennis balls rolls into view, many desert travelers must think they're losing their minds.

The Tree of Utah is made of concrete and stands eighty-seven feet tall. Its massive trunk rises to a series of branches, adorned with large spheres painted to resemble multicolored tennis balls. On the ground surrounding the tree are seventeen fallen tennis ball halves, meant to represent leaves that have fallen from the tree.

The Tree of Utah was created by a Swedish artist named Karl Momen, who was inspired by the vast emptiness of the Bonneville Salt Flats. He spent six years building the piece and promptly moved back to Sweden when it was dedicated in 1986. A plaque affixed to the tree reads A HYMN TO OUR UNIVERSE WHOSE GLORY AND DIMENSION IS BEYOND ALL MYTH AND IMAGINATION.

Few roadside distractions can aspire to the massive scale of the towering *Tree of Utah*. It's a true icon that will stand for generations to come.

A Tale of Two Mighty Big Balls

There is a universal rule: No matter what category of object you can name, only one example can be the largest in the world. Yet a dispute has arisen in the case of the World's Largest Ball of Twine. Residents of Cawker City, Kansas, have for decades gone head to head with those of Darwin, Minnesota, to claim this title.

The two balls began their battle in the early 1950s. The Minnesota twine ball was started when one Francis Johnson began gathering all his extra twine into a ball in 1950. He spent the next thirty-nine years rolling twine for at least four hours each day. Three years after Johnson's start, Frank Stoeber started rolling his twine in Cawker City. The two battled for dominance throughout their lives. Stoeber surpassed Johnson in the late 1950s and held the title until his death in 1974. Johnson kept rolling twine after this, reclaiming the title for Minnesota. His ball topped out at twelve feet.

The residents of Cawker City took up the torch of twine rolling and continued their fallen hero's effort. Kansas residents come from far and wide to add to the ball Frank Stoeber began a half century earlier. It has once again surpassed the Minnesota ball—it now weighs in at over seven tons—but it is beginning to not even resemble a ball. It is too heavy to lift, so twine has built up on the sides and distorted its once spherical shape.

This is one area that fuels the dispute: Cawker City's ball of twine is definitely bigger than the one over in Darwin, Minnesota, but Cawker City's "ball" is so non-spherical that the Darwinians say the title should default back into the hands of their town. Besides, Darwin's ball is more notable because it is the largest ball of twine in the world rolled by a single person—no one but the late great Francis Johnson ever added an inch of twine to it.

So the World's Largest Ball of Twine is out there, somewhere. We can't say where. But at Cawker City you can become a part of the weirdness—while you're there, you can even roll your own twine onto the infamous ball.

Cadillac Ranch

It stands unadvertised on the outskirts of a remote north Texas city and yet remains the most familiar roadside attraction in the state. If it weren't for the Alamo, it might be the most familiar attraction, period. For more than thirty years, Cadillac Ranch has lured sightseers into a dusty Amarillo wheat field with the promise of offbeat nostalgia—a prime example of Route 66 kitsch.

Cadillac Ranch is a tribute to the unmistakably American tailfin. Against the vast panhandle sky, you see ten rear ends half buried in the ground, each taken from a different model year between 1949 and 1963, illustrating the rise and fall of a distinctive automotive style.

This Lone Star icon is embedded not only in the landscape, but in the hearts of its many visitors. Some who first saw the place as children now bring their own kids out for a look. Many visitors leave a little something of themselves behind. Decades' worth of aerosol scrawl covers every inch of the monument. If you could leaf through the immeasurable strata of spray paint, you would see declarations of love, delirious observations, doodles, and countless names and initials. The appeal of Cadillac Ranch is hard to pin down, but assuming the ever-thickening layers of Krylon stay ahead of the rust, it should continue to beguile and bewilder for generations to come.

Carhenge

Stonehenge may qualify as a full-fledged ancient mystery, but a replica of Britain's famous stone circle in Alliance, Nebraska, is just as baffling. This newer, all-American site is baffling in more of a head-scratching way. For this replica is made of dozens of cars and will be known forever as Carhenge.

Carhenge is the brainchild of Jim Reinders, who visited Stonehenge many times in his youth and decided to build a replica of it as a tribute to his recently deceased father. More than thirty members of Reinders's family assembled thirty-eight automobiles in 1987 and welded them together to resemble the ancient British site. All were spray-painted silver. And thus Carhenge was born.

Carhenge has not always been popular in the town of Alliance. Some residents wanted it destroyed, but after lobbying from the Reinders family and residents, the town organizers came to their senses and embraced the site. Now the town sells postcards and apparel related to its odd attraction. Signs on the town line proudly proclaim that Alliance is the home of Carhenge.

Reinders eventually donated the property to an organization known as the Friends of Carhenge, who maintain the site and have added accommodations allowing visitors to park and eat picnics in the shadow of this strange ring of cars. Other sculptures have been placed nearby, making Carhenge a full-fledged art park. It may not be as ancient or as shrouded in mystery as its British counterpart, but Carhenge is undoubtedly one of the strangest roadside stops in the United States.

Stonehenge, Mysterious Ruins of . . . Michigan?

Why should Great Britain have all the good Druidic ruins? That is what one Michigan couple asked themselves. And the answer was, Michigan deserves an ancient—or at least ancient-looking—ceremonial center too! Accordingly, Fred and Pam Levin, of rural Nunica, have turned the front yard of their seven-acre horse farm into the site of a Styrofoam-and-stucco sculpture replicating England's famed Stonehenge.

The Levins went on-line to find the original site's actual measurements, then tinkered with them a bit to bring them into proportion with their yard. The foam megaliths in the Levin yard stand thirteen feet tall, almost the same height as Stonehenge on the Salisbury Plain, but the arrangement's diameter is only about half that of the original set. And although the British Stonehenge took about one thousand years to complete, the Levins' contractor did the work in six weeks, using photographs as a placement guide and working from the family's horse barn. Each foam block is anchored by a metal beam set into the ground below. And the replica is not finished yet. "We'll be adding more stones," Pam Levin told *Weird U.S.* "It's an ongoing project."

The couple is interested in sacred spaces from a variety of belief systems worldwide and has also created a Cretan labyrinth-style meditation path and a Native American medicine wheel garden. "I think they symbolize spirituality and the mystery of life," says Pam. "That's kind of what the theme is." Fred, an orthopedic surgeon, has also enlarged a natural spring on his property to add ponds and streams. "We're just really into gardening," Pam adds, in a classic understatement.

While England's Stonehenge is a favorite spot for modern-day Druids and other New Agers to congregate, the Levins are thankful that local would-be worshipers appear to understand that their site is part of a family home and, so far, have not tried to perform mystical rites in the Levins' backyard. Or perhaps area neo-Druids simply realize that the Styrofoam blocks don't have quite the same geomagnetic properties or astronomical alignments as the solid rock originals. Building a replica is one thing; duplicating serious ancient mojo is another.

The Nunica Stonehenge sculpture is on private property—no trespassing allowed—but it can be seen from the street just south of town on Leonard Road.

Stonehenge II

When Doug Hill gave his friend Al Shepperd a huge chunk of limestone left over from a building project, neither of them imagined it would lead to a replica of the world's most famous stone circle. Shepperd placed the stone upright in a field near his home in Hunt, Texas. He then asked Hill for help adding two more stones to make a doorway. The result reminded them of Stonehenge, so they decided to reconstruct the entire thing in metal and plaster. They dubbed the reproduction Stonehenge II.

A year and a half later, when Shepperd returned from a visit to Easter Island, he and Hill added two giant stone heads. Unfortunately, Shepperd passed away before he could add an Alaskan-style totem pole, but Stonehenge II and its companion heads have remained under the care of Shepperd's family and are still open to anyone who wants to stop by.

Foamhenge

While we were cruising through Virginia along U.S. Route 11 near the Natural Bridge, we stumbled upon something unexpected. It was Stonehenge. What was going on? Had we tele-transported to England? How else could we explain the fact that Stonehenge was standing right before us? We soon learned that this was in fact Foamhenge, a brilliant full-sized replica constructed of Styrofoam. It was the work of a one-man imagination factory named Marc Cline. Our weird world would unquestionably be that much less so were this gentle soul not a part of it. So we met the man behind the magic.

Weird U.S.: Most people don't think of building replicas of Stonehenge in Virginia. We're glad someone did . . . but where did the idea come from?

Marc Cline: I envisioned Foamhenge fifteen years ago when I walked into a foam factory and saw sixteen-foot-tall blocks standing straight up. After joining up with Natural Bridge, I spotted a suitable location, took photos of it, and shared my vision with my new partner, Lenny. The groovy thing about Lenny is he gives me free rein to create, even as he keeps an eye on bottom lines. I told him that I'd pitch the idea to several businesses as sponsorships. My salesmanship worked. The foam, paint, concrete, crane, excavating, timber, everything was donated. It wasn't a hard sell. Every once in a while an opportunity comes around for folks to become a part of something bigger than they are. Foamhenge offered just such an opportunity.

Weird U.S.: Awesome! Please share with us the nuts and bolts of such a vast and utterly bizarre undertaking.

MC: Foamhenge was prefabricated at my Enchanted Castle Studio and trucked a mile and a half down to its present location on March 30, 2004. The next day it was erected and covered with a huge piece of black plastic. On April Fool's Day, I unveiled Foamhenge by yanking down the plastic

to an eager audience of news media, supporters, and friends.

I "phased" through a solid block of foam, much as magician David Copperfield passed through the giant wall of China. I figured going through foam would be easier. If it solidified, it would be much easier to tear my way out!

Weird U.S.: As neat as your replica is, we couldn't help but notice that a few of the stones were lying askew from their original positions. Was this due to a storm or vandalism of some kind?

MC: The trouble is much of Foamhenge is constructed of inferior foam. For about five months, the whole thing was intact, including the much larger twenty-two-foot-tall interior stones. High winds finally forced this cheaper foam down, and plans were made to reerect the larger blocks using the good stuff. With big "stones" lying about, creating an unsafe environment, Lenny and I decided to keep Foamhenge closed until I could once again give it my full attention. Spectators, however, could still get a great view of it from the pull-off on Route 11.

Shoe Trees: Testimonies of Murder or Funky Road Art?

Where do old shoes go to die? In towns all across the United States, they seem to fly into the branches of trees and just hang there. Here at *Weird U.S.*, we hear reports of trees all over the continent festooned with castoff oxfords, hiking boots, Nikes, and ratty old gym shoes. Most city dwellers have seen a pair of sneakers hanging off power or phone lines and know the story behind it—that it's the work of gangs marking their territory. But nobody's entirely sure why certain trees attract shoes, although there's no denying that it happens.

One often told tale gives the origin of the first shoe tree, in which, dangling from a high branch out of sight from the ground, are several pairs of antique children's shoes, thrown there by a serial killer who stole them from the bodies of his young victims. Another legend involves a boy who died in a swamp after bullies teased him by hanging his sneakers high on a branch. Of course the boy still haunts the place, letting loose an unearthly wail when people scream at the tree. Other trees have their own legends, and it's these we've collected here.

One thing's for certain: It's not always easy to find these trees. Their footwear fruit is often harvested by ticked-off landowners or townships. Sometimes the trees are chopped down completely. But if you happen to find one, enter into the spirit of things: Take off your own shoes and leave a bit of the weird behind.

A Pair of Shoe Trees

What's better than a shoe tree? Two shoe trees, of course! Two hardwoods on Highway M33 outside Comins in Oscoda County, Michigan, are festooned with every kind and size of shoe imaginable. The lower branches bear the greatest load, but evidently plenty of folks with either great throwing arms or wonderful climbing skills have extended the range a good twenty-five feet into the branches. People have also reported seeing mysterious shadows emerge from the woods near the shoe trees or experiencing electrical difficulties with their cars while parked nearby.

Those Shoes Are Murder!

I just wanted to tell you a story about the Shoe Tree. Legend has it that a recluse lured a number of young children to his isolated shack, where he murdered them. Before disposing of their bodies, he removed their shoes as mementos, hanging them on a nearby tree. The tree is still there—and so are the shoes! Visitors claim that the tree remains warm to the touch even in the dead of winter. Many report inexplicable car failure when they try to leave the site.—*Dan*

Flying Footwear Is the Fashion in Indiana

At the end of their lives, most shoes end up in a landfill somewhere. A few, sadly, land at the side of a road, usually separated from their sibling. Some, a bit luckier, find their way into a secondhand store, the orphanage of footwear, where they hope to be adopted by new owners.

The truly lucky, however, end their lives in the most honorable way a pair of shoes can: entangled in a shoe tree. Dangling respectably amid their brethren, it's the only place a pair of well-worn kicks may find eternal rest for their soles.

A prime example is the sycamore at the intersection of Knight Road, Devils Hollow Road, and McFelea Lane outside Milltown, Indiana. Well off the beaten path, it can be difficult to find and, after a hard rain, difficult to get to, which makes for a quiet resting place and a more enticing destination for those seeking to cool their heels permanently.

It's known locally as the Legendary Shoe Tree, the legend being that anyone who successfully ensnares a pair of shoes in its branches will be endowed with good fortune. This may explain, incidentally, the record-setting career of Indiana native and former Boston Celtic Larry Bird, whose shoes supposedly hang high above.

The tree reportedly found its funerary purpose as far back as the 1950s, although its growth has evidently been slow-going, as there are fewer shoes than one would expect to have accumulated in five decades. Much of its vintage footwear may have been lost, though, thanks to a tornado in 1991. Reports also indicate that the tree suffered fire damage in 2005, which, if true, suggests that the original shoe tree is not the current sneaker-packed sycamore, but a charred skeleton just across the road.

Nevertheless, recent years have seen a boom, and footwear has metastasized to all four corners of the intersection, a testament to the tree's enduring popularity. Not to mention that it's perhaps the only shoe tree in existence to not only be tolerated, but formally recognized, by local government, as McFelea Lane has been duly and officially designated Shoetree Lane.

Shoe Corner

The intersection of 109th Street and Calumet in Saint John, Indiana, is known as the Shoe Corner. People throw all kinds of shoes there, from baby shoes to boots to athletic shoes to sandals to dress shoes . . . you name it, it's there. Periodically, someone clears the shoes from the corner, but new shoes keep appearing. The best time to visit the shoe corner is in the summer. It seems to collect more shoes in warm weather. It's fun to see how many shoes are there at any given time. If you visit, have fun and don't forget to take some shoes to contribute.–*Anonymous*

OUR Shoe Tree's Better!

I enjoyed reading about the various shoe trees around the U.S. in your books. However, I think the one we saw in the Northwest is more impressive than most others. It is right on the border of Idaho and Washington in the Priest Lake area, near Upper Priest Falls. There are numerous old cedars there in the Roosevelt Grove of Ancient Cedars.—*Joy Ostaffe*

Sporty Footwear in San Diego

The Shoe Tree on Morley Field Disc Golf Course in Balboa Park, San Diego, is home to hundreds of pairs of active footwear from all over the world. Rumor has it that the first pair was tossed up in the branches to celebrate a hole-in-one that decided a close match of Frisbee golf. Little by little other shoes joined them. In the mid-'80s, the city of San Diego decided to chop down the dead tree, but the course pro mounted a campaign to save it. He convinced friends to decorate it with their old tennies and cleats, then phoned the local newspaper telling the reporter that the city was going to do away with the "world famous Shoe Tree." When the story appeared, the city was deluged with pleading phone calls and letters to let the tree stand.

Arizona Shoe Trees Under Oppression

About thirty miles west of Parker, Arizona, just across the border in California, the region's most famous shoe tree once stood. It was called the Rice Shoe Tree because of its location near the uninhabited town of Rice. The tree, a tamarisk, became so laden with footwear over time that a pile began to form around its trunk. Some quietly protested that the shoes were choking the tree to death. Tamarisks, however, are difficult to kill even intentionally, and so the Rice Shoe Tree continued to thrive. Sadly, what finally did it in was arson. Someone torched it. Twice. Then someone buried the stump under a mound of sand for good measure. Shoe tree aficionados have attempted a phoenix-from-the-ashes type recovery by garnishing nearby trees, but with mixed results.

Other shoe trees, like the one along Highway 95 north of Quartzsite, have suffered a similar fate. Reportedly, it was created originally by "some septuagenarian" who decided to memorialize each year's visit to Quartzsite's Main Event by tossing his footwear into a paloverde on his way out of town. Others joined in. Eventually, the Arizona Department of Transportation allegedly decided the tree had become an eyesore and cut it down.

Shoe Trees of Nevada

Three miles east of Middlegate, on Highway 50, the Loneliest Road in America, is a cottonwood tree adorned with hundreds of shoes, draped like Spanish moss across its branches. In local folklore, the shoes are said to represent reunited love. In the early '90s, the story goes, a couple had just been married in Reno and were making their way back to their native Oregon. They had their first fight under the cottonwood tree, where they had decided to camp for the night. Words flew, and the bride threatened to walk all the way back to Oregon. The man took her shoes and threw them into the tree, saying, "If you're going to walk home, you're going to have to climb a tree first." After half an hour of cooling off at the Middlegate Station bar, he drove back to make up with her, but they could not retrieve the forlorn pair of shoes. In a show of unity, the husband threw his own shoes into the tree, and they continued home. A year later they returned, bringing their new baby with them, and threw a pair of baby shoes into the branches.

That is one version of the tale told by Rus and Fredda Stevenson, owners of Middlegate's only watering hole. The specifics of folklore change, even in a town with fewer than twenty residents. What is certain is that the Middlegate Shoe Tree has been "growing" footwear for at least twenty years—including skis, snowshoes, and divers' flippers. The *San Francisco Chronicle* described it this way in a June 2002 article:

> Dangling in the branches of the 70-foot cottonwood tree in a gully a few yards off Highway 50 are what looks like every type of footwear in existence—cowboy boots, tennis shoes, running shoes, sandals, ballet slippers, high-heeled shoes, even Rollerblades. Red, blue, yellow, green, black, striped, red-and-white, yellow-and-black. All sizes, all shapes.

They've all been tied together in pairs or clumps and flung high into the branches, with the lowest shoes at least 15 feet off the desert floor. Most hang from shoelaces, others are linked by bras or underpants. Stand beneath the tree, and you can hear the relentless Nevada wind rustle through the shoes and the leaves like a leather-and-cloth version of a muffled wind chime.

A few plastic soda bottles stuffed with papers and dollar bills are lashed to the tree about 20 feet up, and American flags flap amid the soles here and there. Nailed to the trunk at eye level is a yellow, 6-by-2-foot metal sign that reads "Shoe Tree" in faded black letters.

There's another shoe tree, the Old Shoe Tree, on Highway 95 a few miles south of Schurtz, but this one ain't what it used to be. On our visit, it had been pruned of its fruit and the branches cut down. But there is still hope; new sprouts of leafy branches bloom, and a few shoe clusters have begun to appear on the old tree.

Shoe Tree Grove

Outside of Beaver, Arkansas (close to Eureka Springs, a popular tourist town) is a shoe tree "grove." It was started years ago with one tree, in which tourists and locals would throw their old pairs of shoes for good luck.—*Julie Bivans*

The Five Maples of Lyndonville

New York is proud to throw its hat into the shoe tree arena with a cluster of five shoe trees—the Sneaker Trees of Lyndonville. These five maples stand on Morrison Road in the small Orleans County town. Local custom says that if you make a wish and toss your sneakers into one of the trees, your wish will come true as long as the sneakers catch. Maybe the surest bet of all is to wish for a brand-new pair of kicks.

Nebraska's Shoe Fence

Not every shoe-wearing hunk of wood is still attached to the tree. A few miles east of Northport, Nebraska, the fence posts along Route 26 are capped with shoes for several miles. Some say that this was an old farmer's trick to protect the wood from rotting, but not everyone shares that view: One white tennis shoe we spotted on the post is inscribed to the Gods and Goddesses of the Shoe Fence . . . whoever they are.

There are places in the United States where the laws of physics just do not seem to apply. Water flows skyward, and people can actually walk up walls. So what do you do if you discover a site of such anomalous activity? You charge admission, of course! The great American mystery spot—sometimes given the scientific-sounding name *vortex*—is a time-honored classic among roadside tourist traps. How could you fail to notice places with great names like the Santa Cruz Mystery Spot and the Oregon Vortex? And with their wild but accurate claims that you won't believe your eyes and will experience dizzying sensations, how could these places fail to entice the curious?

Some say that these places are merely off-kilter rooms designed by highway hucksters to disorient the equilibrium of the hapless tourist with optical illusions. Others claim that there's something more mysterious going on—that these places have been shunned for centuries by Native Americans who noticed strange things happening there. Birds refuse to nest on the oddly tilted spot. Horses would whinny and shy away. The local tribes pronounced the ground "forbidden" and refused to go there.

So are there really places in America that belie all that science has taught us about the way the universe operates? We can't really say for sure, but we're always willing to take a walk up a wall and amble across any ceiling to find out for ourselves.

Never on the Straight and Narrow

Visitors to the seaside resort and college town of Santa Cruz, California, have often observed how odd the local culture seems to be. They note the town's many peculiar characters, its eccentric civic politics, its vast array of bohemian subcultures, and—more darkly—its onetime status as the mass-murder capital of the world. But nothing beats the weirdness of a hundred-fifty-foot-wide patch of land on the hill just north of the city. The Santa Cruz Mystery Spot was first discovered in 1939 and opened to the public a year later. It fast became one of North America's most famous "vortices" a place where the laws of gravity, perspective, and even physics are suspended.

Visitors to the mystery spot are taken into a small hillside shack and shown bizarre and seemingly inexplicable sights. Plum bobs hang almost parallel to the cabin floors. Billiard balls seemingly roll uphill. People look as if they are standing at impossible angles, then dramatically change height when they move a few feet.

Some claim that the mystery spot is sitting on an electromagnetic hot spot. Others say that unknown geophysical forces are at work here. The mystery spot's own Web site (www.mysteryspot.com) speculates that a powerful guidance system for UFOs lies beneath the land and warps the laws of gravity . . . and presumably, the local culture of Santa Cruz.

degree angles, and balls suspended on chains swung in only one direction.

We asked Satya if anyone had discovered how the spot produced such miraculous effects.

"The most common theory—some kind of gravitational magnetic force making us lean," she said. "Scientists have been coming up here for sixty-five years; nobody has proven a theory. That's why it's still called the Mystery Spot."

A little research on our own pointed to the spot being nothing more than an elaborately planned optical illusion. By building a crooked house with uneven corners, slightly bent horizons, and other abnormalities, builders are able to fool our brains into thinking everything is normal while in actuality, we are on a steep incline. But even if it is a hoax, mystery spots such as this one in Santa Cruz are well worth the price of admission.

Visiting the Mystery Spot

We here at *Weird U.S.* had a chance to visit the Santa Cruz Mystery Spot while filming for the History Channel. Having heard the decades-old stories of the place, we decided to stop by personally to see if the rumors were true. Our host for this adventure was a young lady named Satya Drew, a tour guide at the mystery spot.

"The Mystery Spot was first discovered in 1939," Satya informed us. "The man who wanted to buy this property noticed some weird things. He noticed when he went up the hill, he would begin to feel dizzy and light-headed."

George Prather founded the Santa Cruz Mystery Spot in 1939, betting that tourists would pay money to walk through a place where the laws of gravity seemingly didn't work. He originally charged five cents a head for the pleasure of feeling sick to your stomach and watching ordinary objects behave in ways they shouldn't. These days, the price has been upped to $5.

Satya took us through a series of trials, and we were amazed to see the results. Billiard balls rolled up hill, hanging from the building's rafters led to our bodies being swung out to forty-five-

Big Mike's Mystery House

Big Mike's main purpose seems to be selling minerals to tourists passing through Cave City, Kentucky. A large fake dinosaur sits out front to beckon in passersby; other attractions include a fossilized skull. But for those who need an extra reason to stop their cars, Big Mike's is also the home of a mystery house. Inside, all of the classic mystery house elements are offered—objects and water roll uphill, you feel nauseous, and objects stand at unnatural angles. And there's an optical illusion room where you and a friend can take turns at appearing bigger or smaller for the camera. If that's not frightening enough, the house is also adorned with multiple black lights and images of aliens. All this fun for just a buck for grownups, fifty cents for kids. If you're itching to defy gravity, Mike's place is at 566 Old Mammoth Cave Road.

The Oregon Vortex

In the small town of Gold Hill, the Oregon Vortex may have more historical background than any other mystery spot in the country. The official Web site, oregonvortex.com, relates tales regarding the area that stretch back to Native American lore. (Apparently, the horses of said natives refused to enter this area, and it was referred to as the Forbidden Ground in their society.) The Web site further relays how many scientific examinations of the area were staged by John Listster, the son of a British diplomat, in the early twentieth century. These days visitors are invited to participate in this grand tradition of weirdness by visiting the vortex to experience "a strange world where the improbable is the commonplace and everyday physical facts are reversed."

Cosmos Mystery Area

"Have you ever experienced a place where the laws of nature seem to have gone completely berserk?" asks the homepage of the Cosmos Mystery Area at cosmosmysteryarea.com. This attraction in Rapid City, South Dakota, offers a thirty-minute tour. The Web site proclaims the tour to be family-friendly, though the banner atop the page aggressively challenges patrons to "See it. Feel it. Survive it!" Nevertheless, the site makes for a fun diversion along a highway full of tourist traps near Mount Rushmore.

Confusion Hill

Piercy, California, is home to Confusion Hill, which has stood since 1949. It was sought out by one George Hudson who wanted to find a spot similar to Santa Cruz's vaunted attraction. The spot features the Gravity House, the Redwood Shoe House, a miniature train ride, and the World's Largest Free Standing Redwood Sculpture. A $5 admission is charged for adults, although Confusion Hill's Web site does say that "just before you get to the Gravity House entrance we have a free exhibit which is a metal rod on a pivot that George set up. It's free because it doesn't work all the time."

Buy Your Own Mystery Spot!

If you're a millionaire looking to own a gravitational vortex, it looks like there's hope after all! The Teton Mystery Spot in Jackson, Wyoming, has been a tourist attraction since 1948. As far as we can tell, it's the only mystery spot to ever be put up for sale on-line. In early 2007, the spot's owners put it up for auction on eBay and were asking for $1.5 million.

The Mystery Hole

Ansted, West Virginia, boasts not only a mystery spot, but the one and only Mystery Hole. The Web site at mysteryhole.com tells the hole's story in a sentence whose grammar is as mysterious as the content it describes: "This mysterious mind-baffling Mystery Hole was unclosed for public view around the middle of the year 1973, and is probably the best kept secret in WEST VIRGINIA or maybe in the whole U.S.A., . . . no one really knows for sure."

What's the difference between a mystery spot and the Mystery Hole? One variation we noticed was that the proprietors of the Mystery Hole tout the hole's medicinal value — claiming that it can cure headaches and implement positive personality changes.

Mystery Spot plus Arrowheads

The mystery spot in the resort town of Blowing Rock in the mountains of North Carolina features all the attractions of other mystery spots, plus an extra incentive for visiting — a collection of over fifty thousand genuine Native American arrowheads. So for one small entry fee, one can glimpse the nation's past and be disoriented by its all-too-weird present.

Spend a Night at Mystery Hill

Marblehead, Ohio, is home to Mystery Hill, a mystery spot with a number of amenities most similar sites don't offer. For one, visitors are also invited to visit the Prehistoric Forest, a companion attraction featuring cartoonish dinosaur sculptures throughout a patch of forest. More interestingly, you can rent a cabin for a mere $55 a night. While this offers a unique opportunity for visitors to have an extended stay in a genuine mystery spot, be prepared — the site's official Web site bluntly advises visitors to "bring your own pillows, bedding, and bath towels."

An Old West Mystery Shack

Calico Town is an attraction located within Yermo, California. It is built on the site of an abandoned town and re-creates exactly what this town looked like during the Wild West era. One-third of the town is original buildings, and the rest are replicas. Curiously, within the borders of this larger attraction is a genuine Mystery Shack. We have no idea whether this is one of the original buildings and many a cowboy used to defy gravity back in the day, or if this is one of the newer additions. We're betting on the latter.

Michigan Loves Its Mystery Spot

Is it a place that somehow traps gravity and magnetic forces to create its own topsy-turvy world, or are tourists the only things really trapped in St. Ignace's mystery spot? Michigan's mystery spot is typical—a slant-walled cabin set into an inclined natural area, where balls seem to roll uphill and furniture can never quite align with the walls. We watched a procession of brave people try to stand upright on a table that appeared to be horizontal, but wasn't. They were able to balance on a chair tilted backward and perform various other feats of gravity-bending

amazement that would never be possible at more ordinary sites. Compasses will spin aimlessly in the area. It was discovered by three surveyors in 1953, when their equipment wouldn't work and they felt "light-headed" within a certain three-hundred-square-foot area. Their brochure claims that even blind people are affected by the physical sensations.

Some speculate that the ground underneath must contain some sort of rock strata with electromagnetic properties; others wonder if it is a window into another dimension. Part of it is admittedly illusion, with the "cabin" walls built at wacky angles to enhance the experience. Still, the crowd seemed to find it entertaining that day, and more than one person became disoriented and dizzy, whether from odd architecture or mysterious earth forces. The mystery spot can be found just west of St. Ignace on U.S. 2.

Like Gravity, Sometimes Memory Fails Us Too

I wish I could send you a picture for the weird place I'm about to describe, but unfortunately, I don't have any. I visited this place with my parents as a young child, so my memory of it is pretty sketchy. I can't even remember its name, but after reading about some of the places in your recent book where gravity seems to go awry, I was reminded of it. It's a tourist attraction in central/northern Michigan. While some of the place is somewhat questionable from an authenticity standpoint, some parts of it are not.

There are two level stones. Two people of identical height stand on them, and they are of equal height. If those people switch places, one person suddenly appears taller than the other.

There is a building where the gravity is so odd, that you have to use handholds to get through it. A chair can be balanced on a ledge on its rear legs, and a person can safely sit in that chair, and it will not topple.

Frankly, keeping your balance anywhere around the top of this hill or mound is no easy feat. What I remember most is that at one point, my mother dropped her purse, which popped open, and the contents of her purse started to roll away—on a level surface. We had a pretty good chase trying to round some of them up, too.—*Thomas Wheeler, Tucson*

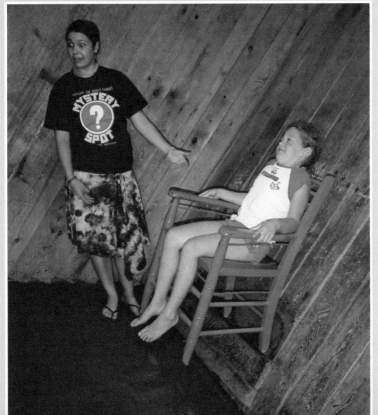

Mystery Solved?

A psychologist writing for the May 1981 issue of *Omni* had a prosaic explanation for what goes on at vortex sites. Ray Hyman examined the Oregon Vortex and described the cabin wherein all the "phenomena" took place as an architectural funhouse. It was filled with horizons that weren't level, corners that weren't squared, and walls that weren't vertical, all of which distorted normal frames of visual reference and created a series of optical illusions that made it seem as if gravity was being violated right and left.

Devoutly Different

Ever since *Thomas Jefferson* pushed through the First Amendment to the Constitution, the United States has officially recognized that its people should be free to pursue whatever religion their conscience tells them to. We at *Weird U.S.* are grateful for that. If you look around the land, you find that people are building many stairways to heaven, each with the earnest desire that only the true faithful can muster.

Like most religious practices, the ways of the devoutly different look odd to the outsider, but we've never dismissed anything just because it looks strange at first sight. Just the opposite. It's almost impossible not to be impressed by the devotion of sincere adherents.

And so we bow our heads out of respect, take a moment to reflect, and begin another journey into the unusual side of these United States—a side that the framers of the Constitution could never have dreamed of.

EVERY DAY CHRISTMAS

INRI

XII STATIO

AMERICA RETURN TO CHRIST

Welcome To Oneida, N.Y. Home Of
CROSS ISLAND CHAPEL
The WORLD'S SMALLEST CHURCH
BUILT IN 1989
Floor Area 51" x 81" (28.68 sq. ft.) Seats 2 People
Non-Denominational And Open To The Public Upon Request
Available For Special Occasions And Meditation
CHAPEL IS DEDICATED AS A WITNESS TO GOD

Homemade Holy Lands

All major religions, and many minor ones, believe in some kind of pilgrimage to a holy place. But not everyone can make such trips. Many people lead busy, hectic lives, and not all of us can travel the world to get in touch with our faith. What are the options for those of us tied to home and hearth? We can always turn to the nation's homemade Holy Lands, places where the devout among us have set up shrines in their own backyards. They might not have the mystical qualities of Jerusalem itself, but they have as much heart and care put into them as one or two visionaries can muster.

Gilgal Gardens

For many years, it was one of Salt Lake City's best-known secrets—tucked between the Wonder Bread factory and Chuck O Rama at 452 S. 800 E.—and most Salt Lake City residents had no idea such a bizarre animal existed. Filled with strange sculptures with a weird Mormon ambience, Gilgal Gardens is the creation of Thomas Battersby Child Jr., former bishop of the Church of Jesus Christ of Latter-day Saints.

Child spent nearly twenty years working on the garden, located on about a half acre behind his home. He filled it with twelve original sculptures and over seventy engraved stones. The most arresting of his creations is a sphinx with the head of Joseph Smith, founder of the Mormon faith.

However, the garden is also loaded with strange carved images, such as grasshoppers and disembodied heads. There is even a life-size statue of Child himself. To view these works of art, a visitor must walk a stone path in which each stone is engraved with biblical and literary quotes.

For years, the park was open to the public only on Sundays. If someone wanted to view the wonders of Gilgal on a day other than the Sabbath, he would need to call a phone number listed on a sign that adorned the nondescript gate guarding the gardens. That didn't stop all curious folk though; they would hop the fence at night. Many knew the place as Stoner Park and had no

clue about Gilgal or how it had come into being. It was just one of those weird quasi-Mormon places that pepper Utah.

The history of Gilgal begins in 1945 after Child retired from his role as a bishop of the Mormon Church. To fill his time and reavow his faith, he had a very special plan. He would create a monument to the church, one unlike any other in Mormonism. He named this wonderland after the fabled gardens near where the Israelites had crossed the River Jordan on their way to the Promised Land. Child enlisted the help of Utah sculptor Maurice Brooks, and Gilgal Gardens was born.

The retired bishop and his sculptor pal often drove into the canyons to acquire the material required to accomplish this mammoth work. Child would haul the

who would listen. When, in early 2000, rumors surfaced that Gilgal was to be razed for a condominium development, these champions leaped into action. The Friends of Gilgal sprang up. Their goal: save the beloved garden.

Bishop Child would have been proud that his little testament to the Mormon faith inspired such zeal. And the Friends succeeded. Money rolled in, including $100,000 ponied up by the LDS church. This enabled the Friends to purchase Gilgal and save it from the developer's bulldozers. The saviors donated the park to the city.

Today Gilgal is open Monday through Saturday. Visitors can browse its strange wonders at will. Ironically, the one day it is not open is Sunday.

—*Clint Wardlow*

stones, some boulders weighing as much as seventy-two tons, in the bed of his truck. He remained active in the church, serving as the director of the bishop's warehouse and cochair of Pioneer Day activities as he toiled on his monument.

Child added to the garden right up until his death in 1963. After that, Gilgal fell into limbo. Rumor has it that he tried to give it to the church, but they didn't want it. Mormonism was trying to embrace a clean-cut image and didn't need any works that emphasized their strange history. So Gilgal sat there for thirty years, pretty much ignored, in the shadow of the Wonder Bread factory.

But as people found out about it, Gilgal's mystique grew over the years. Some folks love the strange side of Mormonism that the church takes such pains to hide. They were Gilgal's champions and spread the word about this mondo weirdo garden to anyone

Holy Land Waits for Archaeologists—or Resurrection

It all started out rather covertly—perhaps supernaturally. In 1956, a Waterbury, Connecticut, lawyer named John Baptist Greco gathered a small group of associates at his home. The details of that original gathering have never been made public, but some say Mr. Greco revealed that God had given him a task to perform. Others say he made a humanitarian appeal for a community project. In any event, Mr. Greco had just returned from a visit to the Holy Land and wanted pilgrims unable to make the trip to experience it for themselves: He proposed a vast, minutely detailed replica of the Holy Land to be built on Pine Hill in Waterbury.

Blueprints were developed from studies of the Bible, maps, photographs, and some say divine revelation to create Holy Land U.S.A. Mr. Greco and his helpers fashioned buildings from anything they could find: plywood, tar paper, plaster of paris, car parts, blown-out boilers, chicken wire, bedsprings, and concrete. Inadvertently, they also created a grand piece of outsider art, full of Lilliputian pyramids, tombs, grottoes, tunnels, and statues. They even located a replica of the Shroud of Turin.

By the end of 1958, there were eleven buildings standing. By 1970, nearly two hundred buildings sprawled beneath a sixty-foot stainless-steel cross (local non-Catholics say Christ was electrocuted on that cross). During its heyday, the 1960s and '70s, Holy Land attracted some fifty thousand visitors a year. However, by 1984 Mr. Greco had grown too old to care for his creation, and the magical site officially closed to visitors.

More than two decades later, it's still there—a diminutive ghost town. Weather and vandals have taken their toll, but somehow Holy Land U.S.A. survives. While locals decide whether to raze it, restore it, or turn it into a hilltop park, people continue to visit—in secret, just like the place began. Whatever fate may be in store for the site, Mr. John Baptist Greco, who died in 1986 at age ninety-one, will be watching over us from high above the sixty-foot cross, smiling down from his miniature Heaven.

Holy Land USA Part II: This Time, in Virginia

Just when you think you've seen it all, an operation like Holy Land USA pops up and shows you the error of your ways. It has the same name as a similar attraction in Connecticut, but this biblical theme park in Bedford, Virginia, is a different animal altogether. Visitors are cheerfully invited to walk its three-mile-long nature path at their leisure. As we moved about the grounds, we uncovered many neat and utterly bizarre things. A whimsical Rube Goldberg contraption called Herod's Idol reveals the folly of worshiping false gods. Farther down the path we came upon a humorous comparison between a wise man and his foolish counterpart. The wise man's house stood tall and proud, as it was built from a strong foundation. The foolish man's looked like the result of an ill-conceived trip to Home Depot.

Faith is an undeniably strong thing—a force that can sometimes move mountains. And the twin forces of faith and remodeling are now at work in Holy Land USA. But even if this wonderfully oddball place stays precisely as it is, you will still find devout people paying it homage. Amen to that.

Desert Christ Park, Yucca Valley

Here on a sweltering, rocky hillside in California's high desert, Jesus is missing his hands, and some of his disciples are missing their heads. It's the result of earthly spite and neglect, and at least one incident of what insurance companies call an "act of God."

Desert Christ Park was the realized dream of artist and former aircraft company employee Frank Antoine Martin. In 1951, Martin fashioned a three-ton concrete statue of his Savior in his Inglewood driveway, hoping to install it at the rim of the Grand Canyon. When that plan fell through, he packed up his family and settled one hundred miles away in Yucca Valley to realize a new dream: the New Testament set in concrete.

On Easter Sunday 1951, the twelve-foot Jesus was installed on a hill overlooking the town, and a ten-year labor began. Martin mixed and hauled the concrete by himself, built armatures of steel rebar to support the statues, and finished them off with plaster and white paint.

The largest group of statues depicts the Sermon on the Mount. Some of the figures in it are obviously moved, while others wear doubting or even hostile expressions. Closer inspection reveals the detail that the artist put into his work: Hands are creased, waves of hair and cloth are sculpted to an astonishing degree.

But there was trouble in paradise: The owner of the land where Martin was working wanted to charge admission to the attraction, and Martin didn't. In a fit of pique, Martin smashed the noses off the Apostles, Mary, and the Almighty himself—but he left Judas untouched as a statement to the landowner.

The appendages were later replaced, but Martin's back-and heartbreaking work took its toll. He died two days shy of Christmas in 1961, at the age of seventy-four. His legacy remains in ten biblical scenes scattered over three acres, damaged somewhat by the 1992 Landers earthquake, the harsh environment, and vandals. Concerned citizens formed the Desert Christ Foundation to look after the statues, but lacking significant contributions, Martin's legacy will, for the present, be left in a state of arrested decay. From Interstate 10, take Highway 62 east to Yucca Valley. In Yucca Valley, turn left on Mohawk Trail and then right on Sunnyslope Drive. The park is on the left.

Pallin' Around with the Apostles

Every piece of evidence seemed to suggest that sculptor Antoine Martin intended Desert Christ Park to be a place dedicated to peace, tolerance, and love. Nevertheless, there's an eerie feel about the park that even the most reverential could not deny. The creepiness may have to do in part with the fact that a 7.3 earthquake rattled the valley in 1992, shook heads and hands off the statues, exposing the rebar and steel skeletal remains.

The *pièce de résistance* in this whole place is no doubt the Last Supper. One hundred and twenty five tons of concrete bas-relief, twenty feet tall and thirty feet wide, it's an interactive replica of Da Vinci's Last Supper, with a square window cut out above the dinner table for the sole purpose of posing with the giant Christ. It seems incredibly blasphemous at first, but it's impossible to resist the temptation to sling your arm around the Savior's shoulder and tip Jesus off to Judas's plans ("There he is, Lord. . . . There's the guy who ratted you out to the Romans.") If you feel the slightest bit guilty or sacrilegious after spending your time in Desert Christ Park doing any of these things, don't worry. . . . He'll forgive you. It's what He does.—*Joe Oesterle*

Renaissance Reverends

Many shrines in this chapter are larger-than-life places dedicated to God. Some have a more distinct kind of artistry in their heavenly displays. The following are homemade holy lands that are the visions of individual reverends who chose to lead their flocks through artistic expression of the weird kind.

Howard Finster's Paradise Gardens

In its heyday, a visit to Paradise Gardens in Summerville, Georgia, offered spiritual uplifting, a lesson in homegrown art, and a healthy dose of weirdness. The four-acre garden was the work of late evangelist and renowned American folk artist the Reverend Howard Finster, and it's a cacophony of religious messages, mixed sculpture, paintings, and horticulture. Between concrete mounds laced with bits of glass and scrap metal, evangelical texts call out from almost every surface.

Alabama-born Finster became a tent-revival preacher at the age of sixteen, but his art work didn't start out spiritual. While living in Trion, Georgia, the pastor began to build miniature edifices that would highlight every last one of man's inventions. It was after he relocated to the Summerville area that he saw a face in a dab of paint on his fingertip that instructed him to "paint sacred art."

Finster took the message to heart, creating a fantastical world made mostly out of scraps and garbage. Trees made of hubcaps, houses made of bottles, and walls studded with television screens and political memorabilia lived happily under garlands of coffee cups and gourds. Scripture and

partial sermons preached to believers and skeptics alike from myriad pulpits—cardboard cutouts, mailboxes, sides of buildings. He even included curiosities like a jar of tonsils.

In addition, Finster continued to create paintings—prolifically. Among the 46,000 paintings he did in his lifetime were the giant Coke bottle shown at the 1996 Olympics and the album covers for R.E.M.'s *Reckoning* and the Talking Heads' *Little Creatures*. During the latter part of his life, Finster allowed the gardens to fall into disrepair as he was working at a frenzied pace on other projects.

Upon his death in October 2001, the gardens were picked over by collectors and the most notable works were sold. However, Finster's survivors (among them his wife, five children, fifteen grandchildren, and fifteen great-grandchildren) expressed an interest in keeping the site open to the public. Recently his daughter Beverly donated the property to a Christian nonprofit organization. According to finster.com, a Web site Beverly set up in her father's honor, the gardens will never be sold and are now open to the public. It won't be the same as having the opportunity to chat with Finster himself on a balmy Sunday afternoon, but it is sure to be well worth a visit.

Prophet Royal Robertson

Royal Robertson was born in Baldwin, Louisiana, in 1936. In his late teens, he apprenticed as a sign painter and traveled to the West Coast for several years. On his return, he entered a marriage that lasted nineteen years but ended badly: His wife left him for another man. This betrayal sent Robertson into a creative rage, which is manifested in the signs covering the front of his house. His fury has gradually taken on science fiction overtones: He believes he is the victim of a worldwide female conspiracy, as told to him in numerous visions of interplanetary travel where alien beings warned him about the dangers of adultery and fornication. They also predict the End Times through complex numerological formulas.

Under his new identity of Libra Patriarch Prophet Lord Archbishop Apostle Visionary Mystic Psychic Saint Royal Robertson, the artist uses as his main focus biblical passages dealing with adultery: His ex-wife is cast in the role of Jezebel, and her betrayal will be the cause of the cataclysmic destruction of humanity. Unfortunately, Hurricane Andrew destroyed much of the existing outdoor environment at Royal Robertson's place in 1992, but the artist's drawings and writings continue to proliferate.

Anderson Johnson

From the streets to the pulpits to the canvas, Anderson Johnson spent his life letting people know about the glories of God. By the age of eight, he was already an established street preacher in several cities, but after he fell ill in the early 1970s he left the streets and founded a faith mission in his modest home in Newport News, Virginia. His flock came weekly for Johnson's impassioned sermons and to see the walls of his home church, which were covered in art that further accentuated the messages he was trying to get across. Most of his art featured women's faces painted on cardboard or plywood.

Johnson's church was demolished in the early 1990s for an urban renewal project, but much of his art was preemptively collected and saved. Although he passed away in 1998, his art still lives on in museums such as the Newport News Peninsula Fine Arts Center and the St. James Place Folk Art Museum and Asheville Art Museum in North Carolina.

Searching for Peace in Peaceville Valley

We'd barely stepped out of the car a mile or two south of Williamston, North Carolina, when a friendly-looking man welcomed us. "Would you like to take a look?" he asked, gesturing to the PEACEVILLE VALLEY sign, or perhaps to the plywood angel beneath it, bearing the slogan IF YOU'RE LOST STOP—FIND YOUR WAY. We were a bit lost, so we shrugged and decided to go on in.

John Lilley introduced himself and led us into a miniature town, complete with a tiny Hardee's hamburger joint, a mini used-car dealership, and about twenty other waist-high buildings. Little plastic trucks and cars added to the charm.

"Here we are in the modern world," Lilley said grandly, dropping into practiced tour-guide cadences, "surrounded by all of life's daily distractions." Actually, given the scale of things, we felt more like Godzilla entering a two-bit Tokyo, but we held our tongues.

"We go through our days hurrying from place to place and errand to errand," he continued, "weary to bed and dreading to rise. But we must rise above it all! We must see beyond our daily existence! We must struggle to see the big picture!"

Suddenly, the fact that we stood above it all in Peaceville Valley began to make a little more sense. Then Lilley pointed beyond the circle of buildings. For the first time, we noticed another little tableau. About twenty feet away, next to the edge of a swamp, stood two other angels.

One had a sweet face clipped from a magazine and was painted with a glowing gown. She held a Bible. The other, masked and bat-winged, clutched a bottle. A sign asked WHICH ONE WILL IT BE? above an open coffin between them. The coffin was labeled MR. AND MRS. YOU OR ME.

"See?" Lilley said in conclusion. "There's the big question right there. We shouldn't get so trapped-up in our daily world that we forget that there's that big question out there, always waiting to be answered! Which one will be YOUR choice?" This was the concluding line of the tour, so he dropped back into conversational tones. He smiled as we thanked him for showing us the place. We asked him why he'd built it. "Well, really it's all kind of a monument to overcoming my own problem with alcohol," he said.

Before we left, we marked our maps so we could find it again. A year or so later we came back to show it to a friend, but found the site destroyed and all the tiny buildings gone. A neighbor told us Lilley had lost his fight and had been reinstitutionalized for alcoholism after all. All that remained of Peaceville Valley was a handprint Lilley had made in concrete, embedded in the ground.

Mitch's Cross House

As you turn onto West Chestnut Street, a narrow neighborhood thoroughfare in Chicago, there's no way to miss the House of Crosses. For almost twenty-five years, the owners have been covering their residence with hundreds of plaques, shields, and wooden crosses, emblazoned with red, black, and silver. Back in the late 1970s, Mitch Szewczyk started making wooden crosses out of material that he found in the street. For some reason, he decided to nail them up all over the front of his house.

Szewczyk wasn't fixated with death or afraid of vampires—he wanted to create an artistic tribute to local politicians and to the movie stars of his youth. So he cheerfully gave Mickey Rooney, Zsa Zsa Gabor, Zorro, Buckwheat, and former Chicago mayor Jane Byrne their places. Unfortunately, Szewczyk became bedridden in the early 1990s and was never able to complete his King Kong cross.

Be sure to take plenty of photos from the sidewalk as you pass by. Szewczyk remains a beloved character in the neighborhood. While he might have dubbed his creation the Cross House, the locals just call it Mitch's Place.

Rice's Miracle Cross Garden

For nearly half a mile along both sides of a secondary road near Prattville, Alabama, you can see thousands of signs, crosses, wrecked cars, and mailboxes festooned with barbed wire. These forbidding and obsessive emblems are bad enough, but each of them bears a sign with such forthright messages as EVERYONE IN HELL FROM SEX USED WRONG WAY and HYPOCRITE YOU WILL DIE. This is the work of William C. Rice, who calls it the Miracle Cross Garden. As Rice explains it, the Lord told him to do it in 1976, and when some of his neighbors complain that it is an eyesore that lowers property values, the reverend claims he is only doing God's work. The insides of W. C. Rice's house and chapel are decorated the same way. Now approaching seventy, Rice continues to work on his Cross Garden and to tell visitors of the divine inspiration that led to its creation, reminding them that "Hell is Hot, Hot, Hot!"

The Big and Small of It

According to the Good Book itself, God is in all things. The good and the bad. The light and the dark. And perhaps most interestingly, the big and the small. Americans have embraced the last of those pairings quite literally. Houses of worship dot our landscape. Some are huge, for those who like to give glory to God. And others are tiny, for those who find faith to be a quiet, private affair. Either way, the following pages are devoted to those houses of devotion— America's biggest and smallest places of worship.

The Big

If you love God, go tell it on the mountain. But if you can't find a mountain, why not go to one of these religious sites that are built to be as big as one?

Some of the World's Largest Biblical Items

All over the world, religions revere the sites where their forebears experienced the visions and epiphanies that nourished their prophets. And that's why a well-manicured hundred-ten-acre park in Suit, North Carolina, is able to take its place alongside the likes of the Dome of the Rock or the Wailing Wall in Jerusalem and the Bodhi Tree in India. Of course, the Fields of the Wood is a relatively recent starting point for a faith. It marks the spot where itinerant Indiana preacher and traveling Bible salesman Ambrose Jessup Tomlinson first found inspiration in 1902.

Tomlinson had gathered a group of followers to start a new church but wasn't sure what form it should take until June 13, 1903, when he came back down from a morning of prayer like Moses from the mountaintop and founded the Church of God of Prophecy (COGOP).

By the time of Tomlinson's death in 1943, COGOP had begun an ambitious project to create a focal point for its half-million members scattered in sixty countries. The land around the Place of Prayer, where their founder had been

inspired, was cleared, and construction began on what would eventually become the world's largest Ten Commandments. The Law of Moses was spelled out in King James English in concrete letters five feet tall and four feet wide arrayed across a mountainside in view of the site where Tomlinson had prayed.

Other record-breaking acts of biblical gigantism to follow at the site include the world's largest altar (at eighty feet long), the world's largest New Testament (a concrete Bible thirty feet tall and fifty feet wide with access to a rooftop viewing area), and the world's largest cross, which is 115 feet wide and 150 feet long and lies flat. A small hangar for a gospel missionary airplane, replicas of the Crucifixion site at Golgotha (with creepy skull-like masonry to commemorate the "place of the skull"), the hauntingly "empty tomb" of Christ, and an outdoor pool with mass-baptismal capability are complemented by picnic areas and a gift shop. It's located on Highway 294, eighteen miles west of Murphy.

Tallest Cross in Florida

Set high above Matanzas Bay in St. Augustine, this metallic cross marks the landing spot where, on September 8, 1565, Spanish explorers planted the first cross of Christianity in the New World. The largest religious cross in Florida, it is lighted at night and is open to the public.

ruci-fixation

Towering over the west end of Groom, Texas, and visible from Interstate 40, is a neck-bendingly big cross. It stands 190 feet tall and 110 feet wide, and is covered in corrugated steel, the same stuff one might use to make a toolshed. It's like someplace you'd keep your rakes — the really long ones. Of course, the big one isn't the only cross you'll see here. Circling the base are a collection of impressive bronze statues depicting the thirteen stations of the cross, including Jesus carrying the cross, Jesus falling with the cross, and Jesus being nailed to the cross. Several yards away stands a portrayal of Calvary, where Jesus and the two thieves hang from crosses. The cruci-fixation extends even to the property's light posts, also crosses. No visit would be complete without a picture next to the replica Shroud of Turin, which the attraction claims is one of only seven in the world.

Sadly, most people miss these bonus features. Problem is, the cross is so enormous, it defeats most attempts to draw travelers off the highway. After all, you really don't have to pull over to see it. And the thing the cross's builders won't tell you is that their 1,250-ton edifice isn't the tallest. The Cross at the Crossroads in Effingham, Illinois, beats it by an entire eight feet. Yet, surprisingly, billboards in Groom still invite you to see the "Largest Cross in the Western Hemisphere." So much for the Ninth Commandment.

Giant Madonna

Behind the parking lot of the Servants of Mary Center of Peace near the town of Windsor, Ohio, stands this gargantuan statue of Our Lady of Guadalupe, whose appearance in the sixteenth century is credited with the conversion of seventy-five thousand Aztec Indians to Catholicism. Although it's not the largest Virgin Mary statue around, the thirty-three-foot-tall Madonna stands on the outstretched wings of an angel perched on a cloud, bringing the statue's entire height to fifty feet. In front of her, a giant, illuminated string of rosary beads made of chain-linked balls of metal surrounds a small lake. Both the statue and the Servants of Mary Center of Peace sit on an organic farm owned by Pat and Ed Heinz.

The Heinzes conceived of the larger-than-life Mary, but she was just a vision until Richard Hyslin, a Texas artist, offered to donate his skills free of charge. The statue, covered with small, colorful mosaic tiles and complete with a huge metal coil conveying Mary's radiance from behind, was dedicated in 1995.

Mary sits far back from the road, so look for her carefully if you're traveling on Ireland Road in Windsor.

This place is still technically open, but it's seen better days. A lot of the "beads" from the rosary have been broken, and the gift shop is now closed.

Giant Jesus

Solid Rock Church seems a fitting name for a house of worship that's home to a colossal sculpture of Jesus—despite the fact that the sculpture is actually made out of plastic foam and fiberglass stretched over a metal frame. The huge Christ looms over the baptismal pool outside the church founded by evangelist Darlene Bishop and her husband Lawrence, in Monroe, Ohio.

The sixty-two-foot sculpture depicting Jesus's head and torso has a forty-two-foot span between its upraised hands (leading some locals to refer to him as the Touchdown Jesus) and a forty-foot cross at the base. Rendered by artist James Lynch at the request of the Bishops, the statue serves as advertising for the three-thousand-member nondenominational church and as a subject of controversy in the community. Many Monroe locals believe it is an eyesore, while others feel it puts the town on the map. Probably the most sensible commentary appeared in a forum on Monroe's community Web site, "There have been so many deaths on that section of I-75, perhaps when people see Jesus they will be more careful."

The statue is actually at the back of the Lawrence Bishop Music Theater, an amphitheater that belongs to the church. If you are riding up I-75 north, there is no way you can miss this thing.
—*Jim Willis*

Jesus Christ, That's a Big Statue!

I am a long distance trucker and have seen my share of roadside oddities but this one takes the cake. I took a U-turn off Route 71 near Monroe, Ohio, to get to the largest statue of Jesus I've ever seen. The Solid Rock Church is more like a place you would catch a sporting event—it's huge. There is a walking path around the giant Christ and man! Do you feel small under his giant sky-raised arms. I half-waited for him to rise up out of the water and start picking up cars of the unrepentant to toss them a few counties away.—*Dave Lounsberry*

More Big Religion

In Eureka Springs, Arkansas, is the Christ of the Ozarks—a seven-story-tall, two-million-pound uncrucified representation of the Messiah, the largest Christ statue in the United States. Passion plays are still put on nightly at the base of the big Jesus.

Ossineke, Michigan, is home to Dinosaur Gardens, a theme park where statues of dinosaurs fight each other in the woods. Outside the park is a gigantic Jesus statue holding a globe. Who says dinosaurs and creationists don't mix?

The Virgin Mary looms large over Catholic traditions. She also looms large in Butte, Montana, where a ninety-foot statue depicting her stands above the Rocky Mountains. That rendition is larger than Sioux City, Iowa's thirty-foot-tall Queen of Peace. And let it never be said that Boston is losing its Catholic roots. A fifty-foot-tall Madonna stands in North Boston.

Redwood trees are the tallest trees in the world and a North American treasure. They're also prime for carving. In Indian River, Michigan, the crucifixion is depicted by the fifty-five-foot-tall, twenty-one-ton Cross in the Woods, carved out of a single redwood tree. Jesus himself weighs seven tons and is made of bronze. And it's not even the tallest crucifix in the country. That honor goes to a sixty-foot sculpture in Bardstown, Kentucky.

While the two crucifixes mentioned above are the largest in America, there are larger crosses; they just don't feature an image of Jesus on them. Groom Texas, Alto Pass, Illinois, and Frankfort, Kentucky, all have some pretty big crosses. But the biggest might just be the 198-foot-tall cross in Effingham, Illinois.

Praying Hands of Webb City

This memorial in Webb City, Missouri, is a wonderful accomplishment. The statue's physical birth took place in twenty-year-old Jack Dawson's backyard, where he constructed the steel and wire mesh skeleton. As soon as the skeletal substructure was complete, it was transported to the elevated site along the northbound lanes of Route 71. There it took on its precise shape, ending up weighing one hundred tons, with a height of thirty-two feet.

The hands were dedicated to the public in 1974. Thirty-three years have passed as of this writing, and the giant praying hands are still drawing the faithful and the curious. There is convenient parking next to the hands, and on a day with just a little wind, you can stand behind them and look past to see the American flag flying boldly in the near background.

Statue of Liberation Through Christ

The Bible Belt has a new buckle, and it is bling. It towers seventy-two feet above the busy intersection of Kirby Parkway and Winchester Road in Memphis, Tennessee, out in front of the World Overcomers Outreach Ministries megachurch. It looks like the Statue of Liberty's born-again cousin. She is the *Statue of Liberation Through Christ*, a less-than-subtle call for America to return to God.

From the top of Miss Liberty's head down to her sandaled feet, the universally recognized image of American freedom has been co-opted with Christian symbology. Her crown is emblazoned with the name Jehovah, with each spike displaying one of seven other names for God. A tear runs down her right cheek, a reaction to the nation's "self-destruction" through legalized abortion, banning prayer in schools, and promoting "Wicca, secularism and humanism." Then, of course, there's the unmistakable gigantic cross held aloft as though to protect Memphis from vampire assault.

The Lord's Lady Liberty is the brainchild of "Apostle" Alton R. Williams, the church's pastor and a prolific writer who's never disinclined to publicize his opinions on world matters. (He contended that Hurricane Katrina was God's retribution for the sinful ways of New Orleans.) He says he selected the easily recognized Statue of Liberty so he could spread his message to the "unchurched" of the world, a choice he defends by pointing out that the statue has been used by others to promote guns, sex objects, and condoms. Not surprisingly, the statue receives unwavering criticism, especially for its price tag of more than a quarter million dollars. The church defends its decision by saying they'll recoup the costs through the sale of Liberty-themed mouse pads, coffee mugs, and foam crowns, as well as a half-dozen books about the statue.

The Small

Humble yourself before God, the Bible recommends. Well, the following churches are about as humble as they get—especially in terms of size!

For Ye of Little Faith: An Appropriate Church

Agnes Harper operated a rural grocery store in coastal McIntosh County, Georgia. A lot of her customers came off U.S. 17, one of the nation's busiest highways, but as she fed their bodies, she worried about their souls. So in 1949, she decided to use her limited resources to cater to their spiritual needs and constructed Christ Church, better known as the Little Church.

The tiny cinderblock chapel measures only ten by fifteen feet. On each side are two elegant stained-glass windows, with three in the back, all imported from England. Set into the roof is a glass star through which a sunbeam is cast through the interior of the structure.

Twelve bench chairs have foldaway kneelers, and up front is a small pulpit. It is said the church is just large enough to accommodate the Twelve Disciples, with Jesus at the pulpit. "It is not the dimensions of the church which is important," Agnes declared. "It is the extent of the faith." The popular slogan for the church is "Where folks rub elbows with God."

Fearing that the church would be sold following her death, Agnes deeded the property to Jesus, but in 1983 the McIntosh County chamber of commerce adopted and refurbished it. In 1998, a tiny bell tower was placed beside the church by a couple who had married there. The Little Church is open twenty-four hours a day. Pause and rest in tranquility, pray, meditate, or reflect on life's journey, spiritual as well as physical. To get there from I-95, take exit 12 and drive south on U.S. 17. The Little Church is on the left.

World's Smallest Real Church

In Iberville Parish, Louisiana, directly across the Mississippi from St. Gabriel, is a tiny structure that locals proudly claim is the world's smallest real church. Unlike a roadside shrine, services are held regularly (once a year, on August 15, for the Feast of the Assumption of Mary), and the vigil light candle is kept burning year-round. But it has

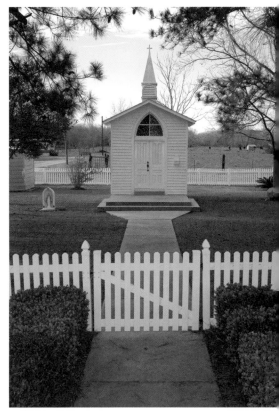

no seats or pews. In fact, during the annual Mass, only the priest and an altar boy or two can cram inside to stand before the altar, while the congregation and participants must stand outside, shielding themselves from the hot August sun (or rain) with umbrellas.

The Madonna Chapel was built to fulfill a pledge that immigrant Italian sugar farmer Anthony Gullo (also spelled Goula or Goullo) made in 1890 when he prayed to the Blessed Virgin to cure an illness that threatened the life of his eldest son. When the son recovered, Gullo donated land for a churchyard, and members of the community began constructing the tiny church in 1903. When the levee was enlarged in the mid-1920s, the church had to be moved and rebuilt, and was enlarged to its current size of eight feet by six feet.

A Little Religion on the Lake

The world's smallest church can be found resting upon a small wooden platform in the middle of a small lake off Sconondoa Road, in the small town of Oneida, near Syracuse, New York. It's known as the Cross Island Chapel, but don't let the name fool you. There's no island at all; the tiny church just sits on a sort of makeshift dock in the middle of the pond. Nearby a wooden cross is wedged into a pile of rocks that do breach the water's surface and may qualify as an "island." The nondenominational chapel was built in 1989 and is open to the public upon request. But you'd better have a pretty small family if you're thinking of booking it for a wedding: At about three feet by six feet, with only two seats, it can barely hold the bride, groom, and minister.

More Tiny Churches

At seven by twelve feet, the Stop, Rest, and Worship Church of Yuma, Arizona, stands just north of the intriguingly named Bridge to Nowhere. It's in a crop field off U.S. 95.

Open twenty-four hours a day and seven days a week, the Memory Park Christ Chapel of South Newport, Georgia, holds up to thirteen people at a time for services. With stained glass windows, pews, and a pulpit, this tiny church has all the accoutrements of bigger religious buildings.

The Traveler's Chapel of Nashville, Illinois, is a log cabin–style church with Bible verses written on the inside walls. It's next to a convenience store, so when you're done praying you can cool down with a Double Big Gulp and snap into a Slim Jim.

Morning Star Chapel in Elk Horn, Iowa, is outside the Danish Immigrant Museum. At only six by eight feet, it doesn't take too much room away from the fascinating exhibits on Danish immigration history for which Iowa is famous.

The Chapel of Memories is part of Waukon, Iowa's House of Clocks. It's been used for a number of marriages and is only six feet by six feet.

The Geographical Center Chapel is in Lebanon, Kansas, and is part of the Geographical Center of the forty-eight continental states. It's not used for services, but anyone is welcome to kneel beneath the cross/stars and stripes combination to get a little praying in.

On the grounds of Thomas More College in Crestview Hills, Kentucky, is the Monte Casino Chapel. It's been around since 1878, and its ceiling is only eight feet high.

The Wayside Chapel of Atwood, Michigan, is occasionally used for weddings, but mostly serves as a highway rest stop. It's open 24/7, and visitors can always rest their feet there.

Luverne, Minnesota's Blue Mound Wayside Chapel holds services on occasion, but has more animal visitors than humans. A group of buffalo tends to congregate around the small building on Highway 75.

Winslow, New Jersey's tiny church isn't even an official church. A Catholic landscaper combined his loves of Catholicism and landscaping and erected it on his front lawn.

Ardmore, Oklahoma's chapel on Durwood Road can fit a handful of people and plays music automatically when the door is closed.

The Wayside Chapel of White Lake, South Dakota, stands on I-90—actually two of them do. There's one on either side of the road for fast-traveling religious fanatics.

America's Smallest Synagogue is located in Honesdale, Pennsylvania. It's been around since 1852 and houses a congregation that met in a member's living room before it was built.

Praise the Lord and Fill 'er Up!

In the town of Long Beach, Washington, there is an old, abandoned gas station. The four holding tanks in back all have pictures painted on them, depicting four different times in Jesus Christ's life. There's an old gas pump that says JESUS IS LORD on top, and CROSS WAY on the bottom. There is also a dedication plaque to THE GOOD CITIZENS OF THE LONG BEACH PENINSULA BY CROSS WAYS MINISTRIES AUGUST 22, 2001. –*Karen Connelly*

Only Spiritual Relief

Too busy to chat with your Maker? If you commute along Washington State Route 2 between Monroe and Sultan, you have no excuse. Pull over to "Pause, Rest and Worship" at the teeny tiny Wayside Chapel. Complete with steeple, pulpit, and seating for eight souls, the chapel was dedicated in 1960 and is supported solely by donations and volunteers. Record your prayers in the notebook provided, but expect nothing beyond spiritual relief . . . as the sign outside states plainly: NO FACILITIES. The Wayside Chapel may be found along the Stevens Pass Highway, just east of Fern Bluff Road, in a small but well-lighted parking lot. Visit it 24/7—"The door is always open; the light is always on."—*Peg Boettcher*

Drive-in Church

There is a place of worship that eliminates those excuses about not having anything to wear to church. This is the Drive-in Church in Daytona Beach, Florida, where the entire congregation never leaves their cars.

Providence Home Geode Grotto

The Providence Home Geode Grotto in Jasper, Indiana fills four city blocks. It was the inspiration of Father Philip Ottavi, the Director of the Providence Home for retarded men. Father Philip's design was based on the Grotto of Lourdes, France, and used geodes as a primary building material. It took a crew of about 10 men from the Home about ten years (from around 1960 to 1970) to build the Grotto.

In addition to the many shrines built within the area, there are fountains, flower planters, benches, lamp-posts, birdbaths, and walls—all encrusted with geodes. Other materials, such as marble, granite, seashells, rosaries and pictures were also embedded into the planters, posts and sidewalks. The cave-like Mother of God Shrine features a marble statue of Mary and a ceiling with faux stalactites.
—*Debra Jane Seltzer*

The Grotto of the Redemption

Iowa is ninety-five-percent farmland, and it looks just about like what you'd expect from the nation's leading producer of corn and pigs. It's sprawling, wide-open, and flat. But near the tiny town of West Bend, Iowa takes on a different identity—as a geological wonder that speaks to the power and glory of God.

This site is an outcropping of gems, agates, and geodes known as the Grotto of the Redemption, and all it took to make it was a little religious inspiration and a few decades of obsessive, backbreaking labor. It's the world's largest collection of minerals and petrified material; its raw materials carry an estimated value of more than $4 million. But it's the story behind the grotto that makes it truly priceless.

In 1893, Catholic priest Paul Dobberstein was diagnosed with pneumonia. Before penicillin, this was more than a matter of medicine, rest, and recovery; it was a matter of life and death. Doctors told Dobberstein that his prognosis was grim. The recent German immigrant made a promise to God: Should God spare his life, Dobberstein would devote it to building a monument in his honor.

Five years later he was still alive, and in his new home of West Bend, he saw a large opportunity to build a grotto and, most importantly, a large amount of open space to build it in. With only a priest's modest salary at his disposal, Dobberstein spent the first decade of the twentieth century crisscrossing America, enlisting help in gathering raw materials. In every town he visited, he found helpers who gathered stones and shells with him. More than a hundred railroad cars full of minerals and

ore arrived in West Bend that decade—including a few geodes from the Carlsbad Caverns, before they became a protected national park. Construction began in 1912 on a foundation of Portland cement and sand.

More than a hundred feet wide, over twenty feet deep, and up to forty feet high, the grotto is actually nine different grottoes, each focused on a different theme and using different building materials. Inside, hand-sculpted Italian marble statues depict various scenes from Christian history and lore. Working without drawn blueprints, Dobberstein built the grotto by hand over the space of

several decades, opening the first section to the public in 1924. He was still working on his great tribute when he died thirty years later.

Over six million people have visited the Grotto of the Redemption since 1924, and tens of thousands still visit it each year. The site is currently owned by the Diocese of Sioux City and is maintained by a dedicated staff of curators. One of those curators, Rhonda Miller, spoke to *Weird U.S.* when we visited.

"It was really all in his head," she told us. "He could envision it in twenty seconds and know what he was going to do." But impressive though this is, it makes maintenance difficult. "Is there a blueprint that we can go on today? Unfortunately not."

The Grotto of the Redemption is not just a religious monument. It's also a monumental expression of one man's faith. And it's all in the place where you'd least expect it—the cornfields of West Bend, Iowa.

Splendor in the Glass

When Father Mathias Wernerus began sprucing up the cemetery of Holy Ghost Church in Dickeyville, Wisconsin, he started by building a not-so-remarkable soldier's memorial. That was in 1919, but within five years he was encrusting cemetery urns with flowers made from broken china and glass. His parishioners chipped in, helping him bridge the gap between cemetery and rectory with fantastically constructed shrines and grotto areas, surfaced with a bewildering array of glass, crockery, shells, and stone.

The altar of the Grotto for the Blessed Mother holds a cross made of pipestone that legend says was made by the first Native American convert of missionary explorer Père Marquette. Many of the pieces of glass and crockery were donated by parishioners, so that the entire grotto, although intended as a devotional area, is also a sort of historical record of the Catholic households of the Dickeyville area. Yet Father Wernerus worked for less than a decade on the place: After his housekeeper and cousin Mary Wernerus died in

1930, he lost the will to live and died within two months.

At one time as many as ten thousand people would visit the Dickeyville grotto on a summer Sunday, and it is still well maintained and a popular tourist and religious attraction. Doubtless it has inspired many a spiritual seeker, but Father Wernerus also has to be congratulated posthumously for his sheer bodacious artistry. He certainly spiffed up that cemetery.

Sanctuary of the Sea

When touring the grounds of Saint Mary-of-the-Woods, Indiana, you will come across many memorials and shrines dedicated to saints. But as you are standing in front of the oldest shrine on campus, the St. Anne's Chapel, you just might find yourself asking yourself, "What's the deal with all the shells?"

It all started back in 1840, when the Sisters of Providence, led by the Blessed Mother Theodore Guerin, arrived in the area. On a sea crossing from France, Mother Theodore experienced a storm so severe that it seemed the ship would capsize at any moment. She began praying to Saint Anne, the patroness of sailors, promising that if she were to make it safely home, she would erect a chapel in the saint's honor. Needless to say, the ship survived the storm and made it into port safely, and Mother Theodore wasted no time holding up her end of the bargain. By July 1844, a small log cabin chapel had been erected. Every year on the anniversary of the feast of Saint Anne, Mother Theodore would lead a procession to the chapel for service.

But over the years, the

logs of the chapel rotted and were replaced with stone. At this point, the sisters got a unique idea. They decided to decorate the interior of the chapel with shells from the nearby Wabash River. All the sisters joined in, and before long the entire interior of the chapel was covered. Some of the shells were pressed into the plaster as it was drying, while others were meticulously arranged to create works of art depicting the state of Indiana and even scenes from Mother Theodore's stormy night at sea. Today it still stands and represents the oldest shrine on the grounds of Saint Mary-of-the-Woods.
—*Roger Manley*

Ultraviolet Apocalypse

Religion comes to different people in many different ways. Some are born into it, while others wake up one morning and just start to see things in a different way. In Indiana, some people say that the Our Lady of Mount Carmel Monastery in Munster is the place to go if you want to see things in a different light—a black light, to be precise.

God-Created Beauty

On the grounds of the monastery is a collection of shrines erected by the Carmelites. Specifically, they were constructed by the Discalced ("barefoot") Carmelites. These were a group of monks who served under Allied command in the Free Polish Army during World War II. After the war, many of the men emigrated to America to spread the word among the American people. After arriving, the monks began collecting unique rocks, stones, and gems from all over Indiana to create shrines that would show the God-created beauty in all things.

The tour begins at the Grotto of the Holy Mother. Completed in 1954, the grotto is a multistoried building constructed from over two hundred and fifty tons of sponge rock from a strip mine in the Ozark Mountains. The focal point of the grotto is a large altar inset into the front of the building. However, off to the side of the altar, barely

visible, is a small opening that leads to the catacomblike structure nestled behind the altar.

The Fluorescent Altar

As you wander through the passageways, you will come across religious icons and statues built into the walls of the grotto. At one stop, you come to the fluorescent altar, which offers a sign of bigger glowing things to come.

Front and center on the altar is an alabaster statue, the Mother of Our Savior, surrounded by stones and rocks. It's a pretty scene as is, but with the aid of a good old-fashioned light switch, you can turn off the lights and activate a black light. This allows some words "hidden" in the stones to pop out in all their neon glory: "hail" and "queen." Just be sure to read the letters from the bottom left and work your way around, otherwise you'll see the secret message as "LIAH QUEEN."

On Your Knees!

As you leave the grotto, you begin your walk along the stations of the cross. To reach a re-created Calvary, the place where Jesus was crucified, you are asked to climb the Holy Stairs. But since these are holy stairs, you are asked to climb them on your knees and be reverent about it too. Should you choose not to, there are a set of ordinary feet-climbing stairs to the left of the Holy Stairs.

hands reach up from graves, all the while yellow crosses fill the sky above your head. It's a strange enough scene until you take into account that all of this is the result of black lights, and then things really get trippy. As you stare at the neon stones and try to take everything in, you half expect to hear Pink Floyd's "Dark Side of the Moon" start coming from speakers hidden within the rocks. But it doesn't. So you take your leave and take the stairs on your left up to the outside world, with the new-found realization that if and when it's time for the second coming of Christ, you better have a black light if you want to see it.

Neon Second Coming

After coming down from viewing the Crucifixion, you enter the Holy Sepulchre Chapel, which is made up to represent Jesus' tomb. It's quite a surreal feeling walking down into the darkness and coming upon a pair of angels guarding the pathway. Farther down the hallway, it opens up into what is supposed to be the tomb, complete with a stone figure of Jesus on his deathbed amid a lot of folding chairs. As you make your way to the back stairs and prepare to leave the chapel, make sure to turn to the right. Tucked away in a corner is the amazingly disturbing Memorial Chapel. The scene itself is a simple one: Jesus rising from the dead and the end of the world. An angel blows his trumpet while

"Get Right with God"

It's amazing what a little bit of faith can do. In the case of Henry Harrison Mayes, it led to a seven-decade-long mission across forty-four American states, all from his home base in the tiny town of Middlesboro, Kentucky. Mayes was born in 1898, and in 1917 he experienced a life-changing ordeal. He was pinned to the wall of the mine he worked at by a huge piece of machinery. He begged God for his life and dedicated the remainder of that life to the Lord's work. He survived and made good on his promise till his death, sixty-nine years later in 1986.

The bulk of Mayes's work involved constructing concrete crosses and hearts bearing the messages GET RIGHT WITH GOD and JESUS SAVES. Over the decades, other phrases popped up, including WHERE WILL YOU SPEND ETERNITY? and ADVERTISING GOD SINCE 1918. These signs were placed without fanfare along the roads of Kentucky and, eventually, forty-three other states.

Mayes also erected a number of wooden signs. He created them all personally and shipped them all over the

world at his own expense. In his later years, when wood and concrete work became too difficult, Mayes wrote his messages out on paper, put them in glass bottles, and tossed them into bodies of water throughout the world. All told, he sent over 50,000 bottles into the universe. He even donated a few signs to NASA before his death, in hopes that his mission, and his signs could make their way to the moon.

Mayes clearly lived his mission. But he also lived IN his mission: His house was shaped like a cross, and the roof was painted with religious slogans for passing planes to see. Mayes's effect on the town was physical as well as psychological. He also built a gigantic cross of electric lights that shines vibrantly at the base of a mountain in Middlesboro. While Mayes himself has been gone for over two decades, his effects still literally shine down upon the town today.

Many of Henry Harrison Mayes's sculptures still remain. Be sure to find the ones you can soon. As highways expand, buildings develop, and time runs its course, more and more of his unique roadside icons are falling by the wayside.

Strange Societies

Wherever like-minded people congregate, some bright spark will come up with the idea of starting a club or society. That's how the Elks, the Odd Fellows, and the guys that hang out down at the fire station got started. But whenever weird people congregate, you can bet that the societies they dream up will be odder than your average club. And if they stick together long enough, their clubs turn into full-fledged weird institutions.

Consider Philadelphia's favored sons, the Mummers. Every January 1 for the past century, this group of fun-loving blue-collar guys have marched down blustery streets dressed in outrageous costumes and makeup, heralding the New Year by trying to pluck banjo strings with frozen fingers and blow brass instruments so cold they stick to their

Z z y z x Rd

...ips. This is a group that is determined to stay merry even if it kills them.

But some strange societies are less benign and much less fun to watch. There are dark and secret fraternities shrouded in mystery in this country. They are dogged by strange reputations and theories of dire conspiracies and covert powermongering. And there are groups that split away from mainstream society completely and live in communes in ways we can only guess at. It's these people we turn to now: the nation's strange societies and the odd folks who belong to them.

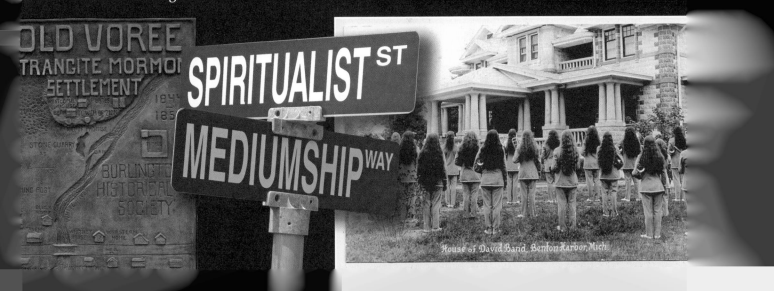

House of David Band, Benton Harbor, Mich.

The Freemasons

Some claim that Freemasonry is a simple fraternal group—nothing more than a social club with a long history. Others see it as a front for something far more powerful and sinister. Rumors abound that upper-level Freemasons form the core of the Illuminati, power brokers intent on uniting the world so that they can control it. The Masons have supposedly sunk their teeth into the United States government since its very inception. Lodges and temples have staked a place in all the nation's significant cities. So what goes on behind those doors with the strange symbols on them?

The GEORGE WASHINGTON
MASONIC NATIONAL MEMORIAL

Is D.C. the Center of the New World Order?

If you ever doubt the influence of the Masons in the United States, take a trip out to 101 Callahan Drive in Alexandria, Virginia. A mile outside the nation's capital stands a massive Masonic temple bearing the name of one of the order's most illustrious members, George Washington. The building's Web site at gwmemorial. org states, "The George Washington Masonic National Memorial was constructed entirely with voluntary contributions from members of the Masonic Fraternity. The Memorial Association is the only unified effort of all of the Grand Lodges in the United States. . . . Each Grand Lodge is a sovereign body in its own territorial jurisdiction but the love and reverence for George Washington by the Masons in this country is amply demonstrated by the collective effort of all of the jurisdictions to keep this Memorial to Washington, the Mason, a living reality."

Heartwarming, perhaps, but it's enough to give anybody who's suspicious of Freemasonry the chills. Those skeptics say that the Grand Lodges came together to build not a memorial, but a central place for the Illuminati to hatch their covert plots, just a mile outside the nation's capital. On *Weird U.S.*'s visit to this hotbed of Masonic propaganda we didn't get any sense of the sinister. But we were impressed by the imposing building and the brief tantalizing glimpse that the tour guide offered us behind a curtain, which revealed a replica of the Ark of the Covenant, "the most beautiful," we were informed, "ever made for Masonic purposes."

But in Washington itself, Masonic symbols have penetrated much farther—right down to the street level. Masonic imagery is everywhere, from the sculptures on the IRS headquarters to the Egyptian-style obelisk that is the Washington Monument.

What is less known is that the city itself could be one large Masonic symbol. The architect of the city, Pierre Charles L'Enfant, was widely known to be a Freemason. And how else can you explain this: The classic Masonic image is that of a compass and a straightedge—and this can be traced on the map of D.C. Connect the White House to the Capitol and the Jefferson Memorial to form the compass. Then join the Capitol to the Washington Monument (via the Lincoln Memorial), and then draw a straight line from the Washington Monument to the House of the Temple and presto! You have a Masonic straightedge.

Then there's the pentagram. Dupont Circle, Logan Circle, and Scott Circle form the three northern points of a pentagram. These three circles also each have exactly six streets entering them—so the center of government has a perfectly spaced-out 666 in it. Washington Circle lies at the leftmost point of the pentagram. And what landmark, you might ask, is at the southern tip of this pentagram? Easy: the White House.

It's clear that Washington was not designed for easy driving or tourism—all the squares, circles, and dead-end roads are enough to disorient any visitor. But perhaps the city planners' original intention was not ease of navigation but rather to honor a mysterious secret society.

Rosicrucians

On a wooded ridge above Philadelphia's Wissahickon Creek, there's a stone-framed cave with what looks like a six-foot gravestone outside it. Everyone who grew up around there calls this place the Hermit's Cave, or Cave of Kelpius, and historical markers explain that a group of German hermits once lived there. The stone marker goes one step further. It is inscribed JOHANNES KELPIUS, PHD, 1673-1708, THE CONTENTED OF THE GOD-LOVING SOUL, MAGISTER OF THE 1ST ROSICRUCIAN COLONY IN AMERICA. The inscription at the bottom reads: LOVINGLY ERECTED TO HIS MEMORY BY THE GRAND LODGE OF ROSICRUCIANS (AMORC) A.D. 1961.

All this raises several questions. Who are the Rosicrucians? What does AMORC mean? And why are the answers a 2,905-mile drive from Hermit Lane in Philly to downtown San Jose, California?

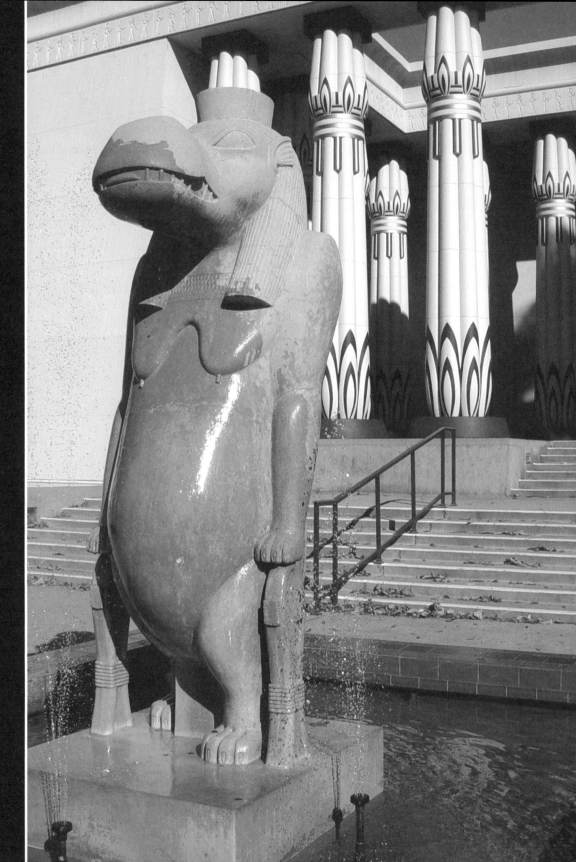

Rosicrucian Park

Sphinxes, pyramids, planetariums, and grand temples all seem strangely out of place in San Jose. But once you step inside the grounds of Rosicrucian Park on Naglee Avenue, it's San Jose that feels out of place. The block-size park, the headquarters of a Rosicrucian group called AMORC, contains shrines and temples, elaborate fountains, tiled walkways, statues, and a museum that houses the largest collection of ancient Egyptian relics in the western United States. There's also a planetarium and, closed to public eyes, a research library with thousands of rare books on mysticism and the occult. Rose-Croix University is here as well, along with the massive, secretive Supreme Temple.

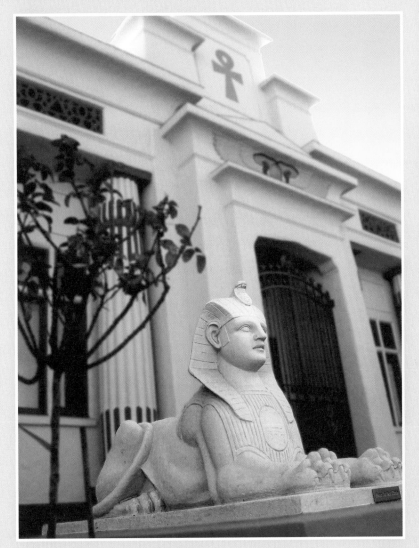

AMORC—the Ancient and Mystical Order Rosae Crucis—gained ground in 1915, when businessman and occultist Harve Spencer Lewis announced to the world that Pharaoh Akhenaton's secret society was now taking applications. As its Imperator (or leader), Lewis claimed that his group began in ancient Egypt and worked its way through 108-year cycles of public and private activity, with many great men in history as members. Other Rosicrucian groups disputed Lewis's claims (English occultist Aleister Crowley claimed that Lewis was a poseur and con man who passed off the teachings of a German "sex magick" cult as AMORC's own), but Lewis persisted and AMORC thrived. Their ads still appear in countless magazines, promising the secrets of "cosmic consciousness" to sincere seekers. Since AMORC denies that it's a religious organization, it avoids the whole process of "converting" recruits—a major factor in its success. And it doesn't hurt that the society is also on the Web at amorc.org.

Thirty-five centuries after Akhenaton introduced ethical monotheism and initiatory wisdom to the world, the San Jose–based Rosicrucians have carried on his work to become the Mystery School for the Global Village. Don't let any doubts you may have about the group prevent you from enjoying the park. It really is an interesting and peaceful place.

Pennsylvania's Pyramids

By the side of a small road between Quakertown and Dublin in Bucks County, Pennsylvania, stands a memorial garden that used to be a place of quiet reflection. Now it's closed down and surrounded by NO TRESPASSING signs and overgrown shrubs. Poking through the undergrowth are two large pyramids, and a mystery that goes back hundreds of years.

The land is owned by the Rosicrucians, a group that has apparently been a secretive presence in Pennsylvania for centuries and that really loves symbols, especially pyramids. At the front of the garden is a yard-high pedestal that turns out to be a topless pyramid. It's lined up with a second pyramid more than five feet tall on the other side of the hedge. This in turn lines up with a large pyramid-shaped mausoleum with tantalizing hints about the order. Memorial plaques list members of the supreme councils of nine, seven, and three, with titles such as Supreme Grand Master, Member Sublime,

and Hierophant. Many of those named are women. And there have been some very influential members, including Benjamin Franklin and Abraham Lincoln.

Looking inside the big pyramid, you get a clearer idea of the symbols of the order. Over the gated doorway stands a circular plate with a winged world crowned with a skull and crossbones, with the word TRY underneath it. The torch, anchor, and triangle in the design only further confuse the uninitiated. Peeking through the gate into the pyramid, however, gives you a jolt of recognition. On two walls of the four-sided pyramid are two very familiar circular designs: an unfinished pyramid topped with an eye, and an eagle holding an olive branch and thirteen arrows. These are the two sides of the Great Seal of the United States, as portrayed on the reverse side of the dollar bill.

So why are these seals hidden inside a Rosicrucian monument? Is the order tipping its hat to the United States? Is it worshiping the mighty dollar? Or is this country actually being branded with the seal of a secret society? Whatever the answer, next time you look at the all-seeing eye in the sky on a dollar bill, remember that there's a similar eye inside a pyramid north of Philadelphia.

Pyramids of the Rosy Cross

Our local cult is a band of people up in the woods who dress in medieval-looking robes and perform strange rituals at night. They have a lot of beautiful, if bizarre, buildings on the grounds: a grey stone pagoda, a tiled pyramid and a utility shed with a giant lightning rod. They have a huge, white Greco-Roman temple way back in the woods. At the summer solstice, they stand around the pyramids in ceremonial robes and chant loudly. I have seen this, and was subsequently chased away. They are strange and unfriendly, but not really dangerous.–Amy McCormick

Death is the greatest mystery of life. It leads to a question that has plagued humans since we first learned how to think: What happens to us when we die? One group of people reason that the only way to get any kind of definitive answer to this question is to go straight to the source and ask those who have died. These people are called spiritualists, and since 1848 when New Yorkers Kate and Maggie Fox first rapped out Morse code in a darkened room, they speak directly with the dead. Even though one of the Fox girls later admitted that she cracked her toe knuckles to simulate rapping from the spirit world, many spiritualists still claim that the dead speak back.

The Most Spirited Town in America

What Vatican City in Rome is to the Catholic religion, the town of Lily Dale is to followers of the spiritualist movement. Since its inception in 1879, this small town a few hours south of Buffalo, New York, has played host to Susan B. Anthony, Harry Houdini, and Mae West. And people still make sabbaticals there today.

Lily Dale is part religious commune, part ghostly summer camp, and all business. For $7 a day, plus up to $75 per consultation with the more than thirty registered mediums, you can meet all your clairvoyant needs. Local temples offer free services: Public group healings are offered twice a day at one, and dozens of visitors gather to attempt to rid themselves of various maladies. Twice daily,

at one p.m. and five-thirty p.m., visitors to the local pet cemetery are treated to spiritualist readings, as they have been since the practice started in 1898.

To become a registered medium in the community, aspiring clairvoyants must pass tests including forty public readings, three private readings, and a reading before the town's board of directors. Potential candidates are then judged on their mystical merits. Only the best of the best pass the test—just one out of twelve applicants is allowed to hang out a shingle.

Cassadaga—A Different Kind of Ghost Town

The quaint town of Cassadaga sits an hour east of Orlando, yet it is one of the most peaceful places in central Florida. To visit this hamlet is like taking a trip back in time, but what makes Cassadaga unusual is that every resident is a medium—that's right, they commune with dearly departed souls. Spiritualism is the main industry here, aside from a couple of New Age bookstores, a café, hotel, and post office.

In 1874, one of the New York spiritualists, George Colby, received instructions from the spirit world to lead a flock to Florida, where they discovered a small lake whose waters apparently cured Colby's tuberculosis. The flock claimed the water was a portal between the worlds of the dead and the living, named it Spirit Pond, and established Southern Cassadaga Spiritualist Camp Meeting Associations around it.

When we visited Cassadaga, certified medium Lawrence Damasio showed us the ropes. He filled us in on the original buildings in town, many of which are haunted. At the church, visitors often see a woman sitting up at a window, and one legendary boardinghouse is occupied by a woman in a white shirt whom Lawrence's friend Harry often encountered. "She looks like she's from the 1800s, and every night as I fall asleep, she gets right in my face, and she wakes me up," said Harry, and Lawrence explained, "She's just checking you out."

Lawrence said the pond is a well-known spot to catch glimpses of ghosts. "It is a really good spot to catch paranormal activity," he told us. "We love this stuff. But I wouldn't be drinking the water, because

thousands of people's ashes have been spread in this very site."

We figured that the only way to see if this was all fake was to experience it for ourselves. So we attended a séance held by a handful of the town's most seasoned mediums, including the Reverend Jim Watson.

"This is something that we do on a regular basis," Jim said beforehand, "and it involves the very core of the religion of spiritualism, which is communication with people who have crossed over. This is a way they've done it since back in the 1840s."

"Anything can happen," he added excitedly. "And it usually does."

The ceremonial room had a solemn air about it. After a brief, tense period of inactivity, the table began to move . . . just a little. Then it began violently tilting and shaking. The mediums urged it on, and the table even began to levitate. As it did, Jim Watson urged us to "work with the energy."

At that point, one of the mediums began communicating with a departed loved one of ours—saying that she left this world fast and needed time to come to terms with it. We asked her if there was beer in heaven, and in response to our levity, she sent the table reeling out of control and eventually up onto its side. One of the mediums, Jean, solemnly told us that, "'Everything in moderation,' she's saying."

Was it all a hoax? Was the table rigged? Did we in fact establish contact with one of our deceased friends? We will never know the answer. But what we can be certain of is that this is one of the most fascinatingly unique towns in the entire United States.

Spiritualists of Spook Hill

The craggy hill looms over tiny Wonewoc like a medieval castle wall. Even the most casual passerby will notice this magnificent ridge in southern Wisconsin, but only those very familiar with the area will know its local name—Spook Hill. It has been the summer home of a cadre of psychics and spiritualist mediums since 1877. These seasonal inhabitants prefer the name Wonewoc Spiritualist Camp, but they cheerfully accept the Spook Hill moniker. As long as camp clients don't mind, the mediums don't either. And with traffic topping fifteen hundred on a good week, the clients don't seem to mind.

Some come to take part in classes or group "circle" readings, others just enjoy solitude in one of the thirty-nine buildings on the wooded campus. There is even a healing tree with legends of miraculous cures. Most, though, are drawn by the desire to have a reading with a trained medium. Thirty-minute sessions at a dollar a minute run nonstop on weekends, with up to eighteen sessions per day. Ordained spiritualist ministers like Barbara Picha and Bradley K. Moore hold court in their simple cabins while clients line up outside. A favorite camp spot for both of them is the wood-paneled chapel, hung with paintings of spirit guides and of early spiritualist Andrew Jackson Davis.

"He received the nine principles we adhere to," Moore told us. "Our creed is called the Magic Staff: Under all circumstances keep an even mind."

Given the camp's long history, it's not surprising that most of the surrounding community seems accepting of it. As far back as the 1850s, even the sons of an area judge were full-fledged members of the Wonewoc spiritualists,

and at one time the group shared a building with the German Lutherans and other denominations. But Spook Hill has not been without its detractors. In 1884, someone attempted to burn the main hall by stuffing straw into the building's chinks and igniting it. More recently, some religious groups have climbed the hill to picket the camp and try to dissuade clients from having readings. "They really just brought us more people," says Moore philosophically. Both Moore and Picha emphasize that everyone is welcome at the Wonewoc Spiritualist Camp, no matter what their background or personal belief system. "We're an all-inclusive bunch," says Moore. "We love everybody."

Utopians

In the 1500s in England, a member of King Henry VIII's court wrote a book that described a perfect society in the continent that Amerigo Vespucci had just explored. It was a place where everyone, male and female, had equal access to housing, health care, and basic human freedoms. It was a stark contrast to the turbulent world where the author, Sir Thomas More, lived. But it all seemed strangely possible in the New World. The book and the land it described both had the same name: Utopia.

The United States has been a haven for people seeking their own personal utopia from the very beginning. But to some huddled masses, this meant more than life, liberty, and the pursuit of happiness. To some, it means setting up a spa in the desert. To others, it means creating a landing pad for benevolent aliens. And to others, it involves moving to an island, crowning your leader king, and letting him take as many spouses as he desires. Whether this sounds like utopia or just more *Weird U.S.*, it's coming right up. . . .

Hollow Earthers

Did you ever think that maybe the earth is not solid, but hollow? In 1818, John Cleves Symmes did, and believe it or not, he convinced many people that he might be onto something. From mathematical patterns of interlocking spheres he had observed in nature, he convinced himself that the world must be hollow, with portals to an inside universe, complete with its own sun, lush vegetation, and a race of human beings descended from the lost continent of Atlantis or possibly the Lost Tribes of Israel. Although many might scoff at this today, in Symmes's time the polar caps had not been widely explored, and the territory seemed as mysterious as Atlantis itself.

He eventually found a rich New York investor to fund an Antarctic expedition, but the S.S. *Annawan* never found entryways to the world within. However, that hasn't stopped people from following in his steps.

John Cleves Symmes Explores Inner Space

If you visit Ludlow Park in Hamilton, Ohio, you can find a stone monument dedicated to Symmes by his son Americus Vespucci Symmes in the 1840s for all to wonder at (and about!). An inscription reads: CAPT. JOHN CLEVES SYMMES, AS A PHILOSOPHER, AND THE ORIGINATOR OF SYMMES THEORY OF CONCENTRIC SPHERES AND POLAR VOIDS; HE CONTENDED THAT THE EARTH IS HOLLOW AND HABITABLE WITHIN. Appropriately, a hollow earth made of granite beckons from atop the memorial. Contrary to popular belief, this monument is not a grave marker. Symmes is buried with several family members in Congress Green Cemetery, which is in North Bend, Ohio.

Journey to the Center of the Earth

In Estero, Florida, there was once a colony of folks called the Koreshans who founded a utopian civilization called New Jerusalem in the heart of the swamps. Established by a Civil War veteran named Cyrus Teed on the notion that the earth was hollow and contained the entire universe at its center, it was large enough to accommodate ten million people, though it never did.

Teed was a medical doctor, but his experiments with electricity took him to another level: He received a severe jolt that knocked him out, and while he was unconscious he saw a vision of a beautiful woman who revealed the secrets of the universe to him and told him that he had a mission to "redeem humanity."

After he came to, he changed his name to Koresh (the Hebrew version of his name), joined a branch of the Shaker community, and began promoting the notion that the earth is a hollow spinning sphere and that we inhabit the inside, held to the inner walls by centrifugal force. The theory appealed to some religious fundamentalists, so he was able to recruit a large number of educated people for what he called the Koreshan Unity.

In 1894, the Koreshans acquired 320 acres of land on the Estero River in Florida to found a utopian settlement. Koreshan-style socialism advocated communal living, sexual equality, and celibacy. Teed's followers tamed the hostile land and eventually developed a self-sufficient community, complete with a sawmill, boatyard, and concrete plant. They even generated enough electricity to power

The New Jerusalem

their city and sell the surplus to neighboring towns.

But this hive of industry still centered on Cyrus Teed's creed: "To believe in the Earth's convexity is to deny God." *Weird U.S.* spoke to Bill Grace, whose great-grandparents and grandparents were Koreshans, and Mike Heare, a park services specialist at the Koreshan State Historic Site. Bill demonstrated an odd model from the site.

"This demonstrates the hollow earth theory," he explained. "The sun was in the center, and the world was on the inside of the sphere of the earth."

"Their belief was that there was a giant ball of gas inside the hollow sphere," Mike added. "The sun was contained in that ball of gas, and it had a light side and a dark side and it rotated, creating day and night."

They also demonstrated a mock-up of the Rectilineator, an instrument devised to prove Teed's theory. The weird contraption consisted of ten huge double T-squares made of seasoned mahogany, set horizontally on ten carefully balanced mounts, all designed to measure the curvature of the earth. The Koreshan Geodetic Survey began on a stretch of beach at Naples, Florida, and it took five months to conduct the experiment, but on May 5, 1897, Teed announced that the end of the instrument had touched the water in the Gulf of Mexico; therefore the earth curved upward and therefore we live on the inside of the earth.

Teed's inspiration included the promise of immortality for all faithful Koreshans—and when he died in 1908 after a brawl with leaders from a neighboring town, his promise was put to the test. He said he'd be back in six (but didn't mention six of what), so his closest aides laid his body in state and awaited his return. After five days, county health officers forced the members to bury him immediately. Within a few years, only a handful of Koreshans remained, and after a hurricane in 1921, not even Teed's tomb remained.

Emissary from the Outer World to the People Within

At a book signing a few years ago at Barnes & Noble in Brick, New Jersey, a curious bearded man came up to Mark and me and handed us a pamphlet that said, "The Hollow Earth Society — Contact Dr. Beard." We met Dr. Beard at his Ocean County home to discuss what the Hollow Earth Society is all about.

Mark Sceurman: For the uninitiated, what is the Hollow Earth Society today?

Well, there are numerous people throughout the world who are members of it. Most of them have the idea that the earth is hollow and has the concentric rings like John Symmes mentioned.

Mark Moran: There are differing theories, like Cyrus Teed's.

Right, it's sort of like a reverse of it. In a similar thought, people have said that they've seen UFOs and flying beings in the upper atmosphere. So there's really no telling what's there. We know very little about our own atmosphere as compared with what we know about other worlds.

MM: So who are these people that live in the earth?

Originally, all life began inside of the earth. Besides being a medical doctor, I have a doctor's degree in philosophy, and I've discussed this with people of mythology and religion. At one time, the earth's shape was quite a bit different on the outside. There were many continents and lands which have sunk. Originally the holes were smaller at the poles, and the original people that were in there came out and lived in the Caucus Mountains of Europe and traveled throughout the region.

Edgar Allan Poe went to the inner earth because he was familiar with Symmes. He went to a land that I visited that's just on the inner side of the North Pole. The outer side to the Greeks was called Hyperboria, but on the inner side, there's an island where the people are black . . . even the whites of their eyes are black. And in several of his writings, which are both factual and fiction, he wrote about that.

MM: So when and how did you first enter through the North Pole?

Well, I have a yacht that I was given by a relative.

MS: So you have to get there by boat, then.

Well, I got there by boat. Admiral Byrd's been there by plane, and my father went near the entrance by submarine. I went up through the Pacific side, and then we came out through the Atlantic. That would be in the early 1980s.

MS: What does the Hollow Earth look like today? Has it evolved culturally?

[There's] Lamaria, that's a continent that sank. And they used flying devices to get into the Hollow Earth. They went directly underneath that, so that they're living on the opposite side of the Pacific Ocean. I've been in contact with them. They've visited the surface. The ones we have to be careful of are the ones that are living in the crust of the earth, and that's a separate realm within the concentric rings. While there's not always bad personages there, they usually are notorious. And that's where we get some of the dark sciences.

MS: But how does the light get in? Is it lit?

There's a sun inside—I have maps available. Long ago, like I mentioned, when the hole was smaller, the top of it broke apart, and there's satellites inside that converge upon each other at different times and make night and day through an eclipse. There's an inner sun, and also it's inhabited as well. There are different types of beings that live on the in and outside of that, and the smaller satellites that circulate.

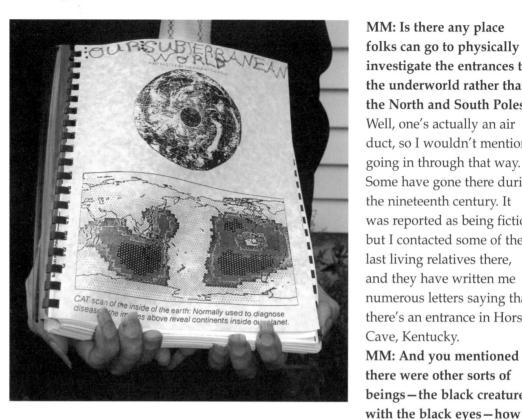

CAT scan of the inside of the earth: Normally used to diagnose disease, the images above reveal continents inside our planet.

MM: Is there any place folks can go to physically investigate the entrances to the underworld rather than the North and South Poles?

Well, one's actually an air duct, so I wouldn't mention going in through that way. Some have gone there during the nineteenth century. It was reported as being fiction, but I contacted some of their last living relatives there, and they have written me numerous letters saying that there's an entrance in Horse Cave, Kentucky.

MM: And you mentioned there were other sorts of beings—the black creatures with the black eyes—how many different species or subspecies are there?

They're all basically human, but they're not from this world. When I was in the Himalayas myself, I saw the Abominable Snowman, and in this area of New Jersey, the Bigfoot. They're actually humans, they just seem to be a little differently evolved from us. The Jersey Devil is a big controversy, and he's a smaller version.

MM: So getting back to the Hollow Earth Society today, how many members do you claim worldwide?

That would be 2,336.

If you'd like to contact Dr. Beard for more information about his Hollow Earth Society, you can write to him at the Hollow Earth Society, P.O. Box 69, Island Heights, NJ 08732.

Beards, Baseball, and Bands at Israelite House of David

The Israelite House of David in the Great Lakes region drew its inspiration from an eighteenth-century English visionary named Joanna Southcott. However, the group's commune in Benton Harbor Michigan, was all the work of Benjamin Franklin Purnell and his wife, and it began in 1903.

The Purnells tagged onto Joanna Southcott's vision that she was the first of seven messengers sent by God to prepare for the second coming—because that allowed for six other messengers and why couldn't the Purnells be among that number? They established a colony on the outskirts of town that called themselves the Israelites—celibate vegetarians who never shaved or cut their hair and who turned over their worldly goods to the Purnells.

Tourists began flocking to the colony grounds on the weekends. To accommodate the throngs, the colonists built an amusement park with steam engines running on miniature railways, a toy factory, a vegetarian restaurant, an ice-cream parlor, and a hotel. The park opened to a public crowd of over five thousand in July 1908; by 1912, ticket sales for the trains were over eighty-four thousand. The park continued to be a large tourist draw through 1968, a full sixty years. The group was famous for its bands and for its baseball teams, which traveled the United States and the world.

After an ugly lawsuit involving religious fraud and sex with minors, Ben Purnell was threatened with exile from the colony, but he died before the sentence could be carried out. On his deathbed, he told his followers he would be back in three days; however, he didn't keep the appointment. Nonetheless, the devoted preserved his body and kept it in Brother Ben's home, the Diamond House, until the early 1960s. It may still be there.

After Benjamin's death, the colony divided in two, with Benjamin's legal advisor in charge of one part and his widow leading the other. Today almost nothing is left of the amusement park, miniature train, or other attractions. The baseball teams are only quaint memories. And yet a handful of believers continue both factions of the colony to this day. Mary Purnell's City of David still serves vegetarian luncheons and hosts vintage baseball matches. They also offer tours of their museum and considerable grounds, two miles north of Interstate 94, exit 28, on Britain Avenue at Eastman Avenue in Benton Harbor. They maintain a well-illustrated Web site at maryscityofdavid.org.

Uriel and the Space Brothers of Unarius

High atop a hill on the outskirts of El Cajon in southern California, thirty miles east of San Diego, a sign sends out a warm greeting to all who pass that way. It reads WELCOME SPACE BROTHERS, and it's the landing site that our space masters have picked for their jeweled spacecraft to land when they return to earth to teach us the ways of the federation of thirty-three planets and other mysteries of the universe.

At least, that's what the Unarius believe, and their name, after all, does stand for Universal Articulate Interdimensional Understanding of Science. The Unarius are America's oldest and most successful alien-contactee group, founded by Ruth and Ernest Norman in 1954. That was the year Ruth changed her name to Uriel (to reflect Universal Radiant Infinite Eternal Light) and began publishing books about past lives, reincarnation, the glorious future, and the outer cosmos. Their spokespeople Kevin and Tracey Kennedy told *Weird U.S.:* "Ernest L. Norman immediately knew that Ruth was incarnated to help him bring this mission forward — to tell people about this better way of life. Shortly thereafter they got married, and he began channeling the books. She began the publication of the books, and then he made his transition in 1971."

By channeling, Kevin meant that the books were dictated by aliens, and Ernest's "transition" is what we'd call dying. However, Kevin explains, "We do not die, just move on to another plane." The Unarius believe Ernest's new plane is on Mars, where he acts as the Moderator of the Universe for the Confederation of the 33 Planets, which entitles Ruth to don the regal robes of an interplanetary princess. These flowing satin frocks, laced with lamé and rhinestones, topped with red or blond bouffant wigs and a jewel-encrusted royal scepter, have been described, rather vividly, as "Las Vegas Elvis meets Liberace in drag — on acid."

But the Unarius Educational Foundation wasn't always so flamboyant. For the first seventeen years, Ernest's lectures on inner contact with higher beings earned the foundation only a small membership. It was after his transition, when his charismatic widow took over and spiced things up, that the movement took off. It didn't hurt that she claimed to be the reincarnation of Confucius, Mona Lisa, Ben Franklin, Socrates, Queen Elizabeth, and King Poseid of Atlantis.

But before you write off the Unarius as just another New-Agey UFO cult, remember that they consider themselves to be a scientific research group, not a religion. And the basic principles of their teachings are quite positive: to research their own past lives through channeling, recognizing their bad karma and purging it all through study, practice, and understanding of one's own self. And they recognize that humans aren't so good at that: "The Space Brothers from all the other worlds live by this science," Kevin told us. "Metaphorically, they're in college, and we're still in elementary school."

"The co-founders of Unarius were very advanced intellects," Tracey Kennedy added. "Their purpose was to once again bring about the teaching that would help us understand ourselves as spirit beings, as energy beings."

From the outside, their academy in El Cajon looks like a large strip mall storefront. The inside is adorned with classical columns and gilded furnishing, pastel frescoes, numerous portraits, busts, and statues of Ruth Norman, and one picture of Ernest. There is also a large-scale model of the future city the Space Brothers will construct and a star chart of the thirty-three federated planets' solar system, complete with blinking lights. But it hardly matches the splendor of Ruth "Uriel" Norman's car, which drove *Weird U.S.* out to the future landing site of the Space Brothers.

The 1968 Cadillac El Dorado was tripped out with spacey imagery and topped with an electrified flying saucer. It may have taken a while to start her up, and she may have stalled a few times, but even if the Uriel-mobile is unfit for intergalactic (or even interstate) travel, it looks pretty good. When we reached the predetermined landing site, we noticed the half-erased numbers 2002 beneath the WELCOME SPACE BROTHERS sign. This was the projected date of arrival for the Space Brothers, Kevin and Tracey said. So what went wrong?

"Well," Kevin and Tracey said, "after September 11, 2001, it must have been pretty obvious to the Space Brothers that we weren't quite ready as a planet to join their federation just yet."

Or perhaps they had already met Ruth "Uriel" Norman and saved themselves the journey. Ruth, you see, had transitioned eight years earlier, back in 1994, and had left her fellow learners with the optimistic message before she left: "The future of the earth world is positive progressive, we promise you, we Brothers of the light and space promise you."

We just hope that if the Space Brothers do finally arrive, they save a seat for us on their cosmic bus.

African Village of Oyotunji

The only authentic African village in the United States is near the town of Sheldon in Beaufort County, South Carolina—or rather, it would be in the States, but it has declared its independence. It was established by a dancer named Walter Eugene King, who traveled extensively with the Katherine Dunham Dance Company in the 1950s and, during a tour of North Africa and Haiti, was moved by a spiritual attraction to the traditions and beliefs he encountered.

After a journey to the Matanzas region of Cuba, King came back to the United States as a Yoruba priest with a new name—Efuntola Oseijeman Adefunmi—and a new mission: to establish the precepts of voodoo-inspired Yoruba religion in the States. In 1970, he acquired a property in Beaufort County and established a community called Oyotunji. Two years later he visited Nigeria and was initiated into the Ifa Priesthood, which enabled him to be crowned Oba, or king, of Oyotunji on his return.

A number of people moved to the village, began to build homes, took up subsistence farming—with no running water or electricity—and settled in to stay. Or at least they tried to. Facing sweltering summer heat and mosquitoes, without air-conditioning or window screens, significantly reduced the number of willing participants. Although Oyotunji reached a peak population of more than two hundred, only about a dozen residents live there now (though some four hundred Yoruba-practicing people live nearby).

And it looks as though it's here to stay. When Oba Adefunmi I died in February 2005, leaving behind some fourteen wives, twenty-two children, and twenty-three grandchildren, one of his sons, Adelabu Adefunmi II, was crowned as the new king. The royal line continues, and religious activities at the ten temples and surrounding shrines go on. A first-time visitor feels a moment of surreal disconnection—like a theme park, the construction may be all plywood, peeling paint, and have a ramshackle ad-hoc feel, but this place is real. It's built on dreams of a better life, and the possibility of that is a fable not one of us can give up trying to make come true.

Case moved the B.O.T.A. to Los Angeles in 1933, where his star pupil, Ann Davies, expanded his doctrines and massively boosted the membership. She took over when Case died in 1956.

Unlike most New Age groups, the Builders' services and studies are based on solidly Western symbolism and teachings. The most commonly used symbols in their literature are the six-pointed Star of David and the Cabalistic

Builders of the Adytum

At first glance you may not even notice the Builders of the Adytum (B.O.T.A.) on North Figueroa in Los Angeles. The architect of this red brick building amid the mini malls probably planned it that way. Because the Builders of the Adytum is what they call a Mystery School, and what better way to keep it a mystery than to put it in plain sight but make it completely unremarkable?

When vaudevillian and lecturer Paul Foster Case founded the school in New York City in 1922, he called it Adytum, after the Greek name for the inner sanctum of a temple. There he taught the divination of the future using tarot, ancient Jewish cult lore from the cabala, and the medieval science of alchemy. His qualifications were strong: At the tender age of twenty-six, he had taken charge of the Order of the Golden Dawn (the occult society Aleister Crowley belonged to), but he left them after a mysterious scandal and set up his own group.

Tree—the representation of universe, consciousness, and body in Jewish mysticism.

The B.O.T.A. provides in-depth classes in tarot, cabalism, and hermetic studies, as well as weekly Sunday morning services for the general public. Their temple is decorated with bright paintings of the tarot cards and banners emblazoned with Hebrew lettering. The black and white Pillars of Solomon flank the altar's centerpiece, a full-color diagram of the Cabalistic Tree. Services feature organ recitals, singing, censing, angelic name-chanting, hand-raising prayers, and sermons on tarot, cabalism, and the other mysteries. The highlight of the ritual is the silent meditation, when the lights dim and the assembled worshipers meditate and send out healing energies while the illuminated Cabalistic Tree glows in the incense-hazed darkness. Dues-paying members can either study by mail, in local groups, or at the temple's Thursday night classes. The B.O.T.A. sells tarot decks and other items by mail, including a six-pound Interlinear Bible. Heavy reading, indeed.

C'mon, Feel the Noyes in Oneida

Today, people know Oneida only as a sedate town east of Syracuse, New York, or as a brand name for silverware and dishes. But the town owes its prominence to a commune known for liberal sexual practices and an outright rejection of societal standards—all during the run-up to the Civil War.

Oneida was the brainchild of a young preacher named John Humphrey Noyes, who made his way throughout the Northeast in the 1830s, preaching fervently and dismally failing to gather a flock. Eventually, he had a nervous breakdown and was abandoned by his lady love, Abigail Merwin, who ended up married to another man. The rejection and his fragile mental state inspired a series of articles that Noyes published in a fledgling publication known as the *Battle-Axe*, which led to the kind of following he had been trying for all those years.

In his articles, he extolled the benefits of a sexually free lifestyle in which no one was bound to any other individual. He also hinted that he was an agent of God himself sent to earth. His articles caught the attention of Harriet Holton, the granddaughter of a

John Humphrey Noyes

wealthy New York politician, whom Noyes married (though he described their roles in such unromantic terms as "yoke-mates," and insisted that they would be living under his progressive sexual policies). Oh, and naturally, Holton would support her husband's goals with her family fortune. Noyes began laying the foundations of his dream with more articles and the beginnings of a communal living arrangement (including arranged marriages between followers).

The commune purchased its compound in Oneida in 1846, by which time they had already begun to practice a series of odd customs, including Mutual Criticism, a practice in which any individual in the commune could be harshly and publicly criticized by anybody else. (The single exception was John Humphrey Noyes, of course.)

But many other Oneidan practices were more shocking. The most famous was known as Complex Marriage, in which every man and woman of the Oneida colony would in effect be married to each other. Every adult was encouraged to engage in sexual activities with everyone else, and sexual exclusivity between couples was highly discouraged. In order to prevent the risk of people wanting to become couples, Noyes and his followers came up with another doctrine to curtail the risk of pregnancy—a system referred to as Male Continence, in which the men were supposed to put down the book before reaching the final chapter, so to speak.

Nevertheless, the Oneida community grew steadily to a late-1870s peak of three hundred people. Naturally, any community this outrageous would attract some strange visitors. One occasional member, Charles Guiteau, ended up assassinating President Garfield, but Oneida's records show that he was often at the receiving end of Mutual Criticism and was seldom if ever at the receiving end of the benefits of Complex Marriage. While

Harriet Holton

The Oneida community c. 1865–1875

the community encouraged universal sexual activity, it wasn't actually compulsory to include everyone.

The Oneida community came to a screeching halt in 1878 when John Humphrey Noyes handed over leadership to his authoritarian son, Theodore. Noyes junior's iron-fisted approach caused dissent, and by the time his father returned to fix things, it was too late. Many of the Oneidans had settled into traditional marriages and were actively rejecting the community's doctrines. And so it was that in January 1881, the community was converted to a company, Oneida Community Ltd., and abandoned free love for free enterprise—building furniture and firing ceramics. And that is why one of America's most outrageous utopian communes now has its name stamped on many dining sets, which are ironically enough used to celebrate traditional weddings and feed conventional families.

James Strang and the Plates of Voree

"*I am eager,* and mankind is frail. I shall act in time to come for my own benefit." So said the only man crowned king within the continental United States, James Jesse Strang. Actually, he didn't say the words out loud. He jotted them in his private diary before embarking on a strange adventure that would end in his assassination on a remote island.

Born in New York State in 1813, Strang didn't seem a likely glory hound. The red-headed lawyer moved to the Burlington area in Wisconsin's Walworth County with his wife and her family in 1843. Short of stature but tall on charisma, Strang made a favorable impression on many people, including Joseph Smith, the head of the booming new Church of Jesus Christ of Latter-day Saints, who took the unusual step of baptizing him into the church personally and conferring elder status upon him.

About a month later, after Smith was killed by a mob in Illinois, Strang surprised his local congregation with a purported letter from Smith naming Strang as his successor and instructing him to found a community called Voree, the Garden of Peace. "There shall my people wax fat and pleasant in the presence of their enemies," the document predicted. Suspicion about the letter's true origins ran rampant, but the letter did appear to be signed by Smith.

Strang promptly planted an eight-foot-tall oak post called a stake of Zion in the center of Highway 11 at the county line and declared that a revelation told him to dig on a nearby rise. When he took a group of elders to witness the excavation, they uncovered a blue clay box filled with three tablets, six inches wide and twelve inches tall. The copper plates bore mysterious markings that only Strang could decipher. Buoyed by the discovery, the group baptized many new converts and settled the area. A marker on a stone house that stands on what is now Mormon Road says that two thousand followers once settled here, but given the small size of the community, the number was probably only a few hundred. One of them was Strang's second wife. Because the church didn't openly accept polygamy at the time, he dressed the buxom girl in men's clothing and introduced her as his nephew and secretary. Later he would openly declare polygamy legal (and provide eighteen more plates from God to back it up), allowing him to marry three other young women. His original wife moved back to New York.

As his flock "waxed fat," Strang moved them to Beaver Island on northern Lake Michigan. Draped in a red robe and wearing a star-studded crown he had purchased from an acting company, Strang proclaimed himself king—and the colony elected him to the Michigan legislature. The fisher-folk who already lived on Beaver Island didn't appreciate any of this. And there was dissension in the ranks, especially over laws requiring all women to wear bloomers and instituting the death penalty for adultery. In fact, after he sentenced a follower to be horsewhipped, the victim ambushed Strang on June 16, 1856, and shot him in the back. The kingdom's fed-up fisher-people then voted Strang's twenty-five hundred followers off their island. Strang himself languished for several weeks, enough time for two of his wives (all four were pregnant) to cart him home to Burlington. He died in his parents' home along the White River on July 9, 1856, and was buried nearby. He was later reinterred in Burlington, where his final resting place is marked by a simple headstone. The town of Voree fared less well: All the bronze plates disappeared as mysteriously as they had appeared, and Strang's followers all either left the church or were absorbed into other branches of the sect. Mankind turned out to be not quite so frail as Strang had supposed.

A Utopia Spelled Z-Z-Y-Z-X

Here's a question to reckon with: How on earth did a desert spring just off Interstate 15 west of the Death Valley Highway become a utopia called Zzyzx? The answer is a testament to the vision of an evangelist and health guru who used religion, ingenuity, and a lot of fast talk to establish a health resort there. And the answer to the other obvious question is, "It's pronounced zeye-zix."

Four and a half miles south off the Zzyzx Road exit on Interstate 15, eight miles west of Baker, California, lie the ruins of Curtis Howe Springer's dream spa. Springer made a name for himself as a radio evangelist in the 1930s, beginning at radio station KDKA in Pittsburgh, but headed west and rounded up derelicts on Los Angeles's skid row and gave them meals and shelter in exchange for construction work on his new desert headquarters. The new town at the foot of Soda Mountain boasted a chapel, a cross-shaped pool with soaking tubs, an artificial lake, a sixty-room hotel, and an airstrip he named Zyport. There was even an old seagoing freighter, whose lifeboat still sits at the site. Free bus rides left every Wednesday from the Olympic Hotel on Figueroa Street in L.A., ferrying the hopeful out in droves.

A day at Zzyzx included meals of goat milk and rabbit meat (the only animals that could live in large numbers on the alkali flats) and twice-daily sermons over a PA system. In addition to folksy Christianity, these sermons marketed his miraculous cures, which included the life-enhancing antediluvian tea, a $25 hemorrhoid cure kit, and a baldness cure called Mo-Hair that involved rubbing a concoction into the scalp and doubling over and holding your breath. When taken to court by a dissatisfied customer, Springer peeled off the $2,500 fine "as casually as if he was taking care of a $2 traffic ticket."

Springer's downfall came when he began to offer lots for sale near Zzyzx that he did not own. In 1974, the Bureau of Land Management informed Springer that he could not sell land that he didn't hold title to. He and a few hundred followers were evicted, and after serving several jail terms, Curtis Howe Springer died in Las Vegas in 1986 at the age of ninety. By this time, the California State University system had begun to use the site for a Desert Studies Center and NASA used the area near Soda Lake for testing the Mars Rover vehicles. Zzyzx became the area's official geographic name in 1984.

Celesta, God's Own Country

Many Americans declare their land is God's own country, but as far as actual real estate holdings go, the Divine Being has only ever held the deed to six square miles of Pennsylvania. And those were repossessed after years of failure to pay taxes. The land in question was known as the city of Celestia, a religious community full of people awaiting the second coming of Christ.

The city of Celestia, also spelled Celesta, was the vision of a Philadelphia papermaker named Peter Armstrong. In the 1840s, he had fallen under the influence of the Millerites, a group that believed the Messiah would return at a particular date in that decade. Armstrong bought land in the mountains, drew up streets and lots, and laid out the foundation of a temple for the Messiah's arrival. After the deadline passed, Armstrong held fast to his belief and continued to recruit believers to populate his city.

He was helped along when the Civil War broke out, because President Lincoln excused one of the brethren from military duty on religious grounds. This appealed to draft dodgers, who soon beat a path to his door. Armstrong then set about avoiding another duty of an American citizen: paying taxes. On June 14, 1864, Peter and Hannah Armstrong registered a deed of conveyance transferring ownership of the land to the "Creator and God of heaven and earth, and to His heirs in Jesus Messiah, for their proper use and behoof forever."

Unfortunately for Armstrong, not all the draft dodgers and tax evaders on his doorstep were true believers, so

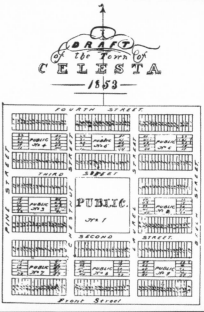

he set up a second village six miles downhill as a proving ground for newcomers. Before being allowed into the holy city, people would serve probation in the village of Glen Sharon to demonstrate their good faith.

Soon Sullivan County tax collectors came knocking. God may have owned Celestia, but his tenants and representatives could still pay his back taxes. So Peter Armstrong spent increasing amounts of time out of town earning money to make his vision come true, and the whole Celestia experiment began to fall apart. The town was almost completely deserted when Armstrong died there in 1887, and within a few short years the area became a wilderness once again.

You can still visit the streets of Celestia by driving along Route 42 from Laporte toward Eagles Mere. There's a Pennsylvania Historic Marker at the right of the road and a small parking area. Stop by the historical society's building behind the Laporte County Courthouse on Route 42 before your visit—you'll need a map to interpret the remains.

Divine Madness, on the Run

Cults are found in all corners of the world. Still, the question, "What is a cult?" is one of the hardest to answer. Many groups labeled as cults fight intensely against being called by the name. The negative connotations of the word reach far and wide.

What is generally agreed upon is that cults are based around charismatic leaders, they attempt to control the thought processes of their members, and there is, on some level, exploitation of members by the group's leadership. Outside of these three basics, the definition of a cult is hazy and can be set forth only on a case-by-case basis.

Many cults clearly have a religious bent. It's not hard to see how groups like the Branch Davidians or Heaven's Gate fall under the banner of the cult label. Cults base themselves around different ideals and activities. Many have wondered if Divine Madness, in Boulder, Colorado, is one of the strangest cults of all—one focused not on religion or politics, but on running.

Around 1991, this group of runners (also known as the community), who follow the coaching and teaching of Marc "Yo" Tizer, began recruiting members to train with them for long runs. The group became regular participants in the small world of ultramarathons, races in which participants run high mileage distances well beyond normal marathons. The Across the Years race is an annual event held in Arizona where competitors sign up to run for an entire 24-, 48-, or 76-hour block. Winners are determined by how many laps they are able to run in this period. For a stretch in the late '90s and early 2000s, members of Divine Madness were regularly ranking among the race's top competitors. In the tiny world of ultrarunners, this group from Colorado was making a huge impact.

But the extent of Divine Madness's influence was not confined to their achievements on the track. In fact, there was a sinister side to the organization. While their success in ultrarunning was impressive, the group's personal lives skewed toward the bizarre. And it was all based on the whims and desires of their guru and coach, Yo Tizer.

Members lived alongside each other in the same compound of rented buildings in Boulder. They would go on fifty-mile runs, after which they would gather together, drink copious amounts of alcohol well into the night, and be encouraged by the enigmatic Tizer to have random sex with each other in couplings of his choosing. Tizer dictated who members of the group could communicate with, the amount of sleep they were allowed to have, and what they were allowed to eat. Most of the group became accustomed to sleeping less than four hours a night and often had to ask Tizer if they were allowed to have things such as a slice of bread. Tizer, though, paid very little attention to the group's needs or requests. Instead, he determined the course of individual members' lives by pulling on their arms, which he claimed allowed him to sense their needs. In another very cultlike move, Tizer required many members to make large financial contributions to the group as a whole, surrendering their financial independence to Tizer.

This strange group managed to stay under the radar for much of their existence. In 2004, though, Divine Madness found themselves under much scrutiny due to the death of one of their most accomplished runners; the examination of his passing put a spotlight on the strange group of runners from Colorado.

Mark Heinemann was a veteran ultrarunner who had completed fifteen separate hundred-mile races by the time he reached the age of forty-six. On New Year's Eve heading into 2004, Heinemann was participating in the annual Across the Years event, which he had won the previous year. In the 2004 race, Heinemann ran 207 miles in forty-eight hours. During the race, he experienced some physical difficulties. He vomited a few times, and at times he was so delirious that he was zigzagging instead of running straight on the track. But these are problems that all ultramarathon runners face, as their chosen activity is both physically and mentally taxing. At the end of the race, Heinemann was no more out of it than he had been after his numerous other long-distance races. The group brought him back to the hotel for some well-deserved rest. That night, visitors to his room found that Heinemann had stopped breathing. A lung disease, bilateral lobar pneumonia, had taken over his body and quickly killed him in his exhausted state.

Heinemann's death brought attention to the unregulated world of ultramarathons, as well as to the strange ways of Divine Madness. *The New York Times* interviewed Dr. A. L. Mosley, who performed Heinemann's autopsy. His opinion of ultrarunners was succinct. "A normal person would say, 'I feel bad; can I sit down?'" Mosley said. "These people are not normal."

A 2003 *SI Adventure* article interviewed some former members of Divine Madness who had left due to the organization's peculiar ways. One was Celia Bertoia, who told of Tizer's strange living and sexual habits.

"There was an entire decade there when I didn't know anything that was going on," she said. "When I got out into the world, people would talk about historical events like the Oklahoma bombing or the O. J. Simpson thing. I had never heard of any of them." Tizer claimed that he had supernatural powers and justified his alcohol abuse by saying that he had to cool down his brain due to his thoughts and his abilities. According to a 1999 *Women's Sports and Fitness* article, he kept a stable of women, known as the Yo Ladies, at his beck and call.

The author of the article, Michael Finkel, trained with Divine Madness in preparation for a hundred-mile run of his own. During his time with them, he was wary of being recruited, although he did run and attend social events with members of the group. Here he describes a Divine Madness party to which he was invited:

The gathering was held in the loft of a renovated barn behind one of the group's homes. The loft was windowless and steam room hot and contained at least 30 people, two thirds of them women. Vinyl records were being played—classic rock, a good amount of Beatles. Many of the men were shirtless and dancing wildly, legs and arms flapping, hips pumping, hair spraying sweat. Women mirrored their moves. A bottle of Maker's Mark whiskey was pressed into my hand. I took a long swig and passed it on. Soon another bottle was in my hand. I drank again.

It took me several minutes to realize what was going on. For 30 seconds into each song, there was regular rock 'n' roll dancing, but this would soon devolve into dirty dancing and then body smearing and then, quite suddenly, passionate kissing. Some of the couples ended up rolling about on the carpeted floor; others sat and fondled each other. No one, save me, seemed the least bit self-conscious.

Some time after Heinemann's death, Marc Tizer began spending less time in Boulder and more at a compound in New Mexico, without other members of the group. While he is still considered the spiritual leader, he exercises less direct control of individual members due to his absence, and their commitment to the group is generally regarded as less intense.

Presently, the group does not refer to itself as Divine Madness. There is very little information as to their current incarnation, although Internet posters often note that an innocuously named runners' group operating out of Boulder is the current incarnation of the Community, also known as the infamous Divine Madness.

Curious Collections

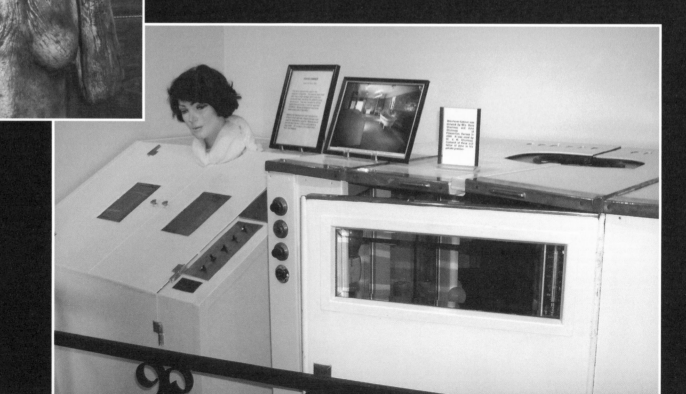

Museums have come a long way from the cabinets of curiosities they used to show in Benjamin Franklin's day. The old collections would cheerfully mix Roman coins and native arrowheads with the dried flatfish carved into bat shapes that sailors used to pass off as sea devils. People knew these artifacts were bogus, but that was all part of the fun.

Somewhere along the line, a lot of the fun got weeded out of most display cases, and the world's a duller place because of it. You'd hardly know these days that the "muse" bit in the word museum used to mean that these places inspired you. But thankfully, there are still some examples of exhibits and whole collections that leave you scratching your head and saying, "What on earth is that about?" And we advise you to get out there fast to see them, because these places have a sad habit of closing down. We're still mourning the demise of southern California's Museum of Death.

Abita Mystery House

If you have time to see only one weird thing in Louisiana, head about an hour north of New Orleans to Abita Springs and the Abita Mystery House and UCM (you-see-'em) Museum. From outside, it looks like a little old 1930s-era gas station, because it is, but through the entrance is a much larger realm of sideshow oddities and slices of bayou life, divided between the main exhibit hall, the House of Shards, and the Shed of Revelations.

The mechanical exhibit called Tragedy on Dog Pound Road sends a tornado through a miniature trailer park, and the miniature version of New Orleans's St. Louis Cemetery #1 features tombs creaking open and the skeletons and spirits of the dead rising. As for Martians Come to Mardi Gras, that speaks for itself. Oh, and then there's the UFO Crash Site, which features a real-life Airstream with a "life-size" UFO stuck in it.

Outside the exhibit hall is the House of Shards, an old horse barn covered with more than 15,000 pieces of broken crockery, and the Shed of Revelations containing such sideshow madness as a bigmouth bass sporting a set of false teeth, a FeeJee Mermaid, and Buford the Giant Bassigator—a half-gator, half-fish horror more than twenty feet long. We could go on describing Darrel the Dogigator, the Gator Girl, the Gatorcycle—there's definitely a reptilian undercurrent coursing through the whole site—but it would spoil the fun. Just take our word for it. It's worth the side trip and the small entry fee. The Abita Mystery House and UCM Museum, located one block east of the only traffic light in Abita Springs, is open every day from ten a.m. to five p.m. Don't miss it.

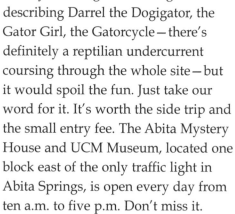

Washington's Wonderful Palace of Wonders

In a truly weird world, the Palace of Wonders would not look out of place on any city street. People in a weird world would expect to watch tattooed acrobats, burlesque acts, fire-breathing lounge singers dressed as Skeletor, all performing live on stage. And in between acts, people would expect to scope out cabinets full of stuffed unicorns, mummies, mermaids, and miniature villages made of human bones.

Fortunately for us, Washington, D.C., qualifies as a weird world, because if you follow the H Street corridor to the Atlas District, you'll find the perfect triple play of strangeness: a vaudeville revival house, a museum of oddities, and a full bar. The Palace of Wonders is a throwback to the nineteenth-century dime museums and Victorian music halls, where people would pay a dime admission fee to marvel at whatever entertainment the carny folk could muster. And in the days before the Hard Rock Café and Cineplex, these were the places to go on a Saturday night.

The heart and soul of the place rests in the display cases, where you find five hundred sideshow exhibits, including Fivey the stuffed five-legged dog and King, the two-headed bull. There's a unicorn that once toured with the Ringling Bros. Circus and the mummy of Devil Man, which once graced the front cover of the *Weekly World News*. Other exhibits have a more illustrious pedigree, such as the head of a snake that strangled a touring performer named Sailor Katzy (his widow had the snake put down, but stuck his head in a jug of formaldehyde and apparently made a fortune exhibiting it as the Head of the Snake that Killed Sailor Katzy). And don't miss the wax model of Joseph Merrick, the Elephant Man.

The exhibits span two floors, with the live entertainment and drinks in the lower gallery and a circus-tent deck. It's open seven days a week, with weekend shows that range from the sublime to the downright transcendent. The Palace of Wonders Web site at www.palaceofwonders.com doesn't do the place justice. You have to head north from Capitol Hill and visit 1210 H Street to get the full experience.

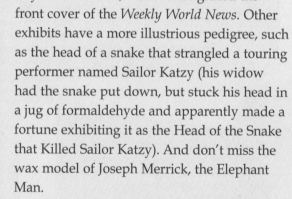

Museum of Jurassic Technology

Museums don't lie to people. Museums are good. My second-grade teacher told me so. But if that's the case, the Museum of Jurassic Technology in Culver City, California, is an anomaly. It takes particular delight in blurring the line between what is real and what is an outlandish fabrication. You know you're being had here, but you can't quite figure out which exhibits are fakes.

There are magnified sculptures so tiny they fit on needles. That exhibit is real, and it's

impressive. There's a diorama depicting the life cycle of the Cameroonian stink ant. Why would anyone make that up? A skeleton of a European mole is displayed right next to a horn that grew from the head of Mary Davis. Now I'm confused again. Just when I thought I could tell the difference, they show me a human horn. And it grew out of a woman with a name so plain it has to be false. Now we begin to doubt that they even have moles in Europe. Brain hurts. Feeling enraged. Curse you, Museum of Jurassic Technology!

Then there is a wing of the building dedicated to old wives' tales. It is here that I assume they are letting me in on their little joke. Such yarns as eating a mouse pie can cure whooping cough or that inhaling a duck's breath helps to heal throat disorders are easy ones to figure out. Those are gags. Right? Next time you think you have life figured out, pay a visit to Venice Boulevard in Culver City. It will change your view of the world.–*JO*

Ye Olde Curiosity Shop's Cornucopia of Curios

On a typical summer day on Seattle's waterfront, you'll hear the organ outside Ye Olde Curiosity Shop before you see the place itself. The century-old shop's founder, Joseph Edward Standley, had two main strengths: an appetite for oddities and a talent for promotion. He stocked baskets made of armadillo hide and tools made of ivory, bone, and jade. Though exotic, these were basically practical items. Less so were the walrus skull with three tusks, the Devil Fish, and the two-headed calf. In some ways, it's like your great-grandma's attic might look if your great-grandma had collected human skulls instead of china and dress patterns. And things have not stood still since Standley's demise in 1940. The family continues the tradition, recently adding Victorian taxidermy of a four-legged chicken and a two-headed bull calf.

But three exhibits stand out in the crowd. There's a real human mummy, which is remarkably well preserved. Nobody's entirely sure who "Sylvester" was, but he was touring carnivals and world's fairs for a century before the shop picked him up in 1955. And he's been closely examined by scientists, who determined he was preserved using fourteen pounds of arsenic, which has kept all his major organs in tip-top shape

1938

for a dead guy. Also preserved are many tall tales of Sylvester's origins. To some, he is a border jumper or desperado who was shot off his horse in the desert and dried out overnight. Some even say he's John Wilkes Booth, the crazed actor who shot President Abraham Lincoln. Then there's a fang-baring mermaid with tufts of ratty hair, who came to the store (along with a great fisherman's tale) in the 1920s. And there are seven apparently real shrunken human heads bought in the 1930s from the collection of George Gustav Heye, founder of the Museum of the American Indian.

Ye Olde Curiosity Shop and its sequel, Ye Olde Curiosity Shop Too, stand side by side on Piers 54 and 55 on Seattle's waterfront. Learn more about them at www.yeoldecuriosityshop.com.–*Peg Boettcher*

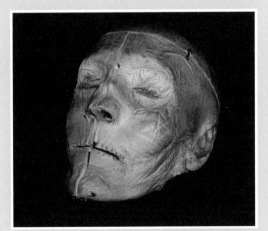

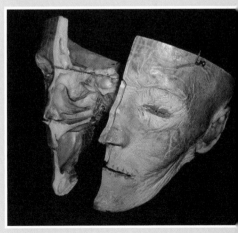

Crypt of Civilization

Oglethorpe University in Atlanta, Georgia, sits at the epicenter of human history. As the stewards of the world's longest-term time capsule, the faculty there have an awe-inspiring responsibility—to guard a repository of all of human history from the beginning of the Egyptian calendar (4241 B.C.) to a point in the twentieth century. And they will continue to guard it until 8113, the year the crypt is to be opened.

The Crypt of Civilization was conceived by Dr. Thornwell Jacobs, who wanted to show the ways of life in the year 1936 as well as the accumulated knowledge of humankind up to that time, or at least as much as he could get into one crypt. The year the crypt is to be opened, 8113, was chosen with a purpose. It is 6177 years from 1936, which is 6177 years from the first recorded date in history, 4241 B.C. Get it?

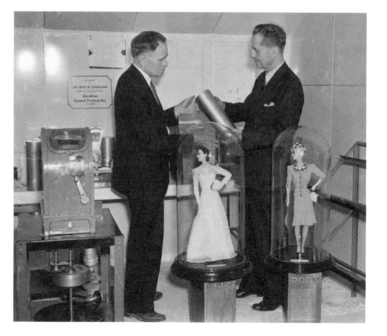

Because of the long lead time, the place is waterproofed concrete, lined with granite and porcelain enamel. The items themselves were to be placed in stainless-steel containment units filled with nitrogen to thwart aging. In case some things manage to rot anyway, Jacobs also had each of them photographed and placed on both microfilm and metallic negatives. The crypt's contents are wildly varied, from the Bible and Koran to the script of *Gone With the Wind* and cartoons of Popeye, with the inevitable declarations from politicians of the time.

In case there's no electricity in 8113 to power the machines inside the crypt, there's a wind-powered generator included, with clear pre-Ikea-style instructions. And in case the English language falls out of style by 8113, there's a machine there that teaches English. Hope that one has long-life batteries in it.

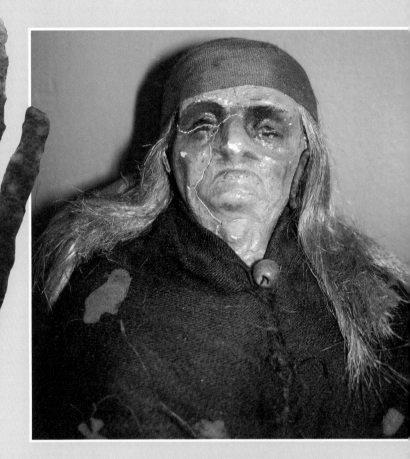

Getting a Head (and More) at This Museum

Next time you're in the vicinity of Covington, Kentucky, head on over to the Behringer-Crawford Museum. Small but amazing, it features all sorts of natural wonders and curiosities. There's a hairball taken from the stomach of a cow. Why? We don't know; ours is not to question. Then there's a striking two-headed calf in all its taxidermic glory, as well as a giant elk and a stuffed specimen of the now extinct miniature breed of English terrier.

What really packs 'em in, however, is the museum's exhibit of a *real* human shrunken head. Such heads are increasingly only in the hands of private collectors. This may well be your only opportunity to view one up close.

The museum is located at 1600 Montague Road. It is expanding both space- and exhibitwise at this time, so make sure you give them a call before you show up, to find out what's open.

Tinkertown Museum

Tinkertown is located just outside of Albuquerque, New Mexico, on the other side of the Sandia Mountains. It is a unique tribute to a man named Ross Ward, who first started carving miniature figures while in junior high school. He continued his hobby into adulthood and began creating intricate little scenes and buildings to showcase his tiny figures. With an exact attention to detail, he filled these scenes with tiny props and even animated some of the figures. His work was first exhibited as part of a traveling show at fairs and carnivals in the 1960s. Later, Tinkertown Museum was built to house his collection.

In addition to the carved miniatures, Tinkertown features a huge amount of Old West memorabilia and odd artifacts. The exterior grounds are just as interesting and eccentric as the interior exhibits. Constructed of all manner of found objects and old timbers, the place gives the impression of an old, rather odd, ghost town.

Over 50,000 glass bottles help form the rambling walls of the twenty-two-room museum. Mirrors, wagon wheels, and a variety of strange artifacts are occasionally inset into the walls.

One complete, comically provisioned covered wagon sits in one of the sheds on the grounds outside. Often accompanied by humorous signs that act as display captions, the wagons are fascinatingly detailed. Another huge shed houses a thirty-five-foot antique sailboat that braved a ten-year voyage around the world. In still another shed is Ross Ward's car, known as the Route 66 car. It is covered inside and out with bits of tourist souvenirs from along Route 66. Ward actually drove this weird, memorabilia-encrusted vehicle every day, and people who saw it would happily donate their own old tourist trinkets to add to his mobile collection.

It is nearly impossible to describe the intricate miniature carved scenes inside this museum. You can spend a huge amount of time looking at all of the little details and comical artifacts in each, and pictures just don't do them justice. The scene of a typical General Store, for example, comes complete with two old geezers playing a game of checkers. The store is painstakingly stocked with authentic goods such as baskets, cooking pots, canned goods, sacks of flour, and more. There is a potbellied stove, a coffee grinder, and barrels of molasses, pickles, and apples. There are even tiny printed posters on the storefront advertising local shows.

The Saloon comes complete with a buxom barmaid and a town drunkard. Bottles of liquor line the walls and bar, and a few of the townsfolk lift their beer mugs at a table in the back. The Indian Trading Post includes tiny examples of Native American crafts such as pottery, baskets, and blankets, and the Blacksmith Shop is another intricate and authentically appointed display. At the town Photographer's Emporium, the hapless photographer is vainly attempting to capture the elusive smile of a

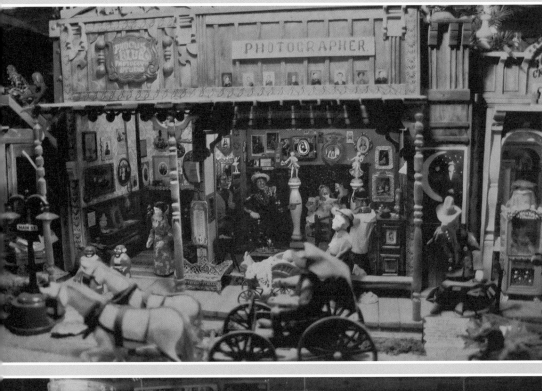

squalling brat under the dire and watchful gaze of the doting mother. Some things never change!

Besides the carved miniatures, interior displays include such wacky collections of Americana as wedding cake sculptures, signs, antique tools, and penny arcade machines. —*Debora L. Carr, Albu-Quirky*

Just What the Heck Is The Thing?

With all the empty desert miles that separate Arizona's roadside businesses from ready consumerism, the key to economic survival is advertising. Highway billboards bombard motorists relentlessly, the least subtle of them all being the bright yellow series stretching from California to Texas that call attention to The Thing.

THE THING? A WONDER OF THE DESERT

THE THING? MYSTERY OF ARIZONA

THE THING? DON'T MISS IT!

Every day, hundreds of visitors passing between Benson and Willcox take the I-10 exit 322 to discover what this enigmatic Thing really is. It only takes a dollar to find out (seventy-five cents if you're under 19). Just pay the cashier, then step through the mysterious doorway and follow the yellow footprints.

On the way, you pass through sheds full of old cash registers, bear traps, and disturbing driftwood sculptures, something labeled "piece of mammoth's front leg." There's a Rolls-Royce "believed to have been used by Adolph Hitler," though admittedly "it can't be proved." Indeterminate credibility is part of the gimmick. And then you see it, encased in cinder blocks and guarded by what can only be described

as Emperor Bigfoot Horsehead. The mystifying . . . the remarkable . . . the unknowable . . . THING.

Although you now know the secret, you feel strangely unsated. But you know your true satisfaction is soon to come. You know what The Thing is. And you now have the power to irritate your friends, to withhold the secret, to goad them into an unwitting trip.

Mystery of the Desert . . . Solved?

It's difficult to discuss the origin of The Thing without giving at least some idea of what it is, so if you want to preserve your uncertainty, skip this article. Otherwise, we'll try not to reveal too much.

In 1965, a former lawyer turned curio shopkeeper named Thomas Binkley Prince moved his business from outside Barstow, California, to a spot just east of Benson, right alongside Interstate 10. He placed The Thing at the top of the bill. He probably acquired the exhibit from a man named Homer Tate, who was building shrunken heads and other bizarre exhibits from papier-mâché, human hair, and the hides of dead animals, produced mostly for exhibition as sideshow gaffs and for his own curiosity museum in Phoenix. Tate distributed his creatures worldwide via mail order, so it's likely Prince had simply ordered it from a catalog.

Thomas Prince passed away in 1969, leaving his wife, Janet, to run things. Janet has since moved away and leased The Thing to Bowlin Travel Centers. Today, a portion of the money brought in by The Thing goes to a University of Arizona College of Law scholarship in Prince's name. Well, ain't that . . . some Thing.

—Craig Robertson

Home of "Old Sparky"

To say Texas loves its prisons is a little bit of an understatement. At the end of 1999, a full five percent of Texas's population was being held in prison or was on parole or probation. One town, more than any other, is associated with the prison system—Huntsville. Three out of four residents of this small town are prisoners. Most of the remaining residents are employees of prisons. The city is home to not one but seven separate prisons, as well as one of the most unusual museums in the entire country—the Texas Prison Museum.

We had a chance to travel to Huntsville, where museum director Jim Willett took us on a tour of the Texas Prison Museum. What he showed us, primarily, was dozens of displays on forms of punishment, weapons, and torture devices dating back to the 1800s.

"The real ball and chain," he said, "that would be something you would use for someone you were going to put to work outside a prison compound. Maybe he had displayed a little rabbit in him, as they call it."

"This thing was called a bat. As you can see, it's on a wooden handle and very thick leather," Jim said thoughtfully. "That was actually a legal means of punishment up until the 1940s in Texas."

But the crown jewel of the Texas Prison Museum is definitely one of the most feared punishment devices in American history. Jim's tone reflected borderline reverence as he took us into a room where a small, well-crafted chair stood. "This is the Texas electric chair," he said quietly. "Inmates dubbed it Old Sparky."

The state of Texas first plugged in Old Sparky on February 8, 1924, and executed its first prisoner, Charles Reynolds. The chair

produced 2,000 volts and eight amps, or enough electricity to light 800 household light bulbs.

Huntsville, Texas, is the most prison-centric town in the most prison-centric state in the United States. If you're a fan of incarceration, there's no better destination than the Texas Prison Museum. It's the closest you'll get to prison itself without actually being behind bars.

Cruel Shoes of Big Nose George

In life, George Manuse was known as Big Nose George Parrot, a criminal who ran with the James Brothers gang. In death, he's better known as "that pair of shoes at the museum" in Rawlins, Wyoming. Because, brace yourself, that's what they used his skin for after they killed the man.

In 1881, Big Nose sealed his gruesome fate by trying to wreck some train tracks so the gang could rob a train.

Unfortunately, a watchman alerted the authorities, and in the ensuing gunfight, two lawmen ended up dead. Big Nose George was captured and sentenced to hanging. Not one to go quietly, he tried to escape and severely beat a guard during the attempt. The local townsfolk were so incensed they took matters into their own hands and lynched him from a telegraph pole.

But being killed by a mob was only the beginning of Big Nose George's indignities. A doctor named J. E. Osborne took his body and sawed his skull in half to see if a criminal's brain looked different from a normal person's. It didn't. At this point, it's fair to say that Dr. Osborne went a little bit overboard. He had Big Nose George skinned and sent his hide to a tannery in Denver to make a pair of shoes. This tough-on-criminals stance seemed to work well for Dr. Osborne. Rumor has it that he even wore the shoes to his inauguration when he later was elected the governor of Wyoming.

Antoine LeBlanc Wasn't Alone

I just saw your show on the History Channel about Antoine LeBlanc, who was hung and his skin was made into some wallets. When I was growing up in a small town in Wyoming called Rawlins, there was a display in the museum with the skull of a man named Big Nose George. Along with the skull was a pair of shoes said to have been made for a doctor from the skin of Big Nose George.—*Winferd J. Schram*

I Got You Under My Skin

You may get crushed by the sheer weight of syllables in Georgia Southern University's Institute of Arthropodology and Parasitology, but you can hardly fail to be impressed by its signature collection. The institute, located in Statesboro, is the home of the U.S. National Tick Collection. This assemblage of bloodsuckers grew to huge volumes after World War II with the addition of Asian and African species. It overwhelmed the Public Health Service, which gave the lot to the Smithsonian, which in turn shipped the million ticks to Georgia, where they can be viewed by an eager public between one thirty and two thirty p.m. on Wednesdays, or by appointment. We'll see you there.

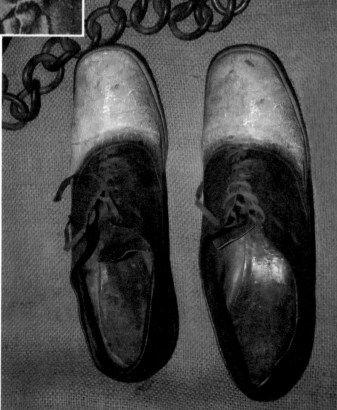

Creepy Cattle on Display

The Samuel Spitler House in Brookville, Ohio, is a charming example of erstwhile architecture, with magnificent staircases, original oak woodwork, elaborate fireplaces, and the first indoor bathroom in Brookville. What's weird about that, you ask? Well, beneath the architectural detail lurk two bizarre creatures from the 1940s. And naturally, they live in the basement.

The Spitler House basement is home to Andy D-Day, a famous freak bull, and his companion, the Two-Headed Calf. Farmers Wilbur and Nettie Rasor charged a dime in 1941 to view the two-headed calf, and stuffed him after his untimely death so they could continue to do so. A few years later, a visitor from Arkansas sold the Rasors his own freak animal, a four-horned, four-eyed bull complete with two functional noses. For the rest of his life, the bull (born on D-Day, June 6, 1944) went on a traveling circuit of sideshows with his stuffed companion, earning the Rasors a quarter a visitor, plus postcard sales.

After his death in 1956, Andy D-Day's head was stuffed and mounted. Eventually, the pair of stuffed freak beasts was donated to the Brookville Historical Society and wound up in the basement of the Spitler House museum—open to the public the first Sunday of every month, weather permitting. We recommend calling first to make sure the museum is open before you head out to rustle up a few (extra) head of cattle.

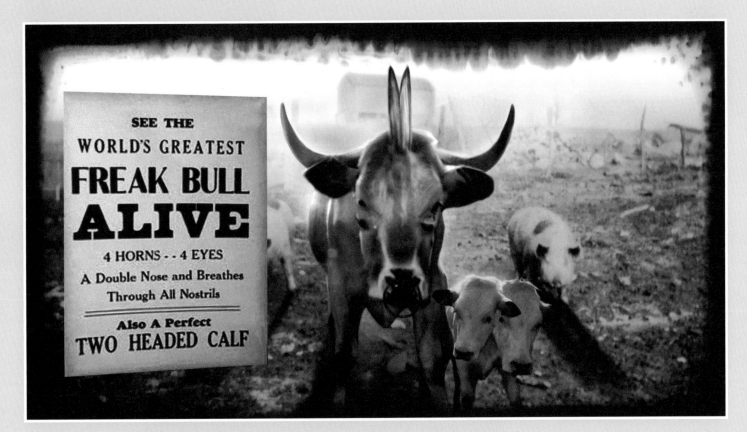

SEE THE
WORLD'S GREATEST
FREAK BULL
ALIVE

4 HORNS - - 4 EYES
A Double Nose and Breathes
Through All Nostrils

Also A Perfect
TWO HEADED CALF

The Three Fingers of Mary Bach

When an old farmer named Carl Bach of Bowling Green, Illinois, showed up at the sheriff's office in 1883, he set in motion a chain of events that would give Wood County Historical Museum its most macabre exhibit. He confessed on the spot that he had killed his wife, Mary, and used a corn knife to reduce the body to bits. When the sheriff looked for evidence in the barn, he found the woman's remains and picked up some evidence to present at trial: three of Mary's fingers, which he put in a glass of formaldehyde.

Bach was eventually found guilty and sentenced to death by hanging, which was carried out on the last day of the Wood County fair, October 13, 1883, in front of a large crowd of ticket holders. It was the last public hanging the county ever held. The courthouse once had a display case of the evidence, including the fingers, the corn knife, and the noose used to mete out justice. They are now part of the historical society's display in the grounds of the old Wood County infirmary.

Bing Crosby's Denim Tuxedo

The Northeastern Nevada Museum in Elko, Nevada, contains an unlikely combination of showbiz memorabilia and fashion: a tuxedo made of denim that once belonged to Bing Crosby. Bing owned a ranch in Elko, and after he was refused admittance to a fancy hotel because he was wearing jeans, the committee in charge of Elko's 1951 Silver State Stampede commissioned the Levi Strauss Company to design him a denim tuxedo. Bing's tux sports a label signed by the president of the American Hotel Association reading, THIS LABEL ENTITLES THE WEARER TO BE DULY RECEIVED AND REGISTERED WITH CORDIAL HOSPITALITY AT ANY TIME AND UNDER ANY CONDITIONS.

Can Can Merman

Since 1934, the Bird Cage Theatre in Tombstone, Arizona, has displayed an exhibit that once sat in the National Museum of China and found its way to Arizona via a San Francisco importer in 1880. Or at least, that's what the sign says. But the fishy exhibit may not be all it's cracked up to be. The Can Can Merman is a strange sight in a museum of Wild West memorabilia, but it's exactly the kind of novelty that P. T. Barnum sent out in his traveling shows to entertain the homesteaders. In fact, the Can Can Merman (who got his name from the Can Can Restaurant where he spent many years), owes a lot to Barnum's 1842 exhibit, the Feejee Mermaid, a patchwork of stitched animal parts. So in a sense, it really is a museum piece.

Albino Animals and Swallowed Objects

The Allen County Museum is currently the only county museum in Ohio accredited by the American Association of Museums—and with good reason. The two-story museum, located in Lima, is filled to the gills with all sorts of historical oddities. Focusing mainly on history, science, and art, with

an emphasis on local county artifacts, there is something weird and wonderful everywhere one turns.

Some of the exhibits include: Albino Animals—a group of pigmentally challenged stuffed creatures has been taxidermied for all to enjoy in the world's largest collection of its kind. Swallowed Objects—by far the weirdest collection in the museum—sits quietly in the basement next to the water fountain. The long, two-sectioned cabinet is filled with well over a hundred objects that were removed from people's esophagi, lungs, and larynxes.

For whatever reason, Drs. Walter E. Yingling and Estey C. Yingling began saving the assorted objects their patients had swallowed. Each object has been lovingly affixed to a piece of paper bearing the name and age of the person it was removed from and the date of said operation. The collection itself includes an open diaper pin, buttons, dentures, coins, and animal bones of assorted shapes and sizes. Some of the stranger items are a key, a pencil eraser, and even a long length of rubber hose, which is often mistaken for a horseshoe.

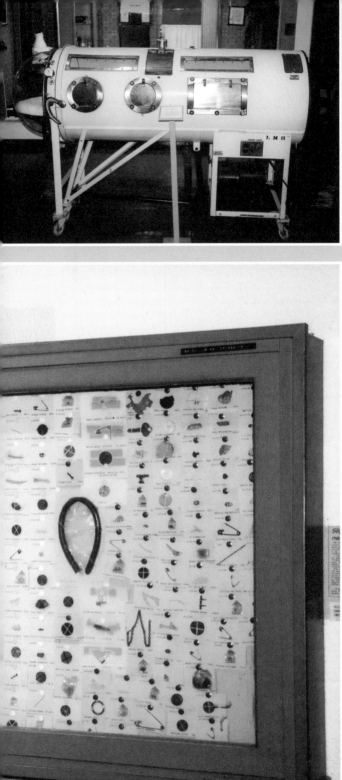

Jefcoat Museum of Americana

Brady C. Jefcoat was one of those obsessive people who seem to have set out to stop time itself by glomming on to near everything they could. Filling three floors of the old Murfreesboro High School in Murfreesboro, North Carolina, are dozens of wind-up Victrolas, antique Wurlitzer jukeboxes, wringer washers, mousetraps of every type, butter churns, cheese molds, mounted ducks, smoking pipes, political posters, a range of church offering plates, and radio chimers. Almost anything of which at least three (and preferably thirty or more) examples could be gathered was folded into the collection.

Raising the Bar of the Bizarre

I'd like to tell you about a weird guy I know. He was my senior year pre-calculus teacher, Ira Fine, from Pitman, NJ. What is really weird is what he collects. Not baseball cards, coins, or stamps. He collects raisin boxes. Yes, I am NOT kidding. This man collects raisin boxes. From all over the world. I know this seems a little unbelievable, but I actually saw the collection. It is the creepiest and oddest collection I've ever seen! He even put his wife's engagement ring in a raisin box!! He used to tell us stories about how he got some of his raisin boxes, and why certain ones are better than others. He would tell us about the history of the Sun-Maid raisin woman.

He has over 300 different raisin boxes of all sizes, colors, and shapes. Some of them are even on display on shelves in his house. He even has a website with all of the boxes in his collection on it. There is also a picture of him dressed up as the Sun-Maid raisin woman on the site. This man is definitely a tad odd.

A while back, his collection was featured on the news around Christmastime. He showed us the interview, and it was just so weird. He is the ONLY man I know that collects anything this extremely odd, and I thought it'd be a funny story for your readers to engage themselves in. —Jacki Gross

Tony Packo's Bun Museum

When Jamie Farr from the TV show *M*A*S*H** signed a hot dog bun at Tony Packo's in 1972, he started an enduring tradition. Although Farr's actual bun crumbled soon after, Tony Packo's encouraged other celebrities to sign Styrofoam buns. The joint, located in Lima, Ohio, now houses over 1,000 examples, including five U.S. Presidents.

Buford Pusser Home & Museum

Who wouldn't want a guided tour of the 1970s-era home of a club-wielding sheriff from Tennessee? Especially when you find out that the sheriff in question, the late Buford Pusser, was the inspiration for the 1973 and 2004 versions of the movie *Walking Tall.* As a former pro wrestler, he knew a thing or two about creating a larger-than-life persona, and the city of Adamsville, Tennessee, knows a thing or two about preserving his legacy.

Marvel at the Buford Pusser Home and Museum's lumpy couch, where the man used to watch *Mannix.* Don't miss his glass-encased report card, documenting all of his F's. And gasp at Buford's famous beating sticks (his motto: "Spare the County, spoil the Town"). And finally, mourn the passing of the late sheriff and his crusade against bootlegging and other crimes. He met his end in a motor vehicle, where two fatal flaws—a legendary lead foot and a refusal to wear a seatbelt—brought this hero to a tragic end.—*Ben Osto*

Where to Go When It Rains

Nestled on 62-B Island Avenue on Peak's Island, Maine, and open by appointment, the museum of Nancy 3 Hoffman (yes, her middle name is 3) is tiny but focused. It is dedicated to what some people call sheaths, sleeves, pockets, and slipcovers from thirty-five countries around the world. Most people here call them umbrella covers, and this is the world's only Umbrella Cover Museum. Some are plain black or blue nylon. Some are multicolored and made of gum wrappers or Kevlar. Some are arranged in themes (such as "the basic black sheath"), some are not. But each cover has its story posted beside it.

The museum's mission statement clarifies everything: "The Umbrella Cover Museum is dedicated to the appreciation of the mundane in everyday life. It is about finding wonder and beauty in the simplest of things, and about knowing that there is always a story behind the cover."

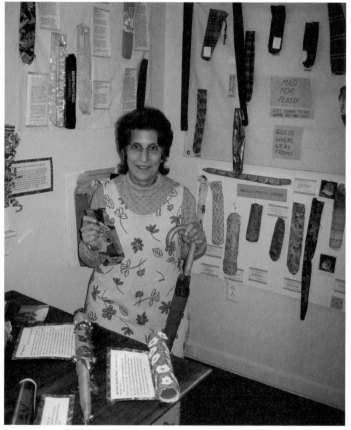

Ed's Museum

Wykoff is a "blink and you'll miss it" stop on Interstate 90 in southeastern Minnesota, but it's home to a time capsule of small-town America. Ed Krueger's tiny general store opened in 1933 and stands as a testament to the habits of the pack rat. For almost sixty years, Ed simply wouldn't throw anything away. Spices that he never sold during the 1930s? They're still there. Movie posters from when he ran the town theater? Available for public consumption.

Ed decided to open his own house as a museum in 1976, and he ran it till his death in 1989 at the age of ninety-one. Traveling through Ed's museum now isn't like leisurely strolling through some big-city series of exhibits. It's like experiencing American small-town culture from the Great Depression through the first President Bush's administration all at the same time. And scope out Ed's own gallstones and gold teeth while you're about it.

"Ed had great foresight," Esther Evers of the Wykoff Area Historical Society informed us. "Here is a bottle that had ammonia in it. That is a very valuable jar. We have a million of them up in the attic." Then it was off to other random items—a tobacco case, an old-time washing machine, a K-Tel record selector. To no one's surprise, the real gems of Ed's strange collection are found in the basement, including the family cat, Sammy. When Sammy passed on, Ed put the remains in a box and put them in the basement, just another exhibit at the museum. Sammy hasn't moved since—literally.

For most of us, "spring cleaning" happens once a year. For Ed Krueger, sixty springs came and went without it ever happening. Instead, his life took on the physical form of the things he owned. And those things remain accessible to us all, even after his death, creating one of America's strangest museums—a museum dedicated to the life of a small-town guy named Ed.

Rodent Resurrection

What do Wisconsin funeral home directors do when they retire? Madison man Sam Sanfillippo avoided golf and shuffleboard in favor of stuffing and mounting albino squirrels in fuchsia Barbie cars, and we're grateful he did.

The basement of Cress Funeral Home is home to the Squirrel and Chipmunk Museum, stuffed with wild tableaux of mounted squirrels and chipmunks, in costume and set into miniature habitats. Gray squirrels play poker. Chipmunks spin on a Ferris wheel or smoke on barstools made of beer bottles. And a suave piano-playing squirrel sits paused at a preemie-baby grand in front of a smoked glass mirror.

The late Wisconsin governor Warren Knowles gave Sanfillippo his start by asking game wardens to pack roadkill in dry ice and ship them to the funeral home. Sanfillippo took it from there, writing to an albino squirrel club in Maryville, Missouri, for any pale rodents they could spare. It's an expensive hobby. It takes $300 to mount each rodent, but it's worth it for Sanfillippo to enjoy the sight of roadkill behind the wheel of their own vehicles. Check it out yourself, free, at the Cress Funeral Home in Madison, but call first to make sure there are no funerals scheduled.

Oh, My Gourd!

Next to the library in Angier, North Carolina, is Marvin Johnson's Gourd Museum, which proves beyond any doubt that even a humble squash can change the world. Here you will see gourds made into hats, furniture, statues, utensils, and musical instruments. It's both inspiring and a little humbling. Thank you, Marvin.

For a Merrier Christmas

Some museums stay small and reflect specialized tastes and interests. One of our favorites is the Aluminum Tree & Aesthetically Challenged Seasonal Ornament Museum and Research Center. Stephen Jackson began it as a joke with a single artificial tree from a trash heap, but the collection soon grew to seven trees, then sixty, and the numbers continue to climb each year. Next Stephen expanded into ornaments made from curtain rings, duct tape, flattened beer cans, and photos of Elvis. The museum is open between Thanksgiving and Christmas each year, and thousands of people now make the pilgrimage to Brevard, North Carolina, to see the aluminum and Mylar trees and everything that goes with them. In recent years, concept exhibits have included redneck Christmas displays and Hollywood themes with tributes to film legends like Marilyn Monroe, John Wayne, and Alfred Hitchcock. A *Gone With the Wind* parody suggests Atlanta would not have burned if Scarlett O'Hara had planted aluminum trees.

Concretion Museum

Byron Buckeridge's rock collection is shaped like nothing else in nature. He has 50,000 in all, ranging from pebbles to yard-tall examples, and he shows them off on Highway 14, one mile west of Arena in Iowa County, Wisconsin.

The Concretion Museum's slogan, "Nothing like it in New York!" says it all. The Big Apple is indeed short on natural rock formations that kind of resemble flute players, parts of the anatomy usually covered by undergarments, or characters from Shakespeare's plays. But that's exactly what this retired philosophy professor puts on display in his museum. You need to squint a bit to make blobby bits of rock fit the fanciful titles Buckeridge gives them ("The Mermaid" and "Anthony and Cleopatra"), but they're still quite a sight.

Geologists will tell you that concretion rocks were gradually formed 10,000 to 20,000 years ago, as water deposited minerals onto the outside of lumps of clay. But Buckeridge has another take on things: Concretions are not accidental; the clay planned and sculpted its own forms, with the help of glacial pressure. He calls his theory "clay energy." The Bad River Chippewas believe that the concretions were created by God, each with a tiny soul, which sounds even better. So get

on over to Arena and see what he's on about. You may not see the face of Barbra Streisand in the rocks, but you'll see something.

Thermometer Museum

Dick Porter, of Onset, Massachusetts, has been building his collection of over 5,000 thermometers since the mid-'80s, though the collection has nearly doubled since 1998 when it was just over 3,000. He calls it the world's largest and only thermometer museum. He's certainly passionate about them, and he's been an invited speaker at more than a few thermometer and weather-related events, like the christening of the world's largest thermometer in Baker, California.

The collection, which Porter values at about four dollars per piece, fills his home's small basement, and visitors should expect him to be an active docent. He has stories about many of the thermometers, even some memories of the day the scientific community decided to honor Anders Celsius by eponymously renaming his centigrade scale. Thinking of scales, Porter even has a few Reamur thermometers. Impressive, yes, though Wikipedia notes a few more temperature scales he didn't mention. I guess it's challenges like this that get a guy through the day.

A visit there conjures first amusement at his passion for thermometers, then a little bit of fear as you contemplate the confined quarters of his basement museum and his refusal to accept your polite excuses to leave.—*Casey Bisson, MaisonBisson.com*

Celebrity Bites

I have become an involuntary collector of partially eaten sandwiches, which were bitten into by celebrities. It all started in September of 1960, when then Vice President Richard Nixon visited my hometown of Sullivan, IL. I was a 14-year old Boy Scout, stationed as security around his picnic table. He took a couple of bites out of his buffalo barbecue sandwich, made a nice comment, then excused himself. I noticed that he didn't finish his sandwich, so I took it . . . paper plate and all. A local newspaper ran my picture and a short story about that incident, and the story lay dormant for almost 30 years.

In 1988, a Decatur, IL newspaper columnist tracked me down to do a follow-up story. Her story was picked up by the wire services, and before I knew it, I was on all of the morning-drive radio talk shows and the Johnny Carson show. Steve Martin, also a guest on that show in December of 1988, gave me something he had bitten in to, as did Johnny Carson. Henny Youngman, Tiny Tim, pro golfers, etc., have contributed to my collection. All half-eaten sandwiches are labeled and safely stored in my freezer here at home in Springfield.—*Steve Jenne*

Pen Pal

Dear *Weird U.S.*

I would like to call your attention to a very unique and weird collection I have right here in Morris County, New Jersey. When I was about 13, I began collecting empty ink tubes from ballpoint pens. To date, I have a little over 400 of them. I have never heard of anyone else anywhere collecting such a thing, and I tried to get into the *Guinness Book of Records* with it . . . but they very rudely turned me down. So be it.

As a lifelong resident of New Jersey and someone who is really devoted to their unique collection, I feel that someone somewhere should at least acknowledge my accomplishment, and perhaps you are the ones to do so. Please don't be mean to me like *Guinness* was.—*Megan Bianchetti*

Presidents Hall of Fame

Oftentimes, the greatest levels of motivation are born out of rejection. When officials refused John Zweifel access to White House blueprints to help him build a replica, he would spend a quarter century and one million dollars to do it himself. This is how the Presidents Hall of Fame in Claremont, Florida, was born.

From the wallpaper in the bedrooms to the books in the library, this White House is accurately represented in every detail. When a bedspread is changed in the original or a rug gets stained, John Zweifel rushes to replicate the alterations.

It all began with a visit to the grand mansion, coupled with a lifelong interest in history. "I cried the first time I went in the White House," Zweifel told us. "I went from room to room and I knew that was Grant's chair, and Garfield sat there." From that moment in 1959, John was inspired with his grand vision. He wanted Americans to be able to experience the White House as he had, and not just the parts that they show you on the official tour, but all 132 rooms. There was only one problem. He would need blueprints, and the government showed no interest in helping.

His first big break came when John F. Kennedy took office, and his hip young wife, Jackie, gave John and Jan Zweifel unprecedented access to the White House. But the Zweifels' dreams were snatched away again in 1963. When President Kennedy was assassinated, the White House was sealed off to them for more than a decade. It wasn't until the bicentennial in 1976 that Gerald Ford let John back in. Ever since then, he has been informed of any changes to the building and its furniture, so he can keep his replica accurate.

The Zweifels' White House is now a traveling exhibit. It's been to every state and has even been exhibited in the Smithsonian. But Claremont, Florida, is the home of this all-access White House. It's also a shrine to what dedication, persistence, and hard work can accomplish.

Ruff!
Clair McLean's

charming collection of
animal memorabilia currently
lives in Annapolis, Maryland,
but she hopes it will be
absorbed into a new national museum in Washington,
D.C. The Presidential Pet Museum celebrates the
pooches, pussies, and other pets who shared the
White House with the commanders in chief of the
nation, the strangest of which must be Coolidge's
bear and pygmy hippo. But the most bizarre exhibit
of all is a portrait of the Reagan family's dog, a
Bouvier des Flandres named Lucky. The painting
itself is coated with tufts of fur that Clair herself
groomed from the dog. What other museum can
boast such an artifact? Check it out at www.
presidentialpetmuseum.com, and unless it's
moved to the nation's capital, book a time to
see it in the flesh (and fur).

Eye of the World Museum

At the south end of the Lone Star Steakhouse in Beaumont, Texas, is a narrow two-foot-wide passageway. If you didn't already know about it, you probably wouldn't even notice. But if you ask someone to flip on the light, you'll be able to see the Eye of the World. It's a twenty-seven-foot-long display case containing a remarkably detailed hand-carved display of . . . well, almost everything.

From the Parthenon and Statue of Liberty to the Tower of Babel and Noah's Ark, this twenty-five-year labor of love was carved by "Poppa" John Gavrelos, the Greek restaurateur who ran the place between 1923 and 1948. Poppa's great-nephew John, who now runs the steakhouse, said Poppa carved his models from whatever timber he had on hand, mostly plywood and vegetable crates. Even today, the passageway with the subtle MUSEUM placard is arranged exactly as Poppa Gavrelos specified. Check it out and leave a generous tip.

Elvis Is in the House—Parts of Him, Anyway

On August 16, 1977, art student Joni Mabe received word that Elvis Presley had died. This event transformed her life. She began creating works in his image and was soon collecting Elvis memorabilia. The obsession grew into a twenty-three-crate traveling exhibit that now sits on permanent display in Cornelia, Georgia. Here, Mabe reigns as "Queen of the King," with 30,000 items that include two actual parts of the King. "Everything in the collection is special," she says, "but the wart and toenail are the most priceless."

Mabe found the toenail in the green shag carpet of the Jungle Room in Graceland on a tour in 1983, where she was on her hands and knees because she "wanted to touch where he walked." The Maybe Elvis Toenail is now locked in a glass case. And the wart was removed from the back of Elvis's right hand in 1957 by a Memphis doctor who later sold it to Mabe. It's visible on a photograph taken before he went into the army, and is clearly missing on later Elvis pictures. This holy relic, which looks like a bit of gross gray gristle, is found in a medicine vial. Of more dubious genetic claim are two commercial products—The Official Elvis Hair Button and a small vial of Elvis Sweat.

Dixie Lee's Exotic World

What was once racy and forbidden has become an almost PG-rated attraction on old Route 66 in the Mojave Desert. Seventeen miles north of Victorville, California, you can find Exotic World, a museum whose walls sag with feathered boas, photographs, and elaborate jewel-encrusted costumes used by such saucy stage characters as the Whip Cream and Cherry Bandit.

Stage props and personal effects of such storied temptresses as Blaze Starr, Lili St. Cyr, and Chesty Morgan are all here. Proprietor Dixie Lee Evans (once billed as the Marilyn Monroe of Burlesque) will tell you the story of what is also known as exotic dancing—from the biblical tale of Salome through the vaudeville years—giving it all a wholesome flavor with tales of old-line burlesque performers who mined their acts for laughs.

Each year, Exotic World hosts a burlesque convention called Miss Exotic World, in which retro performers are encouraged to compete with a coquettish kitsch that focuses more on "what is concealed, rather than what is revealed." Exotic World is open Tuesday through Sunday from ten a.m. to four p.m. on Wild Road just north of Helendale, California.

Weird Science

Most of us would like to keep things simple. We'd like our experience of the world to be boiled down to something that has been proved by the scientific principles of Newton and Einstein. Of course, as the philosopher Jagger once stated, you can't always get what you want.

Cryptozoological Museum

New England is dotted with dotty museums, but none so strange as a two-story house on a quiet residential street in Portland, Maine, that features a hairy eight-and-a-half foot, five-hundred pound Bigfoot on the porch. The International Museum of Cryptozoology is the brainchild of the respected cryptozoologist and author Loren Coleman, who shares his living quarters with replicas of the Dover Demon, Mothman, and Bigfoot (along with Bigfoot's hair, casts of his footprints, and naturally, his droppings).

As you walk past models, masks, miniatures, and authentic specimens, you catch sight of zoological pranks like the horned bunny rabbits called jackalopes, the "Feejee mermaid" sideshow exhibit, and a fur-bearing trout. Then you see museum-quality skulls of Gigantopithecus, Paranthropus, and Australopithecus. And more skulls: Peking Man, Rhodesian Man, Heidelberg Man. And even more, from gorillas, chimpanzees, and rhesus monkeys. All these are offered so you can speculate on exactly where Bigfoot might fit on your family tree.

The good-humored but deadly serious curator puts his money where his mouth is, or rather, he doesn't. There is no charge for visiting the museum. Coleman says, "If people buy a cryptozoology book, read one in their local library, or enter the fields of natural history, anthropology, zoology, or cryptozoology, I will be fully compensated." Like many of its inhabitants, the museum is a little difficult to find. The best place to stake it out is at www.lorencoleman.com.

Macabre Medicine

Aficionados of macabre medical museums swear by Philadelphia's Mütter Museum or the Walter Reed Medical Museum in Washington, D.C. But you can also get your fix of malformed bones, organ specimens, and wince-making medical equipment elsewhere in the country.

Museum of Questionable Medical Devices

Brain not up to par? Bob McCoy, the curator of the Museum of Questionable Medical Devices, can help. His bewildering collection of snake-oil treatments from centuries gone used to occupy its own space, but the Museum of Questionable Medical Devices has now been incorporated into the Science Museum of Minnesota in St. Paul. In the process, some of the raunchier exhibits (such as Vita Radium Suppositories, once touted as a healthy tonic for the pelvic organs) have been weeded out, but many favorites remain. The most memorable is a bizarre Psychograph Phrenology Machine from 1905 that deduces thirty-two personality traits and mental faculties—including suavity and sublimity—simply by reading the bumps on your head.

Many of McCoy's gadgets came from before the crackdown of the Federal Drug Administration, which began regulating drugs in 1906 and medical devices in 1938. As a bona fide skeptic and jokester, McCoy will tell you to have a seat in William Reich's Orgone Energy Accumulator and feel the "orgone" seep through your pores. He warns, however, that new questionable medical devices are still on the market, making instant profits for modern snake-oil salesmen to the chronically gullible.

J. G. HOMAN.
DILATOR.
APPLICATION FILED SEPT. 24, 1917.
1,279,111.
Patented Sept. 17, 1918.

Regular Price $15.00 --- SPECIAL 10 Day Offer $10.00

VITAL POWER VACUUM MASSAGER

A Man Should Be A MAN!

A WONDERFUL INVENTION

WE are offering this invention to our customers after much experimenting and investigation, and because we have long realized the necessity and demand for a reliable Suction Apparatus for men, so designed as to fit over the parts exactly, and by a powerful suction action, to draw the blood in proper quantities to the organs; causing normal, natural nourishment, resulting in A FLOW OF HEALTH, VITALITY and POWER, and complete development of abnormal, undersized parts. The "Vital Power Vacuum Massager" fills these requirements perfectly, being so constructed as to cover and enclose the parts exactly, and exerting a positive suction as strong as may be desired, being regulated to suit the user.

THE EFFECT IS IMMEDIATE, and from the very first time the "Vital Power Vacuum Massager" is used, wonderfully satisfactory effects are noticeable. MEN WHO HAVE BECOME DISCOURAGED WITH THE SLOW ACTION OF DRUGS ARE DELIGHTED WITH THIS MASSAGER, because they can note the improvement from the very beginning.

We call your particular attention to the construction of the "Vital Power Massager." It is made throughout of the very best materials; all metal parts are heavily nickeled-plated and highly polished. The Suction Massager is operated by means of a small crank which gives

Be A Manly Man

It is impossible for a woman to love a man who is sexually weak. To enjoy life and be loved by women you must be a man. A man who is sexually weak is unfit to marry. Weak men hate themselves. Upon the strength of the sexual organ depends sexual strength, in both men and women, furnishing the ambition and energy for all advancement in life. It is a well established scientific fact that musicians, financiers and pugilists are men of exceptionally strong sexual power. Well developed sexual organs manifest themselves in the clear ringing voice, the glossy hair, the sparkling eye, the personal magnetism and force of character. Send your order at once and take advantage of our 10 day offer.

No C. O. D. Orders

BOTTLERS SUPPLY CO.
Springfield, Ill.

Gentlemen:
Send me at once your "Vital Power Vacuum Massager" for which I enclose $10.00 Money Order ☐ Currency ☐ Check ☐

Name..

Address..

Opening the Sluices

We defy you to go to Linthicum, just outside Baltimore, Maryland, and visit the museum named for medical illustrator William Didusch. If you can walk around the exhibits without crossing your legs and bobbing like a kindergartner who needs a trip to the bathroom . . . well . . . you're made of sterner stuff than we are.

The William P. Didusch Center for Urological History features long, thick metal tubes that once opened the floodgates between some unfortunate soul's bladder and the outside world. There are lassoes and nutcrackers on the end of steel tubes, designed to break up bladder stones. There's a fist-size example of such a stone. And there's the excruciatingly named Prostate Punch, which looks like a massively enlarged and curved hypodermic needle designed for the blind resection of prostate tissue. In other words, it reams out your tubes.

About the most tolerable exhibit is a life-size cutout of the wealthy railway magnate "Diamond Jim" Brady and a collection of his canes—all of which concealed catheters that helped with his own floodgate issues. Brady was so happy with the treatment of his problems that he gave a huge donation that established the Brady Urological Institute, a part of Johns Hopkins Hospital, and the museum itself. If you can't handle a free tour of the museum, scope it out online at www.urologichistory.museum.

Fort Crawford Museum of Medical Progress

On South Beaumont Road in Prairie du Chien, Wisconsin, a pair of female twins bare their all to whoever visits. One girl's innards light up organ by organ, while her sister shamelessly reveals her skeleton. An eerie recorded vocal tour of the human body plays as a mannequin in an iron lung lies helpless nearby. Dioramas in another section of the museum, originally from the Chicago World's Fair, show gruesome early medical practices like amputations and operations without modern anesthesia. And then there's the old dental equipment. Welcome to the Museum of Medical Progress.

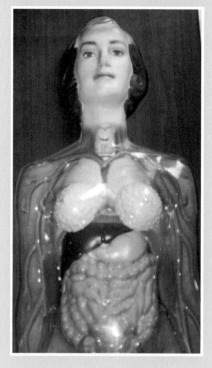

In the military fort that houses the museum, back in the 1800s, one Dr. Beaumont performed live experiments on a man with a hole in his stomach, inserting a sausage on a string into the patient's open belly, then pulling it out at intervals to record the effects of gastric juices. All this and more is fully documented.

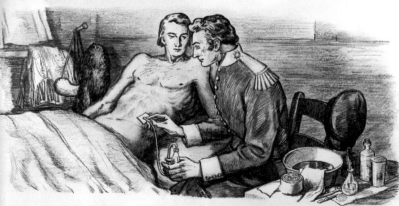

Glore Psychiatric Museum

The State Hospital in St. Joseph, Missouri, served as a psychiatric facility for eighty years before they changed its name from the starkly descriptive State Lunatic Asylum #2. Within a few short decades, the place had closed down. For a while, it also housed a museum of mental health put together by a long-serving employee, George Glore. The museum is now in new digs near the state prison, but the comprehensive collection of the devices and techniques still casts an eerie pall over the place that quickly gives you an appreciation for being born into the age of Prozac.

The treatments used in centuries past seem barbaric today. The Bath of Surprise put the patients (victims?) on a platform that would drop them into a vat of icy water. The Tranquilizer Chair was essentially a chair you could be strapped into for months, developed by a signer of the Declaration of Independence, Dr. Benjamin Rush. O'Halloran's Swing took the chair concept further—this one would spin around at up to a hundred revolutions per minute. Other torture toys include primitive electroconvulsive therapy instrumentation, which is still a legitimate technique, though much better handled and more beneficial today. Then there's the huge collection of items swallowed by obsessive patients: One patient actually swallowed 1,446 items, proudly displayed in a rosette shape in a glass case—the most notable being a Timex watch. Guess you had to do something in State Asylum #2 to pass the time away.

The Country Doctor Museum

You'll find spine-shiveringly antiquated medical gear in this museum in Bailey, North Carolina, including old tools used to bleed patients, fake legs, Civil War operating tables, and an iron lung left over from the polio epidemics of the 1950s.

FRAGILE
DO NOT
TOUCH
OR
SIT IN

Death on Display

National Museum of Funeral History

The caretakers at the National Museum of Funeral History in Houston, Texas, would prefer you to think of their exhibit not as morbid entertainment, but as an educational experience. But that's a little hard to do when its motto is, "Every day above ground is a good one," and their gift shop carries coffin soap and Death Salsa.

Exhibits range from dioramas of Dr. Thomas Holmes—the Father of American Embalming—hand-pumping embalming fluids in a Civil War field tent, to the more ceremonial aspects of death, including a convoy of hearses through the ages and a maze of coffins configured in every size and shape imaginable (Ghanaian lobster coffin, anyone?).

Of course, the gravitas of the funeral experience does sometimes fall victim to real gravity: The 1916 Packard Funeral Bus was designed to carry the deceased, the pallbearers, and nearly two-dozen mourners. But we learn that the design was flawed. It could get so unbalanced that the whole thing tipped backward on the job, tossing about its occupants and casket.

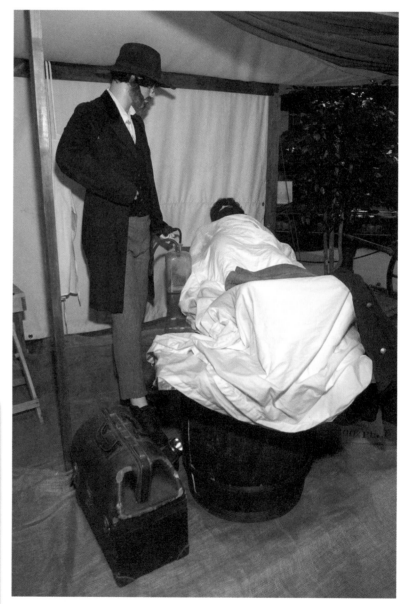

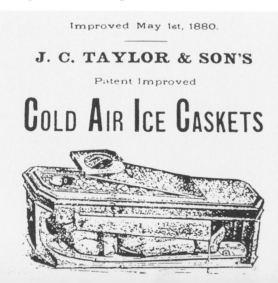

Improved May 1st, 1880.

J. C. TAYLOR & SON'S

Patent Improved

COLD AIR ICE CASKETS

Death Masks

Generations ago making a cast of a dead person's face in wax or plaster was as commonplace as snapping a photo is today. Sculptor Edward Valentine's studio in Richmond, Virginia, displays death masks high up on a shelf, each side by side with its neighbor. One example includes a cast taken from the dead head of General Thomas J. Jackson—"Stonewall" to his friends. If you plan to investigate by stealing a midnight glance through the studio's bay windows, make sure to bring along some hardtack crackers. We hear ol' Stonewall carries a regular soft spot for them.

More Death

The Simpson Mortuary Museum in Newburgh, Indiana, is another place to study the American way of death. Embalming devices, body baskets, and other macabre tools of the trade are all on display.

Keeping the Fun in Funeral

Funeral homes tend to be sad, sorrowful places that people avoid until they are forced to visit one to pay their last respects to a departed one. But that's hardly the case with the three Toland-Herzig Funeral Homes, especially the one in Dover, Ohio. In fact, people of all ages have been known to practically beg to come in. Once inside, they tend to want to linger for hours too. The reason? Famous Endings, John Herzig's incredible collection of funeral memorabilia.

For many years, John Herzig, a third-generation funeral-home owner, was your average everyday autograph hound. But one fateful day, he purchased a Joe Lewis autographed photo from an out-of-state dealer. When the autographed photo arrived, the seller had chosen to throw in an added bonus: Lewis's funeral card. And with that, Herzig's collection of funeral memorabilia was born.

Since that day, Herzig's Famous Endings collection has grown to well over 1,000 pieces. Name practically any well-known deceased people you can think of and if Herzig doesn't have something on display about them at one of his three funeral homes, chances are he's got something in the multiple stacks of items his wife, Joyce, claims he has "all over the place."

Indeed, there is so much to look at that your first thought might be to just scan the items. Be warned, though, because any attempt to do that is sure to make your head spin as you try to take in all the names at once: Tiny Tim, Gregory Peck, Princess Diana, and Pat Morita. And just when you think you've seen it all, there are items from the funerals of Dr. Martin Luther King Jr., Buddy Holly, Rosa Parks, and Johnny Cash. There are even a few that are morbidly fascinating, such as Laci Peterson and Anna Nicole Smith.

Scanning the shelves, you will find memorabilia

from the funerals of such varied individuals as Wendy's founder Dave Thomas, Sonny Bono, and Alfred Hitchcock. Continue browsing and you'll come across the funeral book of Yankee manager Casey Stengel, filled to the brim with signatures that read like a Who's Who of the baseball world. Herzig has such unique and amazing items as one of the yarmulkes handed out to guests at Milton Berle's funeral and even the original temporary marker from Humphrey Bogart's grave.

It seems that everywhere you turn, there's another funeral item with a fascinating story behind it. For example, are you curious as to how much Elvis shelled out for his mother's funeral? Just ask Herzig, and he'll point to the frame on the wall that holds the original 1958 funeral-home worksheets for Gladys Presley's funeral. Aside from featuring the King's signature, the sheets also show that Elvis paid over $19,632 for the funeral.

Or how about this: When James Doohan, Scotty from TV's *Star Trek*, passed away in 2005, a private ceremony was held for his closest friends and relatives. Those in attendance were given a small flashlight bearing Doohan's name, his birth and death years, and the now-immortal phrase "Beam me up, Scotty," one of which is proudly displayed in Herzig's collection.

Look to the left of Doohan's flashlight, and you'll see a bright red hard hat. Seems that for Hunter S. Thompson's funeral, actor and friend Johnny Depp spent an estimated $2.5 million erecting a 153-foot tower from which Thompson's ashes were fired out of a cannon during a private ceremony. Hard hats, complete with Thompson's "Gonzo" logo, were handed out to funeral guests who stood under the tower.

Herzig also has a large number of pieces related to funerals of U.S. Presidents. Mixed into the collection are a pair of funeral vests worn by attendees of President Garfield's funeral, a flag that was displayed during President William McKinley's funeral, and a piece of fabric from the funeral train that carried Abraham Lincoln's body back to Springfield, Illinois, for burial. Herzig even has the original accordion that was used to play a requiem for

Franklin Delano Roosevelt while his casket was loaded onto a train bound for Washington.

Herzig's wife would like to think that her husband's collection is complete, but he doesn't think so. In fact, after being featured in *Ripley's Believe It Or Not!*, Herzig sees no reason to stop now. But as with all memorabilia, there are some items that are considered the holy grails of collectibles. For Herzig, his ever-elusive Fab Four would be items from the funerals of Ed Sullivan, Christopher Reeve, Marilyn Monroe, and Gilda Radner. So if you've got any of those things lying around, give John Herzig a ring. He promises to give anything you send him a nice final resting place.—*Jim Willis*

Far-out Festivals

Every town in the United States holds annual celebrations of some sort to commemorate great events and special times. It's hard to imagine a year going by without parades or fireworks displays or street parties to mark the Fourth of July, Thanksgiving, New Year's Day, Memorial Day, and a welter of other national holidays. It just seems to be a part of human nature to make a big deal of special days.

That's probably why you'll also find that some towns hold annual celebrations of a more unusual nature. Such as the celebration of the death of Bonnie and Clyde, for example. Or the races that commemorate a coffin and its long-dead occupant and their slide down a mountain in Colorado. Or the festival that celebrates the continued low temperature of a cryogenically preserved Norwegian grandfather kept in a storage shed.

You know how it is. Some events in life are just worthy of special attention. Here's a small sampling of those far-out festivals.

Groundhog Day
February Second

Every year on the festival day of Candlemas, thousands of people spend all night congregated at Gobbler's Knob near Punxsutawney, Pennsylvania, waiting for daybreak. Their purpose: to watch an outsize rodent's shadow and forecast the weather. In the center of the same state, AccuWeather makes more precise predictions using state-of-the-art science and computing models. The weird thing? Both reports seem to get equal time on national television news. Go figure.

Frozen Dead Guy Festival
First weekend in March

Nothing quite heralds giddy spring like a celebration of a cryogenically preserved corpse in a storage shed. At least, that's the opinion in Nederland, Colorado, where the annual Frozen Dead Guy Days celebrate Bredo Morstoel. When Bredo breathed his last in 1989, his grandson Trygve Bauge had the body cryogenically preserved and moved to his homestead above Nederland.

Four years later, the U.S. Immigration and Naturalization Service deported Bauge, but his grandfather remains on his Nederland property, chilled with dry ice, awaiting future reanimation—or at least the development of adequate cloning technology. When Nederland failed to outlaw keeping frozen dead guys on private property, the town decided to capitalize on it with an annual three-day festival.

Festivities are generally scheduled for the first weekend in March. An events schedule is posted on Nederland's Web site, www.nederlandchamber.org. If you can't make it, see what the fuss is about in two documentaries by the filmmaking sisters Robin and Kathy Beeck: 1998's *Grandpa's in the Tuff Shed* and 2003's sequel *Grandpa's Still in the Tuff Shed.—Charmaine Ortega Getz*

Sweetwater Rattlesnake Roundup

Second weekend in March

Most festivals are just an excuse for people to party. By way of contrast, Rattlesnake Roundup in Sweetwater, Texas, is just an excuse to kill snakes. It began out of utility—there were too many rattlesnakes in the area—but turned into a full-blown festival and a moneymaker for the local Junior Chamber of Commerce. Today, rattlesnakes aren't as much of a problem in the greater Sweetwater area, so the snakes themselves are often shipped in from hundreds of miles away just to be killed, eaten, and turned into trinkets for sale. Besides serpent slaying, the roundup features all the rides, games, and attractions of your standard state fair.

Saint Stupid's Day

April 1

Most people remember being hoodwinked at least once on April Fool's Day. For the past thirty years, a group of San Franciscans calling themselves the First Church of the Last Laugh have been taking the joke a step further with their annual Saint Stupid's Day Parade.

The event usually involves congregating at noon around the Transamerica Pyramid ("a stupid building"), tossing pennies ("a stupid coin") at a particularly stupid statue in the courtyard, then marching up Columbus Avenue. Why? Because according to Bishop Joey and his acolytes, it's a stupid thing to do. And what better reason could there be for doing it?

Spamarama
April 1

At heart, most festivals celebrate something people hold dear. That's not exactly the case with Austin, Texas's Spamarama. This paean to potted meat was born in 1976 out of a revulsion for Hormel's signature product. Founders Dick Terry and David Arnsberger were lamenting one spring day that chili cook-offs had become routine and played out. They instead decided to devote a celebration to Spam, figuring that there was no food harder to make enjoyable and, therefore, no better food for an annual celebration. Now, over thirty years later, Spamarama is still going strong. What started as a joke between two friends now attracts close to 10,000 people each year.

Conch Republic Festival
Mid-April

Way back in 1776, when a group of American statesmen, philosophers, and rebels came together to found this nation, they recognized a person's right to life, liberty, and most importantly perhaps, the pursuit of happiness. On April 23, 1982, a group of Florida patriots followed that tradition when they seceded from the United States and founded their own nation. This is how the Conch Republic was born and why its independence celebration dominates the middle of April every year.

To these latter-day Minutemen, the pursuit of happiness involved access to a sunny beach with as little hassle as possible. And the federal government made it a tremendous hassle in 1982 by setting up a roadblock on U.S. 1, thirty miles north of Key West. The intention was to stop drug runners and illegal aliens from entering the U.S., but it also created miles of traffic jams, keeping vacationers out of Key West and residents from the mainland. And it forced infuriated locals to prove they were American citizens before letting them enter their own country.

When Mayor Dennis Wardlow and a group of Key West citizens took the roadblock case to federal court, they lost. But Wardlow and his associates didn't take the decision of the federal court lying down. Wardlow told an assembled crowd, "If Key West is a foreign country to Washington, Washington shall represent a foreign nation to Key West." And so they seceded from the United States and founded a new nation consisting of just the Florida Keys. It is known to this day as the Conch Republic.

"It was impromptu," Wardlow told *Weird U.S.* "It was frustration. We walked out of the federal courthouse, and somebody says 'Okay, what're you gonna do now?' And I kinda looked around and I said, 'Friday at noon, in front of the chamber building, we're gonna raise our flag, we're gonna secede and become the Conch Republic. If you're going to treat us like a foreign country, we're going to become a foreign country.'"

On April 23, the rebels went through with their plan. They seceded, declared war on the United States, and entered a battle with the United States Navy. Well, it was more of a food fight with conch fritters and Cuban bread that ended when Wardlow broke a piece of stale Cuban bread over the head of a man in a United States Navy uniform. One minute later, the Conch Republic lay down arms and surrendered to the navy. Then they asked the United States for a billion dollars in foreign aid.

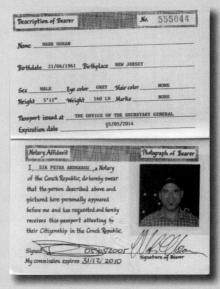

The annual Conch Republic Independence Celebration takes place for ten days every April. Events include a conch-blowing contest, pirate parties, the Great Conch Republic Drag Race (featuring drag queens in hot rods), and the only parade in the world that marches from the Atlantic Ocean to the Gulf of Mexico. The centerpiece of the festival is the Great Battle for the Conch Republic, an annual food fight and drunken celebration held on April 23. Weapons in the food fight generally include stale bread, fish chum, and rotten noodles.

We realize that the Conch Declaration of War against the United States couldn't have been too serious. Yet their compelling combination of style, defiance, and conviction makes them rebels in the finest American tradition. They did it to protect our founding fathers' promise of life, liberty, and the pursuit of happiness for all. And also, they know how to throw a good party.

Art Car Weekend
May

The Texas arts organization Orange Show has been on the leading edge of outsider art for decades, but no endeavor of theirs generates more talk than their annual Art Car Weekend in Houston. Art Cars are just what they sound like—regular automobiles converted into moving artistic pieces with bizarre bolt-ons and creative paint jobs and sculptures firmly fixed on. And since 1987, their creators have converged on the city from around the world to show them off in an annual parade. In recent years, over 250 cars have competed for prizes, compared their techniques, and most of all, shown solidarity with their fellow visionaries.

Art Car Weekend is about as far-out as far-out festivals go, yet more than 200,000 people line Houston's

Allen Parkway each year to catch a glimpse. The weekend involves more than just a parade: The cars visit hospitals and schools to brighten the days of children. The Art Car Museum hosts a symposium for artists to exchange ideas on modifying the automobiles. A local orchestra plays classical compositions using only car horns. Obviously, the entire weekend also has a festive vibe, with many parties and social events spread throughout. In short, the *Detroit Free Press* and *The New York Times* had it right when they called the event "a psychedelic cartoon come to life" and "a retina-saturating extravaganza."

Recent entries ranged from a car covered in tinfoil and plastic fruit, to a mahogany pickup truck, to a van with Pop-Tarts popping out of its top, to a strange go-kart known as the Mordor Mobile driven by a man dressed as the evil Sauron.

Those who seek weirdness in all aspects of their lives know the potential for a simple automobile to be turned into a true original with nothing more than vision—and neon-colored paints, plastic fruits to be glued all over the outside, and a whole lot of welding expertise. (Like many of these festivals, it's a somewhat movable feast, so check out the Orange Show's Web site for exact dates: www.orangeshow.org.)

A Fowl Fest in Fruita
Third weekend in May

In the heart of Colorado's Banana Belt lies the tiny town of Fruita, surrounded by magnificent scenery, dinosaur fossils, agriculture, and wineries. But every third weekend in May, the memory of a former sideshow attraction, Mike the Headless Chicken, has the townspeople run about like . . . well, you know.

The saga of "Miracle Mike" began on September 10, 1945, when Clara Olsen asked her husband, Lloyd, to harvest one of their poultry. Olsen swung his axe and decapitated a young rooster. Not unusually, the critter picked itself up and went on scratching and bobbing as before, so Olsen decided to wait until he stopped before plucking and dressing him. However, Mike was still on the go the following morning.

Anything that determined to live, Olsen figured, should get its chance, so he used an eyedropper to drop grain and water down what was left of Mike's gullet. After a week, he took Mike to the University of Utah in Salt Lake City to get some answers. Scientists determined Olsen's axe had missed Mike's jugular vein, leaving most of the brain stem and an ear intact. A brain stem is all the mentality a chicken really needs, and a blood clot kept Mike from bleeding to death. Apart from a lack of head, Mike remained healthy.

The Olsens took Mike on the road and exhibited him for twenty-five cents a gawk. People from Atlantic City to San Diego flocked to see Miracle Mike. Magazines featured him, as did *Guinness World Records.* Mike was insured for $10,000. Unfortunately, eighteen months later, Mike suddenly began choking and his owners were unable to find the eyedropper fast enough to clear his esophagus and prevent his demise.

Mike was immortalized by sculptor Lyle Nichols with a metal sculpture on Fruita's Mulberry Street, and in 1998 the city's Parks and Recreation Department initiated Mike the Headless Chicken Days. Events vary from year to year but include a 5K race dubbed Run Like a Headless Chicken, a polka band for the Chicken Dance Contest, eating contests featuring marshmallow Peeps or chicken wings, and a game of flag football with a greased rubber chicken.

—*Charmaine Ortega Getz*

Bonnie and Clyde
Third week of May

No pair of criminals has reached the heights of lawbreaking notoriety like the infamous Bonnie and Clyde. For two years in the early 1930s, petite and pretty Bonnie Parker and angry and violent Clyde Barrow led a small gang in bank robberies and daring getaways in small towns across the south and west. Along the way, they murdered twelve people, including nine police officers, until they came to a fittingly dramatic end on May 23, 1934, when Texas and Louisiana authorities ambushed and shot them over 130 times.

Each year Gibsland, Louisiana, where the couple ate their last meal, hosts the Bonnie and Clyde Festival on the Friday and Saturday falling closest to the couples' date of death, May 23rd. The festival features two major reenactments: one of a bank robbery and the other of the ambush of Bonnie and Clyde, held at the actual site of their death.

Gibsland is also home to two separate Bonnie and Clyde museums, which compete for the attention of the gangster fanatics who pass through town each year. The Authentic Bonnie and Clyde Museum sells T-shirts and souvenirs that fund the annual festival. It also provides

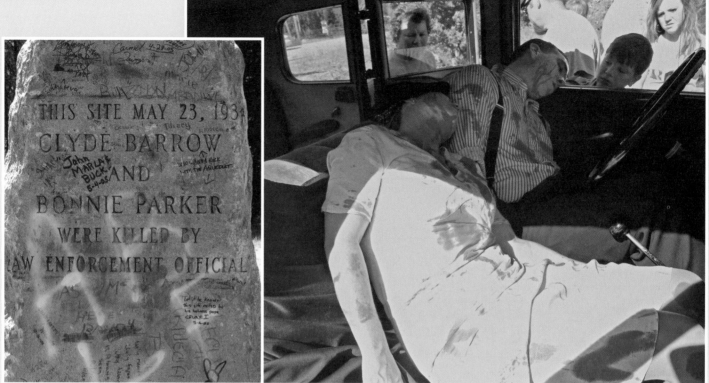

access to historical newspaper articles and photos, as well as genuine Bonnie and Clyde memorabilia. The nearby Bonnie and Clyde Ambush Museum occupies the former site of Ma Canfield's Café, the restaurant where Bonnie and Clyde bought their last meals before getting offed by Johnny Law. "Boots" Hinton, whose father, Ted, was one of the six officers in the ambush, operates this museum. Ted knew the couple from his days as a cop in Dallas and even had a crush on Bonnie from her waitressing days. As Boots tells it, his dad offered up an olive branch to the couple and tried to get them to turn themselves in to the police.

"He tried to get Clyde to come in," Boots told *Weird U.S.* "He sent word to him to come in, he'd be sure he got all the way in, no one would shoot him on the way to the jail. If he got the electric chair . . . he'd walk the last mile with him. Clyde sent word back to him, said,

'Ted, don't try it, you'll just get killed.'"

Boots also told of his father's participation in the surprise attack.

"Car stopped over in the ditch, and he jerked the door open on Bonnie's side. The little lady was leaning up against the door and she fell out. He caught her. And he told me, he said, 'Son, she was breathing when I caught her, and by the time I gathered her up to put her back in there, she wasn't breathing anymore.'"

The Ambush Museum definitely has a more macabre edge than its "authentic" counterpart. Its sign is riddled with fake bullet holes, and the gift shop sells grisly photos taken after the ambush and swatches of blood-soaked cloth from Clyde Barrow's shirt. So go to Gibsland, Louisiana, to see that Bonnie Parker and Clyde Barrow may still be the most beloved rogues of all—at least in the hearts of one small town's 1,100 residents.

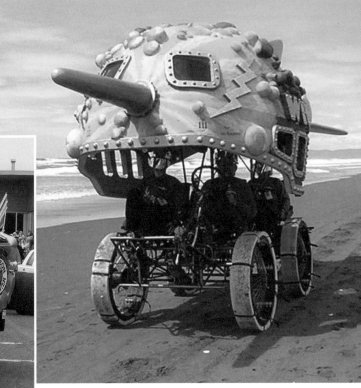

Kinetic Sculpture Race
Last weekend in May

When Ferndale, California, resident Hobart Brown spruced up his son's tricycle in 1969, he spawned one of the most bizarre and enduring traditions in the world of weird art. Hobart's five-wheeled creation raced against altered cycles created by his neighbors, and the Kinetic Sculpture Race was born. It has evolved into a forty-two-mile test of endurance and creative good humor as self-powered vehicles cross Ferndale's pavements, grass, and sand dunes. The race has inspired imitators, including an early-May Kinetic Sculpture Race in Baltimore, Maryland, that's organized by the American Visionary Art Museum.

Skunk Ape Festival
Early June

Don't talk to a Floridian about Bigfoot. Florida has its own big hairy hominid, the Skunk Ape, and that publicity-seeking northerner Bigfoot is stealing his thunder. First sighted in 1957

by a pair of hunters, Florida's Skunk Ape is a seven-foot-tall creature a bit like a red-eyed orangutan, known for stealing food, frightening local pets, and giving off a strong unpleasant odor. Since then, hundreds of people claim to have personally witnessed the beast in action.

So it should come as no surprise that there's an annual Skunk Ape Festival. It's held at the beginning of June at the Trail Lakes Campground in Ochopee. The festival was started by a man named Bill Mitchell to raise money for the local fire company. These days, it's organized by David Shealy, who's largely recognized as the world's leading Skunk Ape expert. Shealy has taken to the airwaves and to the press with his theories on the Skunk Ape, and the festival gives him a chance to gather the troops of loyal Skunk Ape believers who hope to verify the beast's existence. The festival serves primarily as a time for those with a common interest in Skunk Ape research to meet and exchange the latest theories and information regarding the origins and locations of their favorite furry monster.

The event has a real party atmosphere, with live bands and entertainment. Most curious is the Miss Skunk Ape Contest, which chooses a young lady who will help promote Skunk Ape–related activities throughout the following year. (Although we'd have to imagine that women aren't clamoring to be known as Miss Skunk Ape.)

The Skunk Ape stands in American lore as one of the most talked about monsters of the twentieth century. With the Skunk Ape Festival, the amount of talk will only increase.

Blackbeard Festival
June

Pirates. These thieves and murderers who terrorized travelers from shore to sea are regarded still as an unsavory lot. And of all the dastardly crew, one man stands head and shoulders above the rest: Blackbeard. He spent only two years as a pirate, but he left a legacy that is still remembered today. He put bows in his beard, had fourteen wives, and ultimately died at the hands of Lieutenant Robert Maynard—shot five times, stabbed more than twenty, and robbed of his head, which was then hung from the bow of Maynard's ship.

Each June, pirate enthusiasts and fans of the legendary Blackbeard inundate Hampton, Virginia, during the city's annual

When we decided we'd try to get to the bottom of the mystery of Blackbeard's skull, we figured there was really only one person to ask—Blackbeard himself. Since he's been dead and beheaded since November 22, 1718, we went with the next best thing—Ben Cherry, the man who travels the United States and the Caribbean impersonating the infamous pirate of yore.

"My guess is not as good as yours," Cherry told us at the Blackbeard Festival, "and yours is perfectly awful.

"Rumor has it that it ended up being plated with silver and used as a chalice to drink rum from in the Raleigh Tavern up in Williamsburg," he said with a devilish smile. "Old Blackbeard would have liked that of course."

Blackbeard was noted not just for his piracy, but for his personal style. He was known to fight battles with burning fuses tied into his beard. He was a brazen man, and it got us to wondering, Was Blackbeard one of America's earliest Weird trendsetters?

Ben had some thoughts on the subject. "Well, Blackbeard always considered himself a nonconformist. He liked to be different. He was sort of ahead of his time. Because he was different, he was a colorful character." Ben took a moment and contemplated the life and times of the man he spends his life portraying. When he next spoke, it was with a mixture of pride and reverence. "He wore ribbons in his beard to decorate. See, most men were not even wearing beards in the late 1600s or the early 1700s."

Blackbeard made his mark on American colonial society, and it's a mark that is still talked about and discussed today. While Blackbeard's skull may be lost to time, his legacy certainly isn't.

Blackbeard Festival. Dozens of historical reenactments take place, including ships being taken, pirates running reconnaissance on the shores of Hampton, and a Catfight on the Docks (which blackbeardfestival.com describes as "two wenches have a disagreement over a man"). Ever present at the festival is Mr. Ben Cherry, America's leading Blackbeard impersonator.

While the festival is primarily geared toward merriment and celebration, it also opens the door to an obvious question: If Blackbeard's head was cut off to act as an example to all, what happened to his skull? Oral history has long held that when Lieutenant Maynard reached shore, he stuck it on a pike in Norfolk, Virginia, to deter would-be criminals. But to some of Blackbeard's pirate brethren, it served instead as a rallying call. People say that some of them stole his head under the cover of darkness, covered the skull in silver, and fashioned out of it a drinking cup. They engraved into it the phrase "Death to Spotswood," in reference to the governor who ordered the brutal pursuit and execution of the famed pirate.

Blob Fest

July

How can you spin out a festival dedicated to a classic horror movie like *The Blob* beyond a two-hour screening, you ask? The people of Phoenixville, Pennsylvania, where part of the movie was filmed, have the answer: Dedicate two full days to it and see what happens. The annual Blob Fest at the Colonial Theater includes a tinfoil-hat competition, a scream contest, a fire-extinguisher parade, and a re-creation of the scene from the movie in which everyone runs out of the Colonial Theater screaming at the top of their lungs. All this and multiple screenings of a cult classic movie starring Steve McQueen just go to prove that Phoenixville knows how to party, Blob-style.

Ventriloquist Convention

July

Since the first casino opened on the Strip in 1941, Las Vegas has become a paradise for big spenders and a mecca for show business headliners. With Las Vegas being such a competitive showbiz town, only the best of the best in their respective fields can keep the attention of a crowd. It should come as no surprise, then, that Las Vegas is the chosen stamping grounds for the annual convention of some of the most unusual performers of them all—ventriloquists.

The weird aspects of this particular kind of performance are quite obvious to anyone who's seen a ventriloquist and his dummy. After all, what kind of people would choose to express themselves through a wooden human facsimile? But when *Weird U.S.* attended the Las Vegas ventriloquist convention, we were surprised to find a level of weirdness beyond what we had imagined.

Valentine Vox, the organizer of the festival, filled us in on the origins of the art, dating all the way back to the Middle Ages.

"It started as a form of necromantic divining," he told us. "That's divining the future by communication with the dead. And it was a certain kind of necromancer that practiced what we know as gastromancy, divining by the stomach. And what he or she would do, they would talk to the [dead's] stomach, and the spirit was heard to answer them. And they could predict the future. Hence, they were called ventriloquist, from the two Latin words *ventri loquor*—to speak from the belly."

Obviously, spirits speaking from the bellies of dead people gave ventriloquism a sinister reputation. Even the most educated citizens of the Middle Ages were wary of the practice. With pride, Valentine told us,

"Photeus, the patriarch of Constantinople, said, 'It is a wickedness lurking in the human belly.'"

Given these odd beginnings, just how strange are ventriloquists?

"We're not crazy!" one attendee at the convention told us, while wearing an elderly female puppet on her left hand and a bucktoothed plush dog on her right. "Some of us may seem crazy, but no, I don't talk to them whenever I'm by myself."

She then stared at us, smiling, and made sure her googly-eyed creations did the same. It looked pretty unsettling.

"Most ventriloquists are kind of schizophrenic," Tommy Smothers told us bluntly. "You talk to them, they're a little weird. You know, they look at their dummies and their eyeballs are kind of weird. Comedians are twisted enough—but ventriloquists . . ."

Hollywood portrayals of ventriloquists have reinforced the idea that they're off their rockers. The 1945 British film *Dead of Night* features the macabre tale of a ventriloquist who is convinced his dummy is alive. The 1978 vehicle *Magic* stars Anthony Hopkins as a guy who commits murders because his dummy pal, Fats, tells him to. Famous episodes of *The Twilight Zone* and *Alfred Hitchcock Presents* continue the running theme, with *Hitchcock Presents* going so far as having little-person actor Billy Barty portraying a sinister dummy who winds up being the puppet master himself.

And that's just a few reasons why the annual ventriloquist convention in Las Vegas sets the bar for weirdness quite high.

Hemingway Look-alikes
Mid-July

For almost three decades, Key West, Florida, has held a fierce competition in honor of one of its most famous former residents, Ernest Hemingway. Sloppy Joe's, a local bar, welcomes one and all to stake their claim to most physically resembling the deceased author. Besides the look-alike contest, the weekend features a mock running of the bulls, as well as a fierce arm-wrestling contest. Recent years have seen upward of 130 hopeful Hemingways compete for the crown. If you've got a beard, a taste for fishing, and a surly *über*-masculine personality, head to Key West. This might just be the place where you get to shine.

No Bull About It— The Testicle Festival

First week of August

At fifteen dollars per ticket, Clinton, Montana's Testicle Festival may seem to be on the pricey side. But that doesn't take into account that at this event you are given unbridled access to an unimaginable number of bull testicles. And if you've ever tasted a bull testicle, you know that at the end of the day, they're worth their weight in gold.

If you ask us, three Lincolns is a steal, and evidently the festival's 15,000 attendees agree. They consume more than 5,000 pounds of prairie oyster during the event and wash them down with copious amounts of alcohol (as if the testicles weren't enough of a selling point on their own). The festival is held every year at the Rock Creek Lodge. If you enjoy drinking, visiting lodges, eating bovine reproductive organs, or any combination of the three, this is a true-blue can't-miss event!

Hobo Convention

Second week of August

The classic image of the hobo is a lone wanderer riding the rails, looking for adventure. But it seems as though hoboes have a much more social side than any of us imagined. This is proved every August during the annual Hobo Convention in Britt, Iowa. Here, hoboes congregate in one of their most beloved railway towns to touch base, share information on how routes are shaping up, which rail yards have the most aggressive "bulls," and most curiously, to nominate the Hobo King and Hobo Queen for the upcoming year.

Hoboes and outsiders alike also enjoy visiting Britt's Hobo Museum and Hobo Cemetery, where they can learn about their past and pay respect to legendary hoboes of days gone by. This August, if you're clamoring for something to do, why not hop a freight and make your way out to Britt, Iowa? Other rail riders will be there waiting for you.

Elvis Death Celebration

August 16

The Elvis Museum in Cornelia, Georgia, hosts a celebration every August 16, on the anniversary of the King's death, which draws fans with the obligatory fried peanut-butter-and-banana sandwiches. The show hosts ETAs (Elvis Tribute Artists) who perform mini-concerts up to half an hour in length. That's surely worth a visit.

Burning Man
Week before Labor Day

Quite simply the king of all weird events. Each year in Nevada's Black Rock Desert, tens of thousands of people build and inhabit a temporary city, showing off bizarre forms of art for a week before finally setting light to a forty-foot sculpture of a man. It's eight days of survival in harsh desert heat ending in mayhem, and it's our kind of vacation.

Burning Man began in 1986 in San Francisco, when Larry Harvey and Jerry James built a small wooden sculpture on a nude beach and burned it during the summer solstice. Twenty people were in attendance. As the festival grew in reputation, it also grew in size. Within five years, the annual event had moved to the Nevada desert, and within a decade the crowd had swelled to 8,000 people. Now, about 40,000 people spend Labor Day in what they call Black Rock City in the desert, and the attendance is still growing.

The festival itself is a celebration of creative freedom and relies on a number of unusual principles. Each year has a theme, and people design their art to fit the theme. They express themselves by modifying their cars, their clothes (if they wear any), and any strange machinery or sculptures they bring to fit the mood. And the use of money is frowned on: A barter system is in place during the event. Except for payments for such essential services as the pumping of waste from Port-a-Potties, no cash

transactions take place during the eight days. A high priority is placed on not damaging the environment of the Black Rock Desert, so the festival organizers encourage all participants to follow their Leave No Trace policy. The entire event is dedicated to self-expression.

Burning Man has become such a large event, and has so many regular participants, that it's begun to develop its own slang language. Participants refer to themselves as "burners," while trash is referred to as "moop," or "matter out of place."

And of course, like any massive cultural event, Burning Man has begun to bleed over into popular culture. Numerous television shows have included references or visits to the festival, and a number of documentaries have captured the proceedings. If you want to join the swelling ranks of the burners, start modding your car now. And don't forget to pack enough water to survive.

Rayne of Frogs
Labor Day weekend

American cities have some impressive nicknames. Detroit is Motor City. Philadelphia is the City of Brotherly Love. And Las Vegas, of course, is Sin City. All these nicknames are iconic, and there are few Americans who wouldn't know exactly what city you were referring to if you used any of them in casual conversation.

Rayne, Louisiana, might not be as much at the forefront as some of the aforementioned burgs, but it takes its nickname very seriously. Rayne is Frog City, and its annual Labor Day Frog Festival shows just how much the citizens embrace that title.

Rayne became known as Frog City due to the exporting of its locally bred frogs around the world as a delicacy. A group of three Parisian brothers, the Weills, ran the exporting business, and frogs from Rayne were served in restaurants as exclusive as Sardi's in New York City. Rayne's economy came to depend on the frog, so it's no surprise that they've come to honor the amphibian with an annual festival.

The Frog Festival began as the Frog Derby in 1946. This event featured local women, usually of the attractive variety, dressing up frogs in jockey uniforms and entering them in a race. In 1972, this event was held as part of the first full-on Frog Festival. Thirty-six years later, the event is still going strong.

Festivities begin a few weeks before Labor Day, ramping up to the full-on three-day festival held that weekend. The Frog Festival queen is named during a ball in mid-August. A five-kilometer run is held in early September. Labor Day weekend, however, is when the fun really gets going. The whole festival runs alongside a carnival with rides, attractions, and food. Events include pageants, such as the Mr. and Mrs. Tadpole event for kids and the Junior Frog Festival Queen Pageant. A golf tournament is held alongside the grand parade, which runs downtown in Rayne. Musicians take over at night and attract huge crowds to their downtown outdoor venues.

The crown jewel of the weekend is still the Frog Racing and Jumping Contest. Here, frogs compete to see which are the fastest and highest jumpers. These coveted titles are fiercely competed for, with the winners bringing home bragging rights for an entire year.

Even if you can't make it to the Frog Festival, a visit to Rayne at any point during the year shows the town's local pride in its famous delicacy (even though they don't export frogs anymore these days). A local beautification project has led to a series of huge frog-themed murals painted on the sides of buildings throughout town. And many a local business—from Frog's Pub, to the Green Frog Lounge, to Chef Roy's Frog City Café—continues the city's frog-loving theme.

Mothman Festival
Mid-September

Some stories are so scary that they will keep you up long into the night. But it's rare to find a story so chilling, so intense, so downright bloodcurdling that an entire town will spend three days every year examining its every aspect. But that's exactly the kind of story that surrounds the Mothman sightings in Point Pleasant, West Virginia, which throws a three-day Mothman Festival every September.

Like Bigfoot and the Jersey Devil, the Mothman has gone from a figure of fear to a sort of underground pop icon. And his festival brings together all sorts of people, from the most hardcore conspiracy theorists to kids who want their faces painted to look like Mothman. It seems odd that the town that was so terrorized by this mysterious creature has now put him on a pedestal (literally, since there's a metallic Mothman statue in Gunn Park), but each visitor and each plush doll in his likeness is a boon to the local economy. The kitsch factor, however, hides a very real terror of the creature. *Weird U.S.* had a chance to speak with Linda Scarberry, who was one of the first to come forward in the press as a witness to the Mothman.

"I saw it in 1966," she told us. "It was about eleven thirty one night. We come up this road, the lights shined over, and it was standing there in front of the powerhouse. . . . It looked like a man, body of a man. The wings come up over the head and down and around. The wings dragged on the ground.

"We saw it dozens of times. It was at our apartment one day. It was sitting up there on the roof. At first I was really afraid of it, but it had so many chances to hurt us, and it didn't seem like it wanted to. Its eyes would kind of hypnotize you. It acted like it was trying to communicate with us through its eyes."

People thought Linda was crazy, but as more and more people saw the creature, more and more began to fear it. Hysteria gripped the town. One man went so far as to shoot at it, only to find out he had instead killed a rare snowy owl.

When the Silver Bridge collapsed exactly thirteen months from the first reported Mothman sighting, speculation ran wild that the Mothman was a portent of disasters to come. One attendee of the Mothman Festival filled in *Weird U.S.* on some theories, including one about Chief Cornstalk's curse.

"Cornstalk, when he was murdered, put a curse on the town, that the area would be blighted for two hundred years. And Mothman seemed to fall right into the time frame. There's theories about it being an avatar or a spirit, even an extraterrestrial. I think nowadays, most of the common perception is that it is not an alien being."

The reality of who or what the Mothman was will never be fully known. But for those who want to learn as much as they can about all of the legends, the Mothman Festival each mid-September is a can't-miss event.

Bald-Headed Men of America
Second Saturday in September

The Bald-Headed Men of America is a big club. It has enough members to fill a small town, and up to 35,000 of them swoop down to Morehead City, North Carolina, every September for the annual Bald Is Beautiful convention, the world's biggest tribute to the slap-headed, the chrome-domed, and the cranially denuded.

You'll sometimes see a full head of hair there—it is open to any man, woman, or child who is willing to pledge support for the bald—but the pageants and awards are squarely focused on those without enough thatch on their roof. It should be no surprise to anyone that the bulk of the convention takes place on Bald Street.

Roadkill Cook-off
Late September

The state laws of West Virginia allow people to gather roadkill and use it for a variety of purposes, including cooking the critters up for dinner. Not ones to back away from a plan just because some people might recoil at it, the people of Pocahontas County, West Virginia, resolved to celebrate this source of country-road vittles. At the heart of their annual harvest festival, amid the toe-tapping music and baking apples, participants show off their best roadside recipes to their peers. Anyone who enjoys a good road trip knows the danger of accidentally creaming some poor critter on the unforgiving highway. Why not be responsible and turn that next unfortunate highway mishap into a great meal?

Emma Crawford Coffin Fest
Late October

Tragedy and comedy go hand in hand, or so the iconic masks of Greek drama would have us believe. In this spirit, the residents of Manitou Springs, Colorado, throw an annual funfest that pits coffin-wielding contestants against each other in a footrace. Unlike most Halloween-season events, however, this one was inspired by a real-life accident in which an occupied coffin slid into the town.

The Emma Crawford Coffin Races and Festival celebrates the awful fate of a young woman who died at the end of the last century and was buried at the top of a nearby mountain. Years of stormy weather eroded the granite peak, and the coffin slipped free and slid down the side. Rather than recoil in fear and disgust, the residents of Manitou Springs saw the opportunity for an annual theme party.

Each October, dozens register to enter the annual coffin races. They come in costumes and bring with them elaborately decorated coffins mounted on wheels. While many communities mourn their tragedies, Manitou Springs has embraced theirs and turned it into one of the most fun, strange parties this side of any weatherworn mountain.

Local Haunts

If *there's one element* that runs through the folk tales of the United States and Europe, it's the dark place. Forbidding settings, robbed of light, keep cropping up in one form or another in stories and legends. It's no coincidence that the creepiest of *Grimm's Fairy-Tales* are set in forests. Or that monsters are always said to live in caves. Or that visiting an abandoned building or unlit street by night leads to some kind of scary experience. There's something about the Dark Place that you just can't argue with.

But don't dismiss dark places as fiction or old-time folklore just because they happen to feature so prominently in old European writings. America has its own collection of dark places. When Europeans first settled here, they found that many of the native tribes had forbidden areas they called dark places. And even now, centuries later, we hear tales of strange and forbidding places. Some of them are houses. Some are parks. Some are ruined landmarks in the woods. But no matter what they are, the stories that surround them are enough to make your hair curl. Heck, they're enough to make it drop out altogether.

So pack a flashlight and walk this way. Mind your step as you go, though. There are dark places ahead. . . .

Unrest in Cheesman Park

Cheesman Park in Denver, Colorado, seems to be a place of peace and tranquillity. All seems to be well here . . . but is it? Are those shadowy forms moving beneath the shade trees the figures of fellow afternoon sojourners, or something else? Is that woman in the plain dress who sings quietly to herself just an eccentric visitor . . . or could she be one of the park's many apparitions?

Cheesman Park has long been considered to be haunted, and small wonder—it was built over the old City Cemetery. This was more than just a desecration of sacred land. It was a scandal that rocked the city government, outraged the public, and filled the newspapers with lurid tales!

In 1858, a man named William Larimer set aside 320 acres of ground to be used as a cemetery in the new and growing city of Denver. The sites on the crest of the hill were for the rich and influential residents of the city, and were given a suitably impressive name, Mount Prospect. But the first burials to take place here were the victims of crime and violence. A Hungarian immigrant named John Stoefel and the brother-in-law he murdered were

unceremoniously dumped into the same grave. As more murder and accident victims were buried in the lower sections of the cemetery, people began referring to the place as the Old Boneyard or Boot Hill.

In 1873, its official name became the City Cemetery, but nothing helped it gain the respect and reverence that William Larimer had intended. Affluent families started burying their loved ones at the newer Riverside and Fairlawn cemeteries, and left the City Cemetery to paupers, criminals, transients, and unclaimed smallpox

that was part of an Indian treaty that dated back to before 1860. This made the United States the legitimate owner of the property. In 1890, the city of Denver bought it from the federal government for $200. The Jewish and Catholic communities made deals with the city over their grave sites. As for the rest, city hall announced that within ninety days all interested parties should remove their dead for burial elsewhere. Some remains were reburied by concerned family members, but more than five thousand bodies went unclaimed. An unscrupulous undertaker named E. F. McGovern was awarded the contract for disposing of the unclaimed. He specified that each of the bodies would be dug up, placed in a small box, and taken to Riverside Cemetery. McGovern would be paid $1.90 for each box.

It didn't take long for things to go wrong. Onlookers

and typhus victims from the local pesthouse. The Jewish and Catholic sections were well maintained, but the rest of the place fell into disrepair. Lack of interest and care caused the cemetery grounds to revert back to nature. Tombstones fell over, prairie dogs burrowed into the hills, and cattle were allowed to graze among the graves.

With new homes and mansions being built nearby, the city government was pressured to do something about the eyesore. Out of the blue, someone in the U.S. government discovered that the cemetery was on land

and workmen took souvenirs from dug-up caskets. Some fresher bodies were hacked up so they could fit into the tiny new boxes. And stories circulated about an old woman who warned workmen to whisper a prayer over every body . . . or the dead would return. The workmen laughed, but they had a hard time concealing their obvious unease. One workman, named Jim Astor, claimed that he felt a ghost land atop his shoulders. He was so frightened that he threw down a stack of brass nameplates that he had looted from old coffins and ran for his life. People in nearby homes began to report spectral manifestations and confused spirits who knocked on their doors and windows throughout the night. In the darkness, low moaning sounds could be heard over the field of open graves . . . a sound that sometimes can still be heard today.

Before long, newspapers ran front-page stories about atrocities committed at the cemetery and corruption at city hall. There were discrepancies between the number

of reburials being charged to the city and the actual number of boxes being delivered to Riverside Cemetery. The health commissioner brought the project to a halt, and after a long investigation the rest of the bodies were just left. They are still there, under the surface of the park's grounds and gardens.

In 1907, the City Cemetery became Cheesman Park, named in honor of Walter S. Cheesman, a prominent citizen of Denver. In 1950, the Catholic Church sold its adjacent cemetery, and after an orderly removal of its interred remains that portion of the land became Denver's botanical gardens. What was once the Jewish section of the cemetery is now Congress Park.

But despite the ensuing years of peace, the ghosts who were disturbed more than a century ago have returned, or perhaps they never left at all. Many people who don't know the park feel oppression and sadness in these peaceable surroundings. Others claim to occasionally sight misty figures and strange wandering shadows, perhaps wondering what has become of their final resting places. One has to question whether if they will ever find peace.—*Troy Taylor*

"Get the Hell Off of Me!"

I am a thirty-five year old male and a recent transplant to Denver. I've always liked getting out and walking, so I went down to Cheesman Park. After walking all the way around the park about five times, I started getting tired. I decided to cut back to my car to go home. About halfway down the path, I hit what felt like a really cold spot and I had this overwhelming sense of being sad, then really angry. I didn't know what to think about it and just hurried on back to my car. After getting back home, I started feeling really sick to my stomach and light-headed.

I figured that I had overdone it and told my roommate that I was going to lie down. After sleeping for about an hour, I woke up very quickly and found that I couldn't move. I felt like something really heavy was holding me down and the only thing I could move was my fingers. I tried calling out to my roommate but couldn't speak either.

At that time, I heard a voice whispering into my ear saying, "How dare you?" Over and over again. I was yelling in my mind "Get the hell off of me!" This lasted for what seemed like forever but lasted only 30 to 60 seconds. After that, the weight just seemed to disappear and I was able to get up.

I really thought that I had lost it. I came out into the living room and even though I thought he would think I was crazy, I told my roommate what had happened. Growing up in the Denver area, my roommate proceeded to tell me this awful story that the park used to be a cemetery and that there were still people buried there. I've always been a skeptic, but after this, I really don't think I'll be visiting this park anymore!—*S., used with permission from www. RockyMountainParanormal.com*

Lost Souls Still Wandering the Park

It is said if you go into the park late at night you can still hear the muttering of the dead, still confused and dismayed over the mix-up. Local houses are said to be frequented by roaming ghosts who are looking for the bodies, graves, and/or tombstones. I have been in the park late at night, and I have heard the faint incoherent whispering and rants. It is a very odd atmosphere there, almost clammy even during the hottest of summer months.—*G. Haunt Allenbach*

Our Ghostly Neighbors

No question, Cheesman Park and the surrounding area is haunted! My husband and I lived in one of the condo buildings a couple blocks away from Cheesman Park on the west to lower-west side. Our condo, and most of the building, I suspect, was frequented by a multitude of ghostly neighbors. I don't think there was a day or night that went by that we didn't see or hear some paranormal activity.

One entity would come and watch over you if you were sick. She would sit next to you on the couch or bed. You could feel the weight and see the depression this entity made while sitting next to you. Another one liked to take your matches. Days and days later, the matches would show back up in the same place you set them down. We had a lot of ghosts that liked to play with our TV in the bedroom. They would play with the color and brightness controls and some would make visible white smoky swooshes in front of the TV.

One day in the early evening, my husband and I were walking down the hall to the elevator. As we got on the elevator, we both happened to look back down the hall toward our unit . . . and the hall was lined with rose petals. They were only there for a split second. We both looked at each other on the way down in the elevator and asked if the other had seen the rose petals. We both had, the only difference was the color of the petals. His were red with yellow towards the bottom and mine were a deep pink with yellow at the bottom.

We never felt any threatening feelings from our ghosts, it was almost always positive. Every once in a while you would get a touch of sadness, but it was very fleeting.—*Anonymous, used with permission from www.RockyMountainParanormal.com*

Trespassers Beware Pigman Road

Some places in this world seem destined to be the focal points of evil, and Holland Road in the western New York village of Angola might be one of them. This small, quiet, picturesque town is home to only some two thousand people, but the place has attracted multiple

tragedies, multiple legends, and multiple fears. Some of these darker elements are rooted in historical fact. Others are decades-old legends that are harder to verify. But whatever the truth behind the Holland Road stories, they have given the place its more famous name—Pigman Road.

The first time this road came to be associated with death was on December 18, 1867, when a train bound for Buffalo lost its last two cars, which flipped off the track

and threw fifty people to their deaths in the gorge near Holland Road. It was one of the worst train accidents of the nineteenth century. But this wreck, still known as the Angola Horror, is not the only tragedy that made Holland Road infamous.

In the 1950s, the stories say, a reclusive pig farmer lived along Holland Road. He was an ornery man who simply wanted to be left alone. But many teenagers traveled the road at night, looking for a lovers' lane or a place to party. To dissuade them, the farmer stuck butchered pigs' heads on the spiked fence around his property. It was meant to send a clear warning—keep out!—but many teenagers took this macabre message as a challenge. They tested their own mettle and the pig farmer's patience by sneaking onto his property to see just how far he was willing to go. One unlucky group found that the reclusive farmer was far more terrifying than they had ever dreamed.

The next band of visitors to make their way down Holland Road that night made a grisly discovery that has come to define the road ever since. The teenagers who had previously sneaked onto the pig farmer's land were there, staring at them—but only because the farmer had decapitated the kids and mounted their heads on the spikes along his property.

As the legend goes, the Pigman then disappeared into the wilderness, never to be seen again. He has never been caught, and many believe he still lurks in the woods he always regarded as his personal dominion. Today, many people visit the area in hopes of being scared, and many report back that their efforts have succeeded beyond their wildest imagination. Reminders of both the train tragedy and the Pigman murders are often seen by those hunting for the paranormal.

People frequently report hearing the screams of the train victims pierce the night as their ghosts continue to relive the harrowing moment of their sudden deaths. Others have told of seeing ghost trains make their way down the railroad tracks. It is not uncommon for visitors to hear train whistles or loud crashes in the distance, even when it is evident that no train is approaching.

Some people have gone searching for the Pigman, and reports of these nocturnal sojourns into Pigman territory are no less frightening than the tales of the train wreck ghosts. Two bridges cross over Holland Road, and it has

been a long-held belief that the Pigman's house, with its infamous spiked fence, once stood directly between these bridges. Pigman hunters have established a set of rituals to be performed in the area between these two bridges to summon him up. One of the most popular rituals holds that visitors in a car should stop in between the two bridges with their lights off and then flash their high beams thirteen times in succession. After the thirteenth time, the murderous Pigman will emerge, and attack those in the car for bothering him.

Even without a visit from the Pigman himself, the road can be quite the terrifying place. Many visitors have heard sounds in the distance that indicate the murderer is near, including the squealing of pigs or the sharpening of knife blades. Others have found themselves unnerved just by the graffiti painted on these bridges. Legends tell that witnesses often return to the site to spray-paint accounts of their own encounters with the Pigman, so that those who don't see the vengeful maniac with their own two eyes may live vicariously through them.

Creepy Feelings on Pigman Road

Holland Road near where I live is a deserted, secluded road that is crossed by two railroad tracks. The locals call it Pigman Road, after a farmer who placed pig heads on spikes and reputedly killed two trespassing children. Some say his evil spirit still haunts the area. Others believe that the spirits of people who were killed in a horrendous train accident over 100 years ago haunt the bridge. Stories of the road differ a bit from person to person, but there is no denying the creepy feeling one gets on Pigman Road.—*Megan*

The Perils of Pigman Road

Holland Road, or Pigman Road as it is known by the locals, is characterized by the thick forest on either side of the road, and the two one-lane railroad underpasses that anyone driving down the road has to go through. There are variations to the story, which is very old, but the most common one I have heard deals with an old man that used to live in the woods beside the road. This is the story I first heard from a friend of my father's. In the late 1960s, he was offered $100 by a bunch of his friends, which was a lot of money at that time, to walk from one end of the road to the other, and he couldn't do it.

Supposedly, the man who lived in the woods put pigs' heads on stakes on his property to keep children from going there, but they strayed onto the property anyway. The legend says that he ended up catching one of them and put the kid's head on a stake among the pig heads. Local parents found out and burned down his house with him in it. Supposedly, you can still find the burnt-out ruins of the house, but because all of the woods are posted and the area is heavily patrolled by police, I don't know if that's true. The underpasses are covered with graffiti including stuff about the Pigman and there are reports of cult activity in the area.

Either way, I have a strange personal story from the road. About five years ago, a group of four friends and I equipped ourselves with flashlights and video cameras one night, in order to actually go and investigate all the claims we had heard about the area. We had heard a story that someone had stopped on the road, only to almost be hit by a big dark truck that seemed to come out of nowhere without headlights on. That night, on our way to the road, we got into a massive car accident (it was my car so I have pictures of both cars involved to prove it) that almost killed two of us (me and my front passenger). We were T-boned by a large dark pickup truck with no headlights on. Take it for what it's worth, but I get a strange feeling when I'm on that road.—*Jochen Hutzenlaub*

Ghosts of Sensabaugh Tunnel

The abandoned and imposing Sensabaugh Tunnel, off Big Elm Road in Kingsport, Tennessee, was once the site of great tragedies. It is now home to many mysteries. Of all the tales of murder set within the tunnel, many feature the unfortunate death of children.

One says that a homeless man kidnapped a baby from a local family and hid within the tunnel. He soon began to panic and in desperation, he drowned the baby in the creek that runs within the passage. Now the baby's restless spirit resides within the dark expanse. Another story says that a young pregnant girl was kidnapped and murdered within the tunnel. Now both her spirit and that of her unborn child remain behind.

There is another story of a man who lived near the entrance of the tunnel with his family, until he lost his mind. He killed all of his family, including his newborn son, and hid their bodies in the creek inside the tunnel.

All of these legends have attracted thrill-seekers to the tunnel over the years. People report hearing screams and footsteps, as well as the wailing of a baby. If one drives into the tunnel and shuts off their car engine, the car will not start again. People have seen phantoms in their rearview mirrors approaching their vehicles, and have seen strange lights rush towards them down the length of the tunnel. Some people have even said that after driving out of the tunnel they have discovered baby-sized handprints along the sides of their cars.

Protecting the Tunnel's Secret

The road leading to the tunnel is creepy enough, with out-of-the-way little shabby trailers and creepy noises. If you turn your car off in the tunnel, it actually won't start back up, but only if you are driving a stick shift. I have never heard any weird noises in the tunnel.

Also, the tunnel is always so flooded that most people are afraid to drive through it because they aren't sure about how deep the water will be. When we had to turn around in someone's yard, a man came to his door with a shotgun. The people there are really creepy, or else they're trying to protect some kind of secret.—*Ariel Tester*

Saw the Light at the End of the Tunnel

After driving down two of the creepiest roads I've ever seen, we arrived at the tunnel at about 10:30. We didn't stay long because the locals did not seem friendly.

It is seriously the creepiest place I have ever been to. Unfortunately, this time we didn't hear any of the rumored crying. However, there was a light that came from nowhere I could find and illuminated part of the tunnel entrance. We all saw this light and confirmed we had seen the same thing.—*Rev*

"Did You See That Little Girl?"

We sat in the center of the tunnel and did everything we were told to do. We were starting to get restless, and my friend started to joke with us and said, "Did you see that little girl?" But three minutes later, something was at my window and it started shaking the car really hard and fast.—*Kimberly*

Babies' Handprints on the Foggy Windows

Some of my friends and I wanted to find out if the rumors were true or not, so we left Rogersville and headed to the Sensabaugh Tunnel. It was about 9:30 p.m. when we went through the first time. I turned the headlights off and drove in, and once inside I stopped for a minute and my friend freaked out. He said he heard a train, and then I heard it too, so I drove out of there. We drove down the road, built up the courage to do it again, and went back. Once again I turned the headlights off and started through the tunnel. When we

got to the middle, I stopped and waited. Then all of the sudden, the windows fogged up and we could see babies' handprints all over them. Needless to say, we got out very fast. We all laughed at the thought of ghosts before tonight, but I have a change in attitude now.—*Weston Castle*

Tales of Two Tunnels

I live not five miles from the Sensabaugh Tunnel and the stories you write about are some of the ones I heard growing up. You didn't write about it not being the original tunnel, however. The original tunnel is less than a mile from my home. There's a river that always runs through it, unlike the newer tunnel, which only has a river going through it when it rains a lot.

You cannot drive through the original tunnel because of huge rocks and other stuff in it. I know this from experience: I tried one time and got stuck, then almost died trying to get out of the tunnel because I lost control of my car and it went across the street and almost flipped over. Thank goodness an old, fallen tree stopped us.—*Irot*

The Haunted "Big House"

If ghosts come back to places where they suffered in life, as some believe, the ghosts of convicts must surely return to their place of confinement. Is it any surprise, then, that jails breed ghost stories?

Only a short walk away from the museum of art in Philadelphia, Pennsylvania, stands a massive fortress built from enormous blocks of stone. Its vaulted windows and arches look almost churchlike, but its towers and turrets reveal a darker purpose for this building. It is the Eastern State Penitentiary, an innovative prison from the early Victorian era that was in its time the most expensive building ever built. For 140 years, it housed hardened criminals in harsh and controversial conditions, driving many of them into chronic illness and insanity. Hundreds of people still pass through those gates, but nowadays, they pay for the privilege out of their own pockets and tour the place for fun.

Hauntings of Eastern State Penitentiary

Philadelphia's Eastern State Penitentiary was built to further the Quakers' idea of prisoner isolation as a form of punishment. Inmates were confined in windowless rooms and would come into contact with no living persons, save for an occasional guard or a minister. The doorways were

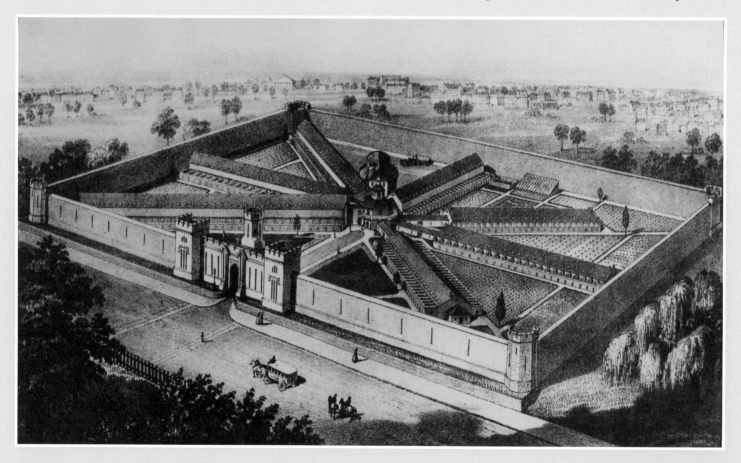

shortened so that prisoners had to stoop down to enter or leave—as a penitent would—because penitence was supposed to be essential for lawbreakers (hence the word penitentiary). The only lighting in the cell was a narrow window in the ceiling that was called the Eye of God.

After the penitentiary closed and the prisoners were removed, the last guards spoke of the sounds of footsteps in the corridors, pacing feet in the cells, eerie wails that drifted from the darkest corners of the complex, and dark shadows that resembled people flitting past. It seemed that the abandoned halls, corridors, and chambers were not so empty after all. Those who left the penitentiary on that final day had become convinced that a strange presence had taken over the building. Most of them breathed a sigh of relief to be gone.

Since the mid-1970s, when the empty prison became a National Historic Landmark, tales of ghosts have proliferated. But does the spooky atmosphere of the place explain the tales as merely tricks of the imagination? Those who have experienced the spirits of Eastern State say that it does not.

"The idea of staying in this

penitentiary alone is just overwhelming. . . . I would not stay here overnight," stated Greta Galuszka, a program coordinator for the prison.

Over the years, volunteers and visitors alike have had some pretty strange experiences in the prison. In cellblock 12, several independent witnesses have reported the hollow and distant sound of laughter echoing in certain cells. No source can ever be discovered for the noises. Others have reported the presence of shadowy apparitions in the cells and the hallways, as though prisoners from the past can find no escape from this inhuman place. Several volunteers believe that they have seen these ghostly figures in the "six block," while others have seen them darting across corridors and vanishing into rooms. Eastern State's death row has also been the scene of strange encounters and chilling visitations by the same shadowy figures encountered by others.

A locksmith named Gary Johnson had his own encounter during a restoration project. "I had this feeling that I was being watched," he recalled, "but I turned and I'm looking down the block and there's nobody there. A couple of seconds later and I get the same feeling. . . . I turn around shooooom . . . this black shadow just leaped across the block!" Johnson still refers to the prison as a "giant haunted house."

Angel Riugra, who has also worked in the prison, agrees. "You feel kinda jittery walking around because you feel something there, but when you turn around, you don't see anything," he said.

One of the most commonly reported specters is a dark, humanlike figure who stands very still and quiet in the older cellblocks. The figure usually goes unnoticed until the visitor gets too close to him and he darts away. The sightings never last for long but are always accompanied by a feeling of anger and malevolence.

Another of the penitentiary's most frequently seen

spirits is a figure that stands high above the prison walls in a guard tower. It has been assumed for many years that this is the ghost of a former guard. One has to wonder why a guard, who was free to leave this place at the end of the day, would choose to remain behind. Perhaps he's guarding the restless spirits within.

As intimidating as this all sounds, though, it is the hauntings that bring people back. Many of the staff members, while unsettled by the occasional strange events, are nevertheless fiercely protective of the place. They are determined to see that it is around for many years to come. Even so, they can't help but feel that forces are at work inside the prison.

"So much did happen here," Greta Galuszka added, "that there's the potential for a lot of unfinished business to be hanging around. And I think that's my fear, to stumble upon some of that unfinished business."

So is the Eastern State Penitentiary haunted? In the end, that is up to the visitor to decide. If the events of the past really do create the hauntings of today, Eastern State Penitentiary is a very haunted place.—*Troy Taylor*

Ghosts and Gangsters at Eastern State Pen

In high school, my sociology teacher took us to the Eastern State Penitentiary on a field trip. I got the eeriest feeling. It looked like all the prisoners had just recently left. Cell doors were left standing open, and remnants of beds and chairs were left in some of the cells. The cell doorways looked like they were made for dwarves. You had to bend over to get inside. I felt like someone was going to walk out of one of the cells at any moment. We all huddled together, whispering.

We eventually made our way to the prison's prime exhibit, Al Capone's cell! Apparently he had served time there at one point. His cell was huge with carpeting and a nice bed—the only cell of its kind in the whole prison. He got the "special treatment," so to speak.—*Jenn*

Abandoned and Haunted

The Glenn Dale Hospital is a sprawling complex on 216 acres of Maryland's Prince Georges County. It was originally built as a tuberculosis hospital and remained in operation as a general hospital until 1982. Today the many buildings in the complex sit crumbling and abandoned, and vandalized heavily.

One of the most enduring rumors about Glenn Dale is that during its later years it was used as a hospital to house the criminally insane. Stories are told that upon the hospital's closing, some of these deranged lunatics were simply released onto the streets. With no family to speak of and no idea of where to go, they found their way back inside the abandoned buildings and live there to this day. Another tale claims that the hospital itself is contagious—touching anything inside could expose you to tuberculosis. (Actually, it could expose you to asbestos, so the place really is a health hazard.)

Although the complex is posted as a no-trespassing zone and is regularly patrolled by law enforcement, late-night explorers do get in and report hearing strange noises and even seeing the spirits of patients who died there. We'd not recommend trying it out for yourself. To see why, read on.

A Police Escort into the Belly of the Beast

I'd like to share the story of when my friend and I visited the Glenn Dale Hospital. I forced my friend to take me there for a photo shoot. Eventually I talked him into walking up a small path towards the main hospital building, which was lacking a warning sign. And wouldn't ya know it? A cop showed up. He was pretty nice and explained that the building we were going to wasn't haunted, but the children's ward on the other side of the road was.

So he took us through the gates and into the belly of the beast. He motioned for us to get out and brought us to a darkened doorway. Eventually he brought out a high-powered flashlight to take us inside, but the bulb burnt out as soon as the beam hit the doorway. He still let us go a little ways inside, telling us, "Go ahead, you first." Something fell off a shelf in the room behind the door. That was too much. I turned around to leave when I caught sight of something through a large open doorway. I saw something run by at the landing of the basement. I was out of there in an instant.

After chatting with the policeman for a bit, he told us a story of another officer who was checking out the area alone. Someone across the street heard gunshots and called it in. When backup arrived, they found the officer standing in the middle of the area, not moving, just staring straight ahead and not saying a word. He had shot all of his rounds at something they never found.—*Zev*

Inside Glenn Dale

The Glenn Dale complex consists of seven or eight buildings. There are still gurneys in the storage areas, a chair at the solid wood reception desk, prosthetic limbs, trash that never made it into the incinerator, and the Board of Trustees plaque in the facilities building. Apparently there is a maze of underground tunnels connecting all of the buildings. I have never seen them. Another rumor has it that Satanists used to worship down in the basement of the main building. I have seen evidence of that by way of plenty of spray-painted upside-down crosses. Yet another rumor was that junkies would take their dead and dump them throughout the buildings. And yet another rumor was that people would go to the top of the main building, where there is an atrium that runs across the width of the building, to commit suicide.

There are fences up, guard dogs, security cameras, motion sensors on the grounds, and the guards are zealous. This is obviously for good reason. The buildings are now very unsafe. Broken glass and debris are everywhere. Asbestos hangs from the ceilings; there are holes in the floor. Also, hundreds of bats nest inside, so there is the distinct chance of walking into a room, feeling your foot sink into something and hearing a lot of fluttering overhead. I did that!—*Pete Monaghan*

Sledding Through the Glenn Dale Tunnels

One night, naturally, we got the idea to explore the tunnels of Glenn Dale Hospital. Several hundred yards in, we found a child's Flexible Flyer sled, which I thought was truly bizarre. I couldn't imagine why or how that sled got to where it was.—*LH*

Not Just the Buildings Abandoned at Glenn Dale

I lived in Bowie, Maryland, in the 1970s. I can tell you a little bit about Glenn Dale Hospital, as I went there many times as a child. In the 1970s, it was an institution for people with mental retardation and developmental disabilities. In fact, I have fond memories of the place, because my father would take us to Glenn Dale on Saturday afternoons and we'd bring a whole bunch of toys with us. We'd go in and find some kids and just start playing with them. These people would literally go days at a time without another human actually touching them. We would light up the place with our presence, simply because we were their only visitors. The institution closed around 1982, but it's still standing. The buildings are certainly not safe, though. I drove past it a month ago, and there's a tree growing right up through the middle of the roof.—*Chris Privett*

Glenn Dale's Barking Hounds

I've been to Glenn Dale Hospital several times with my boyfriend and two of our friends. After about five to ten minutes, we started hearing a dog barking. It was really odd: the exact same bark about every three seconds, as if it were timed. It lasted for a few minutes, but it was definitely coming from within the building.—*Sky Pegasus*

Poked in the Throat by an Inhuman Shadow

So last night, some friends and I explored the Glenn Dale Hospital and I have some stories! As soon as we got there and started to explore, our brand-new flashlight started dying on us. It happened all night long: The flashlight would be perfect, and then would just die out. Sometimes it flickered. At one point, the light was getting brighter and dimmer, off and on.

In one of the buildings—I believe it was the adult ward—we all huddled together, and one of us said, "Everyone turn out their lights!" So we did. As I turned my head to look out a window, I swear something poked me square in the middle of my throat. My heart was racing and I was shaking, it was so scary. I thought someone was messing around with my head, but nobody 'fessed up to it. In fact, they all looked at me like I was lying about the whole thing.

We saw something else as we were climbing up a hill to get to this other crazy building that I believe was the children's wing. I was looking at the ground to make sure I didn't fall and missed this, but they saw this inhuman-looking shadow moving around from side to side and up and down.—*Beth*

Screams and Slamming Doors

I was there two years ago. I saw light-green lights coming from the woods. We went inside and my brother had to go to the bathroom, and as there was no one around, he used the nearby steps. All I heard next was a loud scream from my brother, and then we all ran back to our car outside. When he calmed down, my brother said the door near the stairs had opened and slammed shut right in front of him. We have never been back.—*Tiffani*

Welcome to Hotel Hell

I would like to tell you about one of the creepiest, scariest, and downright weirdest places that I have ever been to. It is an abandoned hotel that I visited once with some of my friends that is located near where we live in the town of Maribel, Wisconsin.

Maribel is a very small town, home to less than 400 people. Next to Maribel Caves Park stands a burnt-out three-story structure that was once the Maribel Caves Hotel. Knowing locals refer to it as Hotel Hell. The hotel was billed as a place where nearby natural mineral waters and the open air promoted relaxation and healing. But even then, stories were whispered that the operation was actually a front to mask the activities of the infamous gangster Al Capone. Maribel lies directly between Chicago and Capone's hideout in Couderay, Wisconsin, making the hotel the perfect spot for America's number one public enemy to lay low. Furthermore, the spring-water bottling operation run out of the hotel was the perfect cover for moonshining.

The building has reportedly burned down three times throughout its existence, on the same date in three separate years. Sometime between the fires, while the hotel was still operating, a patron lost his mind and murdered a number of his fellow guests. He then killed himself. Later down the line, when the final fire broke out at the hotel, a small child who had been playing on the roof of the building was trapped and died atop the structure.

The tales get even more bizarre and macabre. The building itself is said to glow whenever a new moon comes out. People have been chased by white specters that patrol the area around Hotel Hell. When nighttime visitors shine their flashlights at the second-floor windows, they are answered by flashing lights from within the vacant building. People who have gone inside Hotel Hell have seen blood on the walls, have felt cold hands touch them, and have heard strange footsteps, screams, and bells ringing. People have seen objects levitate down hallways or burst into flames. Two different children supposedly haunt the hotel. One is a small girl in a black dress who appears on a stairway inside the structure. The other is the

little boy who perished in the final fire; he has been seen running around on top of the building.

One of the most audacious legends about Hotel Hell involves a coven of evil witches who managed to open a portal to hell through the fountain in front of the building. A good witch caught wind of what was going on and came in to undo the damage they had wrought, but the property is still said to house something evil from that time. Beware the evils that lurk near Maribel, Wisconsin—they have been growing stronger for decades now, and there seems to be no end in sight.–*Erik Bender*

The Many Mysteries of Kay's Cross

The explosion was loud. It echoed through the town of Kaysville, Utah. Many residents heard the boom. It was ten p.m. on Tuesday, February 25, 1992. Someone had sneaked down into Kay's Hollow and filled up one of Kaysville's oddest structures with explosives and set it off. Kay's Cross was no more . . . sort of. Unless you are from Kaysville (a suburb about twenty-five miles north of Salt Lake City), chances are you have never heard of Kay's Cross. An imposing stone and mortar structure that loomed twenty feet high over a remote hollow, it is the stuff of legend in Davis County. A large letter K adorned both sides. To get to it, most folks had to first hike through the Kaysville Cemetery and then trudge over scrub-oak–covered hills.

A lot of Kaysville teenagers made the trip through the years. Kay's Cross was just too irresistible. The spook tales surrounding it are varied and many. During a full moon, the cross gives off an eerie glow. Or a strange spectral woman haunts the cross, chasing away visitors. Or satanists perform sacrifices at its base on Halloween night. Or the face of a murdered woman appears in the cross on the anniversary of her death. Or the cross will burn anyone who touches it during its glowing phase. Or mysterious dog-men guard the cross. Pretty wild stuff.

The most popular myth is that the cross was built as a monument to the landowner's murdered wife or family. Some tales say they were the victims of marauders, but in one version, it is he who murdered his wife—or seven wives, depending on the teller—and hanged himself near the cross in remorse. In its most grisly form, he buried six of his wives around the cross and one standing upright in its base. Another legend is that he sealed only the heart of his wife in the cross. The center has been hollowed out over the years, evidence of curiosity seekers excavating for this gruesome trophy.

As dramatically satisfying as these stories are, no news stories can be unearthed concerning such murders taking place in Kaysville. One of the few stories written about Kay's Cross, a 1981 *Lakeside Review* report by Maggie Holmes, relates a legend in which a series of malevolent spirits guards the cross. In this spooky tale, anyone who wants to visit Kay's Cross must sneak past these specters who reside in the Kaysville Cemetery, or the ghouls will make them pay. One gets the feeling that the teenage sources for this bizarre ritual were pulling Maggie's leg.

A less ghost-oriented story is that an irate farmer, probably the landowner, guarded the structure. He would chase away any visitors with a shotgun loaded with rock salt. Many firsthand witnesses have verified this, so it has the ring of truth.

Though no official history exists for the building of Kay's Cross, there are some theories. The least likely explanation is that it was constructed by Kaysville's founding father, an acolyte of Brigham Young named Bishop William Kay, as a boundary marker or burial place for his wife. Most longtime residents, though, believe that polygamists built the cross in the 1940s and the letter K stood for the family name of Kingston. (In 1992, a non-bylined story in *The Ogden Standard-Examiner* reported that Charles and Ethel Kingston owned the land.) Some have suggested that Kingston's followers built it as a monument to their leader. Others have postulated that Kay's Cross is nothing more than a property marker for Kingston land. Is this irrefutable proof that the Kingstons built Kay's Cross? Not by a long shot.

The explosion that took out Kay's Cross was pretty spectacular. It obliterated the base and hurled ten-pound chunks of rock up to eighty feet. The only known casualty was a pheasant roosting in a tree some forty feet away. An investigation failed to reveal what type of explosive was

used. The sheriffs dutifully sent evidence to the Bureau of Alcohol, Tobacco and Firearms. No one was ever arrested and the case remains open.

Though toppled, the ruins of Kay's Cross still lie in the hollow. Development is making its way towards Kay's Hollow, but for now it is untouched by builders. Shattered bottles around the cross's ruins testify that it remains a teen hangout. As long as an aura of the unknown hangs about, folks will be drawn to this oddball landmark, whether Kaysville residents like it or not.—*Clint Wardlow*

Devil Worshipers of the Cross

In Kaysville, UT, there is a place known to some of the locals as Kay's Cross. It's a field with a lot of trees and there are some small houses around. Over the years devil worshipers and such would go there and do animal sacrifices and other weird things. To get these actions to stop, the town members blew up the cross. This was a very long time ago, but at night weird things still happen. I have seen tall figures in black that seem to hover and teleport, glowing eyes, and clothing and tents that have been ripped apart. My friend has a story about sitting in his car with one of these black-cloaked figures coming towards them, and the car wouldn't start or lock.—*A.K.S.*

Weeping Woman of West Virginia

Parkersburg, West Virginia, is home to the *Weeping Woman,* a graveyard statue that is the focal point of dozens of local legends. The following are a few of the messages we've received detailing this impressive statue's fantastic tales.

Weeping Woman Watches

In Parkersburg, West Virginia, there is the legend of the statue of "The Weeping Woman." The statue is located in Riverview Cemetery, and watches over the family plot of the Jacksons, a prominent family in Parkersburg who were cousins to famed Civil War General Stonewall Jackson. A number of unexplained powers are associated with this curious statue. Some say that at night during a full moon, the statue stands up and walks through the graveyard, weeping over the conflict between North and South. Others claim to have seen her move and have photographed her hands in different positions. We love this graveyard. Let it thrive.—*Hellface*

She's Got You Figured Out

The Weeping Woman is said to be a good judge of character. If a person is up to no good, she can be a mischievous presence. She's been known to tear people's clothes, trip them, pull on their hair, and unbutton or unzip their shirts and pants. On the other hand, if someone has a strong character and is pure of heart, they should visit the Weeping Woman—legend says that for these do-gooders, the statue can grant wishes! So, whether nefarious or true in spirit, the Weeping Woman has got something to offer everyone.—*Scott Koolb*

Weeping Woman Makes Babies!

I'm sure that you've heard about the world famous Weeping Woman statue in Parkersburg. I think anyone who grows up within 50 miles of that cemetery is legally required to visit it at some point. One of the stories about the statue says that any woman who touches the Woman will become pregnant within a year. My wife and I visited the statue and she did indeed touch it and we did indeed conceive within the year. Of course, we were trying, so keep that in mind. If the Weeping Woman had anything to do with it, then my thanks are with her forever!—*W. H. Kostel*

Puzzles of the

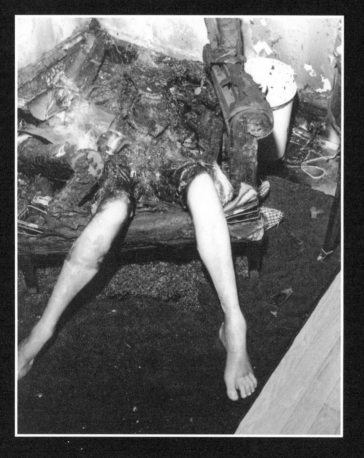

Some questions in life have no easy answers. If a tree falls in the forest, and nobody is there to witness it, does it make a sound? How many roads must a man walk down before you call him a man? What is the sound of one hand clapping?

These famous imponderables pale next to some of the things we've run into on our *Weird* field trips across the United States. No matter how hard we think about it, we just can't understand how ancient Romans, Vikings, and medieval knights managed to find their way here—yet in states as far west as Oklahoma and Minnesota, there's evidence that they may have.

We don't quite get how a spark plug could embed itself in a fossilized rock. And try as we might, we can't understand why some mysterious character or characters have spread a message on crosswalks across the nation explaining that the dead are being resurrected on Jupiter. And as for people spontaneously bursting into flames . . . well . . . how can you explain that away?

It is indeed a puzzling world out there. It's a good job that we're not seeking the easy answers, because unlike the strange puzzles spread across this land, they're NOT out there.

TOYNBEE IDEA IN KUBRICK'S
MOViE 2001 — ALONE AS
RESURRECT DEAD
PLANET JUPiTER

HELLION S AND NEDS NFILTRATE
AND HARVEST YOU TO PRISON

LAW ENFORCEMENT CENTER
Sheriff's Department
Marshall County Minnesota

CONFIDENTIAL

FILE No. 79-1405

INVESTIGATION REPORTS

Person Reporting: VAL JOHNSON
Res. Phone: 695-5281
Res. Address: OSLO, MN.
Bus. Address: MARSHALL CO. SHERIFF'S DEPT.
Bus. Phone: 745-5411

Owner if Other than Person Reporting: MARSHALL CO. SHERIFF'S DEPT.
Address: LAW ENFORCEMENT CENTER, Warren, Mn. 56762
Bus. Phone: 745-5411
Res. Phone:

Classification: PIMV (Pass. Vehicle & all others)
Date of Occurrence: 08-27-79
Time: 0140-0219 am
Area of Occurrence: 1.10 mi. South of Co. #5 on Hwy #220
Report Received By:
Date Received By: 08-27-79
Time: 0219 am
How Reported: ( ) In Person ( ) Phone ( ) On View Other __radio__
Report Investigated By: DENNIS BREKKE AND EVERETT DOOLITTLE
Theft Loss Value:
Damage Loss Value:

DETAILS:

SYNOPSIS: PATROL VEHICLE 407 ON PATROL IN THE NORTHWEST AREA OF MARSHALL COUNTY, NOTICED A LIGHT AND UPON GOING TO INVESTIGATE, SAID VEHICLE WAS INVOLVED IN AN ACCIDENT WITH AN UNKNOWN OBJECT.

INVESTIGATION:

08-27-79

0225, ON OR ABOUT, THIS OFFICER WAS NOTIFIED AT HIS RESIDENCE THAT DEPUTY SHERIFF VAL JOHNSON HAD CALLED IN A 10-88 (OFFICER NEEDS HELP). THEREAFTER, THIS OFFICER CALLED THE SHERIFF (401-DENNIS BREKKE) AND PICKED HIM UP AND WERE ENROUTE TO SAID LOCATION. AN AMBULANCE FROM STEPHEN, MN. HAD ALREADY BEEN DISPATCHED.

0305, ON OR ABOUT, 401 AND THIS OFFICER MET DEPUTY SHERIFF GREG WINSKOWSKI AT THE SCENE WHICH IS LOCATED APPROX. 1.4 MILES SOUTH OF CO. HWY #5 ON STATE HWY #220. AT THE SCENE, THIS OFFICER OBSERVED THE FOLLOWING:

1) On or about 1.1 miles south of County Hwy #5 on State Hwy #220, at Mile Marker #68, there was glass on the road. It was in the south-bound lane.

2) From this area, Sheriff Brekke paced off on or about 854 ft. south where skid marks started. These skid marks were in the south-bound lane and then a sharp turn to the east ending in an easterly direction. Said skid marks were approx. 99 ft. (these were also paced by Sheriff Brekke). (See picture #1.)

3) This officer noticed the following:
   a) front head light, left pair (driver's side) right light was broken out
   b) Small dent on hood (driver's side)
   c) Windshield (driver's side) broken
   d) Top antenna bent toward rear of vehicle
   e) Rear antennae also bent toward rear of vehicle

THEREFORE, THIS OFFICER AND SHERIFF BREKKE WENT TO MARSHALL COUNTY SHERIFF'S OFFICE TO MEET WITH DEPUTY SHERIFF VAL JOHNSON.

0455, ON OR ABOUT, THIS OFFICER AND SHERIFF BREKKE TOOK A TAPE STATEMENT FROM DEPUTY SHERIFF VAL JOHNSON. MR. JOHNSON STATED THE FOLLOWING:

(Signed) Everett Doolittle
Investigating Officers

Mystery Stone

When you think about it, we owe a debt of gratitude to rocks. The Ten Commandments, carved on heavy stone tablets in biblical times, have been keeping us out of trouble ever since. The Rock of Gibraltar, sturdy and unyielding, has given us a convenient metaphor for stubbornness. Asking little in return, they protect, support, steady, surround, contain, crush, mark, destroy, and preserve. And some of them, special ones, intrigue.

Nestled within an arroyo in Hidden Mountain in central New Mexico, secluded and accessible only by foot, the so-called Mystery Stone has that talent. Across the flat, north-facing surface of the stone, someone has inscribed a set of characters that are similar to those in Phoenician or ancient Hebrew alphabets. Running parallel with the downward angle of the rock, the 216 individual characters are precise and ordered. There's some evidence of sloppy penmanship in the chunks of rock broken from the face by the strike of the scribe's tool, as well as in the crowded spacing between the topmost of the nine lines of text. But overall, the characters have been chiseled with a degree of care that is almost delicate.

Thus, to solve the Mystery part of the stone's name, we should ask not only "What?"—the inscriptions are clearly meant to be a message—but also "Who?" As in, "Who on earth stole all the way out here in the hot New Mexico sun to carve a missive on a rock?" And, following closely on the heels of that, "Why?"

Linguists and historians of all backgrounds have offered a variety of answers. Epigrapher Dixie L. Perkins, for example, suggested that the inscription was left by an ancient Greek explorer named Zakyneros, exiled from his home on the Island of Samos around 500 B.C. for refusing to pay a debt. "I, Zakyneros," he supposedly wrote of his plight, "just as a soothsayer or prophet, out of reach of

mortal man, I am fleeing and am very afraid."

That's just one explanation, though. Other researchers have suggested that the inscription is the work of a member of the Ten Lost Tribes of Israel; still others, a Mormon emigrant heading west. Even if some of these explanations are far-fetched, they invite us to add "What if?" to our list of questions about the Mystery Stone. What if visitors from the rest of the world reached North America much earlier than we know? What if an ancient Greek explorer really did venture this far into this desert, so distant from the home he loved, and what if he bewailed his fate for eternity in a series of chiseled strokes on the side of a rock? Can you blame him?

Many scholars believe the inscription to be a version of the Ten Commandments themselves, though they're unsure exactly when the words were carved or by whom. In fact, the stone is often called the Ten Commandments Rock, or the Los Lunas Decalogue Stone for the nearby city of Los Lunas.

Then, of course, there's the possibility that it's all a hoax. For one thing, the location is suspect. If you want people to see your message, which presumably you do if you're carving it on a rock, why not put it somewhere with greater visibility? Also, it's been done before. The Mystery Stone may be similar to the Newark Decalogue Stone near Newark, Ohio, inscribed with a shortened version of the Ten Commandments. Or the Kensington Runestone, found near Kensington, Minnesota, with writing that suggests a visit by Vikings to the area in the fourteenth century. Historians regard both stones with suspicion.

Perhaps the only decisive victor in this battle is irony. Because even if you believe the Los Lunas Mystery Stone is a hoax, you're still left with your original questions: Who wrote it? And why? The Mystery Stone, taciturn as only a rock can be, reveals nothing.–*David Pike*

Heavener Runestone

Heavener is a small town in Oklahoma close to the border of Arkansas. It's home to three thousand people—and a slab of sandstone that challenges everything we believe about the settling of the United States. When the Choctaw tribe first discovered what we now call the Heavener Runestone, inside its ravine atop Poteau Mountain, they had never seen the writing before. True, they were from Mississippi, but they knew the languages of other tribes—but not these strange symbols, etched six inches high on the rock face. When white settlers made their way to the area in the 1870s, they were equally baffled. By the turn of the century, the stone had been nicknamed Indian Rock, despite local tribes' insistence that they had no idea what it was.

The first step to solving the mystery came in 1923, when a local man, Carl Kemmerer, copied the inscription and sent it to the Smithsonian Institution in Washington, D.C., which determined that the symbols were ancient Norse runes. This has led to an explosion of speculation. Many believe that Viking explorers visited the North American continent before Christopher Columbus, but this rune hints that they actually explored the continent—at least as far west as Oklahoma.

Could it be some kind of fake or fraud? Well, the inscription is worn and eroded, which makes it seem old, but it's in sandstone, which erodes quickly. However, this slab sandstone is protected from the elements in its ravine on three sides. The rest of the stone erodes at a very slow pace, so the letters seem to have been there for centuries.

Six of the eight letters carved into the Heavener Runestone are consistent with a set of ancient Norse symbols known as the Elder Futhark runes. The two others, the second and last letters in the series, look like mirror images of symbols from the same set. Much effort

has been put into deciphering the meaning of the runes.

In the 1960s, researchers thought they had the answer—they were graffiti representing a date (November 11, 1012) scrawled by Norse explorers. This was the generally accepted explanation until the mid-1980s, when an expert in runes, Dr. Richard Neilsen, began research on the Heavener stone. By this time, similar stones had been discovered in the area. One of them, the Poteau Runestone, gave Neilsen the key to translate what was written on the Heavener stone.

Neilsen's theory is that the Heavener Stone spells out the words "Glome Dal." This, in the language of the ancient Norse, would translate to Glome's Valley, which seems to indicate that Scandinavians didn't simply pass through here, but actually settled. The Heavener Runestone, it is inferred, was the boundary marker for the property of one of these settlers.

Both theories have some merit, but neither is conclusive. These days, the rock is the centerpiece of the Heavener Runestone State Park. A small wooden house has been erected over the stone, and a glass case has been built around it. The Heavener Runestone and its many riddles may never be solved, but it will certainly be preserved and pondered for many generations to come.

It's Stone Heavener

Are you familiar with the Heavener rune stone, in Oklahoma? Most historians disregard it because of its distance from known Viking sights. But to my knowledge the Heavener stone (and the other smaller stones found nearby) are the only rune stones found in North America that have not been proven a hoax. I visited the sight expecting to see an obvious fake. I left thinking that it might be real.—*Wolfemark*

Mystery of the Kensington Runestone

Eight Goths and 22 Norwegians on an exploration journey from Vinland to the west. We had camp by 2 skerries one day's journey north from this stone. We were to fish one day after we came home found 10 men red of blood and dead AVM [Ave Maria].

We have 10 men by the sea to look after our ships 14 days' travel from this island Year 1362.

This was written on a huge slab of graywacke stone dug up in the farm of Olof Ohman in 1898 in Kensington, Minnesota. At last! We finally have proof that Scandinavians explored the area 130 years before Columbus!

Or is it actually proof? Skeptics point out that settlers had been faking all kinds of artifacts to make a buck. Just two years earlier, a "Petrified Man" was discovered underground in Bloomer, Minnesota. Later, so were molds for making a concrete human. Besides, Ohman was a stonemason and his friend Sven Fogelblad had studied runes. Much later, in 2003, the National Historical Museum of Stockholm, Sweden, analyzed the runes, and declared they were similar to a secret trade language used in Scandinavia in the 1800s.

But the stone was tangled in the roots of a large aspen tree—how could that have been "planted" by Ohman? If he was in it for the money, why did he sell the slab for only $10? If he was in it for fame, why did he face public mockery about the stone and not take credit for tricking the world?

Many experts have weighed in on the stone, but nobody's come up with a definitive answer. Even though the Smithsonian has kept its distance from the controversy, they wanted to include it in an enormous

touring exhibit on the Vikings—as a curiosity, not a true artifact.

Perhaps more interesting than the arguments for and against the stone's validity are the theories that it has inspired. The translator of the words on the stone, Hjalmar Holand, hypothesized that its tale was of an expedition led by Paul Knutson sent by the evangelical Catholic King Magnus Erickson of Sweden and Norway in 1355 to his colonies in Greenland and Vinland (North America). The colony in Greenland was deserted, so Knutson continued on to Vinland, searching for years for the colonists. One winter, the explorers were icebound in Hudson's Bay, and in the summer a small party went down the Nelson River into Lake Winnipeg and on to the Red River. After a fishing trip, part of the group returned to find ten comrades killed "red of blood." Holand assumed that the rune-stone was a memo left for the others in their party, who couldn't find their way home and settled in North Dakota with the Mandan Indians. He speculated that this explains the Mandans' European-style villages, the runic images found on old Mandan animal bones, and their blue eyes and fair skin.

In 2001, author Thomas Reiersgord hypothesized that the "Goths" of the stone were actually Cistercian monks from the Swedish island of Gotland, who were often literate stone carvers. He argues that the "red of blood" meant the ten men were hemorrhaging from the bubonic plague, which was ravaging Europe. Reiersgord suggested that the Dakotas carried this stone with them after the white explorers carved it. He wrote that this Dakota tribe "identified themselves as the Isanti, meaning the people who possessed 'isan,' the cut stone," or the rune-stone.

The possibility that Ohman's stone is valid has helped fuel Scandinavian fervor across the state. Walker has a huge Viking ship mural on a downtown building, and Spring Grove has a replica Viking ship perched on a hill, along with a bronze Viking statue in town called *The Quest*. Statues of Norse explorer Leif Erikson have popped up all across Minnesota. Duluth has a Viking in Leif Erikson Park; St. Paul even has Leif Erikson next to the capitol building, as though he were one of the state's founders.

Pecked Pictures of Petroglyph Point

Lava Beds National Monument in California, a volcanic cone of rock rising above the surrounding farmlands in Siskiyou County, is covered with petroglyphs: abstract shapes, animal figures, and human outlines pecked into the rock about seven feet above the ground. Extending for hundreds of feet, the petroglyphs are fenced off to protect them from vandals but can easily be seen from behind the barrier.

Their age, origin, and meaning are a mystery. Though they're attributed to the Modoc Indians, other theories abound. Perhaps the most colorful one is occult writer H. Spencer Lewis's claim that refugees from the lost continent of Lemuria made them. Lewis was obsessed with the idea that the Lemurians were the common ancestors of both the local Indians and the classical civilizations and insisted that many Modoc words and place-names were almost identical to the equivalent Greek and Latin words.

Roman Artifacts in Kentucky

Roman artifacts tend to turn up in North America with alarming regularity. A Roman figurine head popped up in a sixteenth-century Mexican burial site. Burrows Cave in Illinois was discovered to contain artifacts of Roman, Greek, and Egyptian origin that were clearly left there in antiquity. Roman coins were unearthed in an Indian mound in Texas, and a Roman-style ship's remains were found at the bottom of Galveston Bay.

In 1963, as workers began construction on the Sherman Minton Bridge in Louisville, Kentucky, a large cache of Roman coins was dug up. According to one source, the coins were arranged in a way that suggested they had originally been buried in a bag or a pouch, which had long since rotted away. One of the coins bore the likeness of Claudius II, circa A.D. 268. Two of the coins

ended up on display in the Falls of the Ohio Museum in Clarksville, Indiana, but were ordered removed in 2004 by the state of Indiana. Apparently the state has a specific policy forbidding the suggestion that pre-Columbian contact with other cultures occurred, and so the coin exhibit was packed up and has presumably been filed away in a forgotten box in some dusty storage room.

Some years after the Louisville find, Roman coins were discovered in a cave in Breathitt County, Kentucky. Interestingly, these coins were from the same general time period as those dug up in 1963—known as "antoniniani" coins, they're from somewhere between A.D. 238 and 305.

What does it all mean? Did the Roman Empire actually visit America? Perhaps, but even today, anyone can purchase ancient Roman coins, and they were no doubt more plentiful in centuries past. It's possible that some later travelers brought these coins here, although they were probably still pre-Columbian travelers and thus still flying in the face of historical decorum in Indiana.

The Westford Knight

Medieval knights make most people think of Europe and stone castles, but they make some of us think of the town of Westford, Massachusetts. It has a mysterious, centuries-old carving clad in shining armor that shakes up all our preconceptions of the medieval era.

On the side of Depot Street near the center of town is a rock—noticeable only because some stone pillars and a headstone-shaped monument mark the spot. Step close and you still might notice only a large, flat rock—for this mystery requires visitors to get very close to the ground. Your knees may get a little dirty, but it's a small price to pay to look back over six centuries.

Penny Lacroix, director of the Westford Museum, said, "It's believed that Henry Sinclair and his men voyaged over to North America and they traveled up the Merrimack River, which was bigger at that point, and visited what is now Westford."

Henry Sinclair was the Earl of Orkney, a Scottish nobleman. Some say he was also a member of the Knights Templars, that band of men who fought for Christendom during the Crusades. Many believe that Sinclair made a voyage with other Templars to North America in 1398, when the Templars had fallen out of favor and were being hunted down by the pope and the king of France.

What did this group of men do when they got to America? How can we be sure they were here? Many believe the Westford Knight holds the answer. The first mention in print of the mysterious carving is in the Reverend Edwin R. Hodgman's book *History of the Town of Westford, Mass 1659–1883*, published in 1883. Bob Oliphant, a member of the Westford Historical Society, said, "When Hodgman mentions it, he describes it as Indian carvings. It's difficult for me to understand how they could be seen as Indian carvings. It's so obviously not an Indian carving."

When the rock carving was first discovered, no one rushed to form a preservation society or to alert the archaeological community. Locals shrugged their shoulders and went about their business, and New England weather continued its erosive work on the exposed slab.

Although today many of the lines are faded, visitors can see how parts of the etching were made by drilling into or puncturing the rock. The T-shaped sword with a break through it (indicating the death of a knight) is still evident, but the rest is left to the imagination.

One theory is that this place is a memorial to one of the knights who died on the voyage and his body is buried nearby. "Some people think the knight is from the Gunn family," said Lacroix. This theory is based on the faint initials "J. G." carved into the rock. James Gunn—a Templar. But not everyone agrees. Some scholars think the carving is graffiti that may be only 150 years old at best. Others feel this rock offers a glimpse into the last days of the secretive Knights Templars and clearly shows that Europeans were here before Columbus.

Westford has a second mystery rock in town, but this one currently resides in the town library. The Boat Stone, as locals call it, is an egg-shaped rock measuring about eighteen inches in diameter. Carved onto the rock is an etching of a fourteenth-century ship, the number 184, and an arrow. This rock was discovered in the latter half of the nineteenth century while forest was being cleared for roads. It sat inside the barn of one Westford resident until the family decided to donate it to the library. Some speculate that this rock is a map to where James Gunn may be buried; others think it may be a key to buried Knights Templars treasure. Like the Westford Knight, this rock offers a challenge to those who claim Columbus was the first European to discover America.

Coso Spark Plug Still Sparking Debate

Debate has raged for more than forty years about a twentieth-century artifact discovered in a half-million-year-old rock. When three rock hunters found a geode in the Coso Mountains on February 13, 1961, they uncovered one of the most inexplicable archaeological finds in California history. After a good morning's collecting, Wally Lane, Mike Mikesell, and Virginia Maxey dumped their finds into a sack that Mikesell was toting and headed home.

The next day Mikesell pulled a likely-looking specimen out of the bag and went to work with a diamond saw. One rock encrusted with fossil shells split apart to reveal what looked like a porcelain cylinder surrounding a shiny metal rod. It also contained what looked like a washer and a nail. Maxey spoke to a geologist who informed her that the rock would have taken 500,000 years to form. Maxey was at first quoted as declaring the find "an instrument as old as Mu or Atlantis. Perhaps it is a communications device or some sort of directional finder or some sort of instrument made to utilize power principles we know nothing about."

The bizarre artifact defies easy explanation. The few who have ventured to identify it say it's a clay-coated piece of mine machinery debris; this is unlikely, since the "Coso Geode" was found several miles from the nearest mineshafts. At any rate, clay concretion processes don't happen in dry, rocky desert regions like the Coso range.

In the mid-1960s, Ron Calais, a scientist with a heavy creationist bent, was allowed to examine the Coso Geode. He took pictures and X-rays of the cut halves (which was a great stroke of luck when the object later went missing). The X-rays showed a cylindrical structure with a metal ring at one end and a flared metal cap at the other. A threaded, screwlike area topped the assemblage.

In 1969, International Fortean Organization (INFO) journal editor Ronald Willis published a careful and thoughtful article on the Coso artifact. Following the skeptical but interested teachings of Charles Fort, the legendary investigator of the paranormal, he commented on the structure of the anomalous object, but stopped short of calling it an advanced piece of technology. He simply wrote that it was "the remains of a corroded piece of metal with threads." He finally went out on a limb and guessed that the thing might be a spark plug.

Pierre Stomberg, a skeptic, contacted the SPCA (that's the Spark Plug Collectors of America) and asked them to look at the X rays. President Chad Windham responded with a letter and two examples of Champion spark plugs from the 1920s era. Everything matched up, allowing for corrosion of the metal and other components. Creationists

soon latched onto the find, since if authentic it calls into question the ordered pageant of history that the steady march of mainstream science has presented to us. It was a prime example of an OOPArt (Out Of Place Artifact). The creationists responded that the certain parts of the "spark plug, particularly the spring or helix terminal . . . do not correspond to any known spark plug today," but many readers of the Creation Outreach Web site tended to agree with the skeptics. So much for faith.

In the late 1990s, various skeptic organizations reopened investigations into the Coso Geode. They looked at the claims of researchers who started with the premise that the rock was in fact a bona fide geode. Skeptics pointed out that just because the original rock-hunting trio was looking for geodes did not necessarily mean that they found one. Since there were other modern objects (the nail and washer) embedded in the surface, along with fossil shells, at some time the rock may have been covered with mud, picked up hitchhikers, and finally hardened in the desert sun.

Perhaps the Coso artifact has returned to the space-time transient realm from whence it came. It was on display for a while at the East California Museum in Independence, but was reclaimed by the owner in 1969. After forbidding any further dismantling or examination of the relic, he tried to sell it for a reported $25,000, but couldn't find a buyer.

Recent attempts to trace the owner, the original finders, or the "geode" have been unsuccessful. All that's left of this archaeological anomaly are a few photographs, yellowing accounts in some obscure journals, and a tantalizing mystery that may never be resolved to anyone's satisfaction.

World's Slowest Racetrack

When you're tired of sand dunes, dangerous abandoned mines, and interpretive signs, there's only one place left to go in Death Valley: the Place Where the Rocks Move. A few rough miles from the end of the road (the paved one) lies one of the weirdest and most beautiful locales in this most desolate of national parks.

Most packaged tours stop at the spectacular Ubehebe volcanic crater at the north end of the valley. Just before the start of the short loop to the lip of the crater, a track cuts off through the lava and heads southwest. An unassuming sign posted at the intersection reads THE RACETRACK—27

(miles, that is). It's slow going. About an hour of heavily washboarded gravel road rewards your vibrating eyeballs with the sight of a beige smear along the bottom of a huge valley. A sizable conglomeration of uplifted bedrock called the Grandstand juts up from the center of an ancient dry lake. The blackish brown outcropping, about one hundred by five hundred feet, still resembles the island it once was. The demarcation between dry mud and hard rock is gradual and rings the formation like a soft halo.

Don't look for the traveling rocks here. This is just the prelude. Drive almost due east across the lakebed for about fifteen or twenty minutes until the floating, shimmering black dots on the horizon resolve into hundreds of very dark, scattered rocks. No one has ever witnessed the things actually moving. The mysterious race that takes place here apparently moves at glacial speeds. But the evidence is clear: Smeared depressions all end at a rock — some of the tracks are hundreds of feet long. It's as if some spectral hand decided to use the mud as a doodling pad. A few of the trails are ramrod-straight; others curve, zigzag, and even turn back on themselves. It's both creepy and exhilarating. Many of the rocks have even pushed up a lip of dried mud in front of them, and only a few appear to have moved in the same direction.

How did these things get out here anyway? Selective winds? And where are they from? Some are at least a half mile from the nearest mountain — they must have been traveling for millennia.

Some of the tracks stop in mid-slide, with no rock to be seen, which suggests stupid human activity. Apparently someone has moved a number of the rocks. If the ranger catches you, there is a heavy fine, and don't think they won't impose it. Rangers often hide in the hills and appear out of nowhere if they see any scofflaws. —*Greg Bishop*

Tulsa, Oklahoma: The Center of the Universe

My wife, who is from Tulsa, took me to this bridge in downtown that the locals refer to as the center of the universe. She told me that there is a certain spot on this pedestrian bridge where a person can stand and hear an echo whenever someone else speaks. Stand anywhere else on the bridge and you won't get the same effect. Apparently scientists have studied the phenomenon and cannot come up with a reason for why this is happening. The bridge itself is very simple, just a concrete expansion that traverses railroad tracks that run parallel to East Archer Street. I was pretty amazed at the echo, although it was fairly subtle. And to be quite honest with you, I never would have guessed that the Center of the Universe would be in Tulsa.—*Paul Campanell*

On Spontaneous Human Combustion

Imagine walking into a room and being assaulted by the acrid smell of smoke. You look around, expecting to see charred ruins on all sides, but the room seems to be mostly intact. But wait . . . there in the corner is a square yard of scorch marks. The floorboards have been burned away, revealing the basement below. As you move closer to the gaping hole, another smell reaches your nose — something foul that appears to be coming from a yellow oil around the charred floorboards. You recoil from the smell, but move closer, and as you do, you see something horrific that makes you want to run from the room. At the end of a charred stump, you see what's left of a human body. You have just walked into a case of spontaneous human combustion.

SHC is a favorite subject of both the fans and debunkers of unexplained phenomena. These cases tap into the most dreaded of human fears — a deadly fire that you can do nothing to prevent. Victims of this phenomenon are often reduced to ashes, with the torso completely missing and only a leg or arm left intact. The site of the fire is usually contained — most cases spread no more than a few feet from the body, leaving furnishings, paper, and other combustible materials unscathed. It looks as if the victims suddenly grew unbelievably hot and, as their bodies vaporized, cooled down again before a real fire could take hold. It's possible that smokers' falling ashes could ignite clothes and cause a very local fire. But experienced firefighters sometimes find this so-called rational explanation inadequate. If pyro-professionals are willing to consider the possibility of spontaneous human combustion . . . why shouldn't the rest of us?

Fires Spread in Florida

One of the world's best-documented cases of SHC is that of Mary Reeser, sixty-seven, of St. Petersburg, Florida. On the morning of July 2, 1951, the landlady went to Mrs. Reeser's apartment to deliver a telegram and found the door handle extremely hot. Fearing that the apartment was on fire, she yelled for help. Two painters working next door heard her pleas and ran to her aid. They opened the door and were hit with a rush of hot air. The two men immediately went inside to rescue Mrs. Reeser, but she was nowhere to be found. Strangely, there was only a little smoke coming from a small flame burning on a wooden beam separating the kitchen from the living room. The fire department arrived and quickly extinguished the flame, but there were still no signs of the tenant. When the fire chief arrived and began investigating, he was shocked by what he found. In the middle of the floor was a four-foot-square scorched spot with the remains of a chair and the incinerated remains of a human body. Mrs. Reeser had been reduced to a pile of ashes, except for her skull and one foot, which was still wearing a slipper.

The coroner came in and removed the remains for examination. An investigation was launched involving

the police, state fire marshal, arson experts, pathologists, and even an FBI agent. The experts were left puzzled; there seemed to be no heat damage beyond the four-foot area containing the victim's ashes. Close by were flammable items, newspapers, and linens. All were intact and untouched. Investigators observed that the heat had been intense enough to melt a candle on a table twelve feet away and crack a mirror on the wall.

Forensic results indicated that the 170-pound lady had been reduced to less than ten pounds of ashes. Analysis ruled out lightning, electrical malfunctions, or smoking as a cause of the fire. It appeared that Mrs. Reeser had simply exploded into flames and burned up. The fire experts estimated the temperature must have been three thousand degrees in the room, yet there was hardly any other heat damage. The final conclusion was that Mrs. Reeser had died from a fire of unknown origin. The official report referred to the incident as "unusual and improbable."

The Burning of Dr. John

It was December 5, 1966, in Coudersport, Pennsylvania. Don Gosnell came to the house of retired Dr. John Irving Bentley to read his meter. Because the ninety-two-year-old physician had limited mobility, part-time firefighter Gosnell had permission to enter by himself, so he made his way down to the basement to take his reading. He noticed a strange sweet smell, but thought nothing of it until he found a cloud of light blue smoke and a pile of ashes on the dirt floor of the basement. Looking up, he saw a hole in the ceiling, revealing the ground-floor bathroom.

He ran upstairs to investigate and found Dr. Bentley's bedroom filled with smoke. In the bathroom, beside a hole measuring two and a half by four feet burned into the floor, lay the walker that the good doctor needed to move around. The walker's rubber feet were still intact, and beside it lay all that remained of Dr. Bentley—the lower half of his right leg, its intact foot wearing an undamaged slipper.

What could have caused this gruesome scene? Gosnell thought at first that the frail old man might have had a pipe accident—his robe was typically dotted with tiny burn marks from hot tobacco ash. But the doctor's pipe was still on its stand in the bedroom. Perhaps some mighty surge of energy had exploded from within the old physician, consuming his body in a brief and horrific burst of flame. Or perhaps there's a more scientific explanation for the event.

There were remnants of a broken water pitcher lying in the toilet at the scene of the conflagration. Perhaps the doctor had gone to the bathroom to douse a small clothing fire that started in his room, but he simply had not made it in time. Perhaps as the fire took hold, he resorted to a stop-drop-and-roll in a last-ditch attempt to quell the flames. At that point, his burning clothing could have ignited the linoleum on the bathroom floor, spreading to the hardwood flooring and wooden beams of the basement ceiling.

Such arguments don't win over the true believers, however. Their rebuttal pokes a neat hole in the rational explanation. If the linoleum and floorboards were as combustible as this explanation argues, why did the fire not consume it all? The hole in the floor was small, and there was plenty of combustible material elsewhere in the small bathroom. Why was that unscathed by the fire?

The Flames of Helen

The case of Helen Conway's death by fire in 1964 is so intriguing that it even became the focus of a television documentary filmed by the British Broadcasting Corporation. But this resident of Drexel Hill, Pennsylvania, does not look like a poster child for the SHC cause. At first glance, she looks like a classic case of death by

misadventure. Mrs. Conway was a firefighter's worst enemy. She was a heavy smoker whose room was dotted with cigarette burns. She was elderly and somewhat careless. And shortly before her death, her granddaughter had brought her a new book of matches. So. . . case closed, right?

Not necessarily. When firefighters, summoned by a 911 call, made their way through the thick smoke on that November morning, they found very little of Mrs. Conway. All that remained was a pile of melted flesh and her two legs intact from below the knee, as if she had been sitting down when consumed by the flames. The fire chief who attended the scene, Paul Haggarty, has gone on record as saying he believed that this was a case of spontaneous combustion. And his opinion is shared by one of the first volunteer firemen on the scene, Robert Meslin, who later became fire marshal. The key factor in their conclusion is the speed at which the fire took hold.

Larry Arnold's book *Ablaze* quotes Meslin's reasoning. Meslin estimates that Mrs. Conway's granddaughter made the call to the fire department within a few minutes of talking to her grandmother; it came in around eight forty a.m., and firemen were on the scene within ten minutes. This would mean that the fire lasted no more than twenty minutes; some estimates go as low as six minutes. The idea that a match fire could consume a body so completely and so quickly does not sit well with fire-fighting professionals.

The most likely type of fire that a seated woman would experience from natural causes would be a "wick effect" fire, in which flames melt the body fat, which fuels the fire. According to experiments made by the makers of the BBC documentary, such a fire would take at least seven hours to consume a human body.

Skeptical Inquirer magazine takes another tack, which pooh-poohs the BBC's results. If the fire started at the base of Mrs. Conway's seated body, they reason, it would have been more intense and consumed the body faster. Perhaps so, but are they seriously suggesting that Mrs. Conway accidentally sat on a lighted match to precipitate that fatal fire? That seems to us less likely than the existence of a subatomic particle that spontaneously bursts into flames.

Whose side do we at *Weird U.S.* take in these mysterious cases? We're inclined to sit on the fence—and nowhere near any lighted matches or burning pipe tobacco.

You Must Make and Lay Tiles! You!

Of all the graffiti slogans that have appeared in American cities, the strangest and most confusing of all must be the Toynbee Idea. This message is not simple graffiti—it's not painted, but carved into floor tiles and somehow set into the asphalt. Each of the tiles is skillfully made and laid. And yet, they are completely incomprehensible.

Toynbee tiles contain a main message, written large and clear: "Toynbee Idea Movie 2001: Resurrect Dead Planet Jupiter." What could that mean? The obvious Toynbee is British historian Arnold Toynbee, and the movie is clearly *2001: A Space Odyssey.* But how does a famous historian fit in with a science fiction movie? And what's this about resurrecting the dead?

Who knows? And who knows why the message has spread across cities in Pennsylvania, Ohio, New York, Maryland, and elsewhere. The message gets even weirder as you read in the margins of these tiles. In smaller text, the person responsible for the tiles has left other messages—rants, really—about a conspiracy between the feds, the Mafia, foreign powers, and the media. The tiler (or tilers) calls this conspiracy the Cult of the Hellion. And many tiles claim that the tile maker has a fatal disease and that his readers must carry on the fight on his behalf. Many carry the powerful directive "You Must Make and Lay Tiles! You!"

As we've studied the Toynbee Idea over the years, we've come to some conclusions: First, it is not Toynbee's idea. Arnold Toynbee never wrote about reanimation of the dead or space travel. In fact, his only connection with science fiction comes from a Ray Bradbury story called *The Toynbee Convector,* published in 1988, around the same time the tiles began appearing. So whoever wrote the original tile slogan seems to have mixed up ideas from a few science fiction stories and thrown in some paranoia for good measure.

The Toynbee Idea first appeared on red-white-and-blue plaques the size of license plates in the 1980s or early 1990s on South Street, Philadelphia, and other South Philly locations. (As of the beginning of 2008, there was still one on South and Fourth, but the road's a real mess and will

tile first appeared, Toynbee enthusiasts took a sharp intake of breath. Could this be the home of the tiler? But the answer was no—at least, not anymore. The man living there knew nothing about Toynbee tiles, and soon stopped answering the door when strangers came knocking. When we went to South Seventh Street, number 2624 was empty and boarded up.

So it was time to hit newspaper archives to see if anyone had ever written about the tiles. The earliest written connection between 2001 and Toynbee appeared in the May 14, 1983, edition of *The Philadelphia Inquirer,* when columnist Clark DeLeon opened a column under the headline WANNA RUN THAT ONE BY ME AGAIN? this way: "Call me skeptical, but I had a hard time buying James Morasco's concept that the planet Jupiter would be colonized by bringing all the people of Earth who had ever died back to life and then changing Jupiter's atmosphere to allow them to live. Is this just me, or does that strike you as hard to swallow too?"

The article identified James Morasco as a social worker who had uncovered a connection between Arnold Toynbee's ideas and the end of the movie *2001: A Space Odyssey.* He contacted DeLeon to spread the word, and even founded a Jupiter colonization organization called the Minority Association. The only James Morasco in Philadelphia at the time was a carpenter who would have been in his late seventies when the first wave of tiles appeared and who died in 2003.

So even if Morasco was the original tiler, the newly arrived tiles prove he's not the ONLY tiler. And so the trail has gone cold. To this day, who is responsible for Toynbee tiles—and what it all means—is anybody's guess.

probably be paved over soon.) At the start of the new millennium, smaller tiles about the size of index cards began to take their place. There are plenty of examples near City Hall on Chestnut Street, especially at Broad and Chestnut. In late fall 2007, a new tile appeared near Reading Terminal Market. But Toynbee tiles have spread far and wide: Examples in downtown Pittsburgh are at a couple of crosswalks at the corner of Oliver Avenue and Smithfield Street. There are more at Smithfield Street near Forbes Avenue and at Forbes near Ross Street. And there have been literally hundreds more in New York City, Washington, D.C., Baltimore, and various towns in Ohio. They've even moved from urban crosswalks into busy highways: on the northbound lane of Route 476 in Delaware County (just past Milepost 12 near Villanova and St. David's), on I-76 and I-95, and even one at the entrance to the Holland Tunnel in New York.

The most exhaustive clearinghouse of Toynbee lore is at www.toynbee.net, which has listed tiles as far afield as Santiago, Chile. The Santiago tile seemed to contain a key to unraveling the Toynbee mystery—the street address 2624 S. 7th. Phila, PA 19145-4610, US. When news of this

Val Johnson and the Infamous UFO Car

Deputy Sheriff Val Johnson was making the rounds through Marshall County, Minnesota, as usual on August 27, 1979. But that night's events wound up being far from routine. In fact, they made headline news, and even now remain hotly debated—because Val Johnson ended up in the hospital, his car strangely damaged, after what he described as a face-to-face run-in with a UFO.

At one forty a.m., Johnson saw a bright light among the trees to his south. He sped along Highway 220, hoping to get to the light while it was still visible, believing it might be a crashed light aircraft used by smugglers along the Canadian border. But before he could get to it, the light came to him. It rose up from the trees, nearly a mile away, and bathed his car in light in a matter of seconds. Before Johnson could even comprehend what was happening, he heard the sound of smashing glass. That was the last he remembered of the incident itself. The rest of his recollections took place only after he woke up.

At two nineteen a.m., Johnson awoke, disoriented and far away from where he left off. He was now facing east and was on the other side of the highway, close to one thousand feet from where he had been. He was in a state of shock, with his eyes burned and covered in a strange pink film. Both the clock inside his car and his wristwatch were now exactly fourteen minutes off from the actual time, and they had been accurate before the incident. Johnson was immediately taken to a local hospital, where he was treated for the burns and sent home.

Johnson's car was severely damaged, and it is preserved at the Marshall County Historical Museum, where it is referred to as the UFO Car. A crack runs from the top of the windshield vertically down to its bottom. Along the crack, four impact points appear, as if small objects had been launched at the car. A strange, small circular imprint was left on the hood. Both radio antennas, front and back, are bent back at sixty-degree angles. The bulk of the damage seemed to be intentionally focused around the driver's side of the car. An engineer from Ford who inspected the car said he had seen nothing like it. In his estimation, it appeared that something had impacted the outside of the car at the same instant a force had been generated from within.

Val Johnson described the incident like this:

I was rendered either unconscious, neutralized or unknowing for a period of approximately 39 minutes. From the point of intersection, my Police vehicle proceeded south in a straight line 854 feet, at which point the brakes were engaged by forces unknown to myself, as I do not remember doing this, and I left about approximately 99 feet of black marks on the highway before coming to rest sideways in the road with the grille of my hood facing in an easterly direction. At 2:19 a.m., I radioed a 10-88 (Officer Needs Assistance) to my dispatcher in Warren.

UFO investigators immediately traveled to the scene. Their excitement over the strange event helped fuel it further into the national spotlight. Val Johnson appeared on *Good Morning America* alongside a UFO researcher; skeptics immediately began rallying against Johnson's case. It has become one of the most controversial UFO sightings in American history, and was one of the core issues at a debate on the subject at the Smithsonian Institution.

Many have claimed that Val Johnson was a known practical joker, so the incident could be nothing more than a joke that spiraled out of control. But believers counter that Johnson's eyes were burned, and no practical joker would put his own eyesight on the line for kicks.

That August night in 1979 is one of the most well-researched, most thoroughly investigated UFO reports in history. While it may be impossible to discern for sure whether the incident was a genuine phenomenon or simply an elaborate hoax, there's one thing that isn't up for debate—something strange happened in Minnesota in August of 1979. And whatever it was has resonated for decades with all who have encountered it.

Jesus in the Light Beam

If you're looking to tempt an encounter with the unexplained, your first step is not usually to take a trip down Interstate 40 in Arizona. Yet on November 8, 2003, witnesses traveling the highway east of Holbrook reported seeing a powerful shaft of light descend from the sky and down onto the pavement. It was almost eleven p.m., but the roadway lit up with a light so intense that many drivers on the highway were forced to pull over.

Among the vehicles was a bus heading to New Mexico, whose passengers stepped out onto the shoulder to get a better look. One quick-thinking person grabbed her camera and snapped a couple of photographs.

Though the photographer reportedly saw nothing unusual about the light beam at the time, she later noticed a figure standing in the cloudy haze on her photograph. The figure appeared facing the camera, wearing robes and a beard. He was either the ghost of Alec Guinness reprising the role of Obi-wan Kenobi or, the more popular choice, Jesus.

Others believe the light and the subsequent picture to be mere coincidence, as more photos have surfaced revealing almost identical phenomena that took place on two other occasions. The first allegedly happened two years earlier at an unknown location outside Mexico City, Mexico. The second, which has caused even more of a stir, was photographed in March 2005 in McAllen, Texas. The woman responsible for the Texas photo has remained anonymous, but her photograph has apparently inspired a series of miracles at a nearby church.

Unfortunately, the name of the bus passenger who took the Arizona photos has remained a secret, so a proper inquiry will have to wait until the unexplained spotlight appears again.

A Haunted Hum

Shadows in the corners, a chill when you enter the attic, a dark figure ahead of you in the woods.

We are haunted by many things. Usually we give shape to these fears and call them ghosts or spirits, because it's easier to deal with something we can envision. But some unfortunate people are haunted by something they can neither see nor feel. They are haunted by sound.

Starting in the early 1990s, residents of the village of Taos in north-central New Mexico began reporting something odd. At quiet times, often in the dead of night (though it never seemed to go away entirely) these folks could discern in the air around them a strange, low-frequency rumbling sound. This was not the hubbub of white noise that might be explained by wind or the neighbor's television set, but a throbbing, low-grade drone. Those who heard it described it as the sound of a diesel truck idling softly in the distance—albeit a truck that never ran out of fuel. On the scale of annoying sounds, it ranked somewhere between "Scotsman playing bagpipes" and "cat coughing up hairball." The auditory antagonist was quickly dubbed the Taos Hum.

Not everyone heard the hum, but about two percent of Taoseños said they did, when surveyed by researchers from the University of New Mexico in 1994. According to the same study, the sound didn't discriminate between men and women, nor among age groups, with most hearers between ages thirty and fifty-nine. Sometimes scientists researching the hum claimed to hear it themselves, thus probably creating some weird sort of acoustical infinity loop.

Like junk mail, acne, and other things persistent and unwanted, the hum interfered in negative ways with the lives of those who heard it. It kept them up at night. It gave them headaches. Worst of all, it made them wonder if they might be—literally in this case—hearing things.

More theories arose than explanations. Perhaps the hum was the buzz coming from high-tension telephone wires. Perhaps it was caused by plate tectonics and shifts in the crust of the earth or was the result of hypersensitivity among some hearers to otherwise imperceptible electromagnetic fields. Maybe we were all becoming victims of our advancing technology—a karmic conjecture that would no doubt be in vogue at a neo-Luddite convention.

Of course, there was also the suggestion that the hum was part of some clandestine government mind-control project. And while that theory is unlikely, let's stay with it for a minute. If the government did have plans to control our minds for some nefarious purpose, say to create a race of zombie androids, then sending out a subversive subliminal audio message would be an effective way of reaching a mass audience. Advertisers have been doing just that with commercials for decades. Anyway, the government consistently claims to have no such plans and that, furthermore you can't prove anything.

If misery truly does love company, those who heard the hum might have found some relief in knowing that they were not alone in their suffering. For years, other "hums" have been reported throughout the United States and overseas, in England, Canada, Australia, and Wisconsin. In fact, the word "hum" has now come to describe a whole class of similar auditory occurrences worldwide, with the term "hearers" sometimes used to describe those affected by them.

In New Mexico, the case raised interest among scientists, researchers, and other people who make a living taking these things seriously. A team comprised of personnel from Los Alamos National Laboratory, Sandia National Laboratory, the Phillips Air Force Laboratory, and the University of New Mexico descended on Taos in May 1993, measuring, recording, and analyzing, using

a special microphone to try to capture the sound. A momentary burst of unusual underground noise caught by the microphone turned out to be just a gopher. Though the scientists were able to create a sound on their own technical equipment that hum hearers found similar to the original, the elusive source remained so. "As a result," wrote Drs. Joe Mullins and Jim Kelly of the research team, "we are left with a mystery. There are no acoustic signals that might account for the hum, nor are there any seismic events that might explain it."

Still seeking answers, the same research team began to think—or rather, listen—inside the box. Possibly, they reasoned, the sound was not external to the hearers, but rather internal, the result, perhaps, of vibrations within the ear. This opened the possibility that the hummees weren't haunted by sound at all; rather, they were haunted by themselves.

Normally, this would be the point in the story when the mystery would be revealed, the culprit named, and the readers proclaim that they knew it all along. Unfortunately, the mystery of the Taos Hum has no such decisive ending. Though the hum itself quickly rose from kooky phenomenon to pop culture icon, becoming a favorite among reporters looking for an offbeat story, it never quite reached the status of its brethren at the Area 51 or Bigfoot level. Reports of the hum have declined in recent years, but they haven't gone away entirely.

Thus the mystery, like a karaoke singer who has forgotten the lyrics to a song, continues to hum right along.—*David Pike*

Grave Matters

They call it Slab City. Cold storage. Necropolis, the City of the Dead. The final resting place. But no matter what they call it, a cemetery is a great destination for *Weird* spotters. You don't need a morbid fascination with death to appreciate the subtle beauty and fine art you can find in one of the garden cemeteries that sprouted up around American cities in the late 1800s. They're more like public sculpture parks than reminders of death. And they celebrate the lives of some of the nation's more colorful characters.

Don't look for plain old slabs in this chapter. If it doesn't have a giant marble fort around it, a puzzling epitaph on it, or eighteen statues of the occupant and family staring out over the rest of the graves, you won't find it here. And really . . . would you want it any other way?

IN LOVING
MEMORY
FROM THE FAMILY

BENJAMIN
SIEGEL
FEB 28, 1906
JUNE 20, 1947

Memorable Monuments

Anybody can have a tombstone. If you've got enough money socked away, you can even raise a Celtic cross or fancy statue above your final resting place. But for a truly weird graveside experience, you have to reach a little higher than that. And after you've looked over some of these examples, you'll realize just how high some people have set the bar.

Deathstyles of the Rich and Famous

If you can't catch a glimpse of a real-life movie star on your trip to Los Angeles, why not take a long look at the final resting place of dozens of them? That's what Hollywood Forever Cemetery is there for. It's been around since 1899, and it has amassed an unrivaled collection of celebrities from the movie industry.

Where else can you walk six feet over Douglas Fairbanks, Peter Lorre, and even mob boss Benjamin "Bugsy" Siegel? And wonder if Bugsy's epitaph, IN LOVING MEMORY FROM THE FAMILY, came from Mrs. Siegel and the kids or from *that* family. Where else could you find out whether the silver-screen sweethearts Darla Hood and Alfalfa from the old *Little Rascals* and *Our Gang* movies were laid to rest together? (They were, sort of. Darla is entombed in the Eternal Life mausoleum, while Carl "Alfalfa" Switzer is on the lawn a few hundred yards away.)

Fast-forwarding a few decades and cranking up the speed a couple of notches, Hollywood Forever also houses two members of the classic punk band the Ramones. Bassist Dee Dee Ramone and guitarist Johnny Ramone are buried under their real names (Douglas Clovin and John Cummings). Dee Dee has the Ramones' presidential seal logo on his grave, with a tongue-in-cheek epitaph: OK . . . I GOTTA GO NOW. Johnny had more time to plan his memorial, and it shows. A bronze statue of him rises from a granite block, clutching a low-slung guitar in the quintessential rock-god/axe-man pose. Directly in front of the serene duck pond, Johnny's grave assaults your sense of decorum, and no doubt Johnny meant it that way.

In an age when most large cemeteries are feeling a financial pinch and occasionally falling into disrepair, Hollywood Forever has a brilliant scheme for keeping the cash flowing. They screen

The Granite Grand

You probably wouldn't expect a graveyard in Smith County, Texas, to be a must-see vacation attraction. But if you're visiting family in Tyler, Rose Hill Cemetery is exactly where your relatives will take you, because nobody gets out of town without seeing the way-out gravestone of Madge Ward.

Now, unless you have a serious electrical short between your left and right hemispheres, it's easy to figure out what Madge Ward did for a living, because she was laid to rest in an eight-foot-tall, twenty-five-ton grand piano, the largest single-person monument on the grounds. The granite monument took more than a year to design and build, and according to the piano's designer, Ward said she had been saving for it for thirty-five years. Sadly, she never got the chance to see it for real. The monument wasn't set in place until after her death. But it's just as well, since she didn't have to hear the catcalls from some Tyler residents. Apparently, the granite grand monument struck a sour note with some. Our reaction, on the other hand, is to call for an encore.

movies on the wall of the mausoleum. Some of them are spooky to fit the setting, some of them star people who are buried nearby. Up to 3,000 viewers pay their ten bucks, haul their blankets and folding chairs, and enjoy slide shows and spinning DJs and picnics there among the graves. A few families feel it may be disrespectful, but the revenue helps keep the place pristine for everyone.

For a last word, we'll leave it to Mel Blanc, the man who gave voice to Bugs Bunny, Daffy Duck, and Barney Rubble. He read the epitaph that is now set in stone at Hollywood Forever at the end of thousands of cartoons in the excited voice of Porky Pig: THAT'S ALL FOLKS.

World's Smallest Tombstone

Missouri is home to a unique attraction vouched for by *Ripley's Believe It or Not!* — the world's smallest tombstone. This tiny memorial in Oak Hill Cemetery in the city of Butler, Bates County, is about the size of a stack of index cards. Conveniently, the cemetery has been kind enough to place an obvious sign pointing the way to the diminutive marker.

A Hell-bent Clothespin

This handsome granite clothespin grave marker, made for the owner of the clothespin factory in Montpelier, Vermont, can be found at the back right of the Middlesex, Vermont, cemetery. *—Eurovancation*

Frozen Faces of Mt. Nebo Cemetery

An isolated dirt lane in the woods of Clarke County, Alabama, leads to a tiny, picturesque white church. Nearby is the burial site of late members of the church, some of whom stare blankly back at visitors through concrete eyes molded into grave markers. Four graves in Mt. Nebo Cemetery are marked with death mask headstones crafted by Isaac Nettles, Sr., an inventor born in the 1880s. The exact dates of his birth and death are unknown, because in an odd twist, he is buried in an unmarked grave.

No one is sure why or how Nettles created the stones, though local lore says he made his impressions by pressing the subject's face into wet sand and used concrete and wire to create the masks. Sadly, only two of the four markers are intact, and even those are eroding. One marker has three faces on it and is marked MOTHER. There is a legend that the woman died while giving birth to twins, but Kerry Reid of the Clarke County museum said the marker bears the faces of Nettles's three daughters—Pauline, Marie, and Clara—and that the stone marks the burial site of his wife, Korea Nettles.

Nearby, an oversized bust missing its head marks the grave of Nettles's mother, Selena. Concrete troughs flanking the bust's head were inlaid with locks of the woman's hair to add realism; but by the 1980s, the hair was no longer visible. The head itself went missing after that, but no one knows what happened to it.

A few graves away, Angel Ezella Nettles's stone bears a woman's likeness and the words SIS. DOLLIE beneath, and still another reads MANUL BURELL. DIED 1946. HE IS AT REST. The National Park Service designated the stones as historic sites based on their artistic and ethnic significance that "represent a unique burial tradition" in the community. They are the most enduring testament to Isaac's creativity— although he was widely known locally as an inventor, none of his inventions survived. Local lore has it that he invented a perpetual motion machine that drew the interest of the Ford Motor Company, but who knows what became of that?— *Kelly Kazek*

Crystal Shrine Grotto

By now, it should be obvious that there's more to cemeteries than headstones and angel statues. But even we were surprised by what was in store at Memphis, Tennessee's Memorial Park Cemetery. It's fairly new as graveyards go—it was opened in 1924—and it's the final resting place of the man who discovered Elvis: Sun Records's producer Sam Phillips. But that's not even half the attraction this place holds.

It's the only cemetery we know of with a man-made oak tree bearing a plaque that declares it's made "entirely of concrete, reinforced with steel and copper bar so as to insure its existence for many centuries to come." This remarkable bit of sculpture accurately portrays broken-off branches, realistic bark with evidence of insects boring into it, and a massive hole in one side that's thankfully not occupied by any giant mutant squirrels. It's called *Abraham's Oak,* and it's the work of a Mexican folk sculptor named Dionicio Rodriguez, who worked in the cemetery for three years in the 1930s. He used concrete that he sculpted with twigs and cutlery, and stained with chemicals like sulfuric acid, muriatic acid, and lampblack. But it's not the only thing Rodriquez built during his stay there. Nestled beyond the fake tree, next to a pond surrounded by real trees, is a Rodriquez-made cave that glimmers with crystal-encrusted concrete and houses the work of a dozen different sculptors, all of whom use the life of Jesus as their theme. It's called the Crystal Shrine Grotto, and the minute you walk into it, you feel different. It's not just that the place maintains a steady cool temperature even in the sweltering Memphis summers. It feels peaceful. Even if you don't share the belief, as stated on the plaque near the entrance, that Jesus had "The Most Beautiful Head in History," you can appreciate the odd look of the semiprecious stones inlaid in concrete, and compare and contrast the styles of sculpture that fill the space. Rodriguez wasn't responsible for the statues—the most recent of which is less than thirty years old—but it's hard to separate the art on display from this cool underground gallery that displays them. And it's hard to imagine why it was ever built in a cemetery in Tennessee.

One thing's for sure: It's a one-of-a-kind place that's never going to be reproduced anywhere else. Rodriguez is long dead, and although he trained people to help with his commissions, he never shared all his secrets and left behind no preparatory sketches. So if you want to catch a peaceful respite in a jewel-encrusted cemetery grotto, you'll have to get on over to 5668 Poplar Avenue in Memphis and catch the one and only original.

A Bear Grows in Brooklyn

Brooklyn's *Green-Wood Cemetery* attracts its fair share of visitors. It's as large as nearby Prospect Park and stands as a quiet landscaped oasis in the middle of the hustle and bustle of the busy borough. This, coupled with its many fascinating monuments and the dozens of New York celebrities-gone-by buried here, has turned Green-Wood into a quasi-tourist attraction.

While there are guidebooks that point to the Soldier's Memorial, the graves of the famous, and to notable tombstones, there is one grave in Green-Wood that flies under the radar but stands out for its odd nature. The Beard grave is in the middle of a field of nondescript stones, but it certainly makes its mark—perched upon the stone is a large, life-size bronze statue of a bear. There is no explanation on-site for the strange memorial, but research reveals that it's completely appropriate for the man it memorializes.

William Holbrook Beard was a nineteenth-century artist who achieved fame in his lifetime largely for his paintings depicting animals behaving as humans. From the very beginning of his artistic career, bears were one of his main subjects. His painting entitled *The Bulls and Bears in the Market* is the impetus behind the stock market lingo denoting when the market is going well or going poorly. Needless to say, the artist's professional and artistic life was tied intrinsically to bears.

When Beard passed away in 1900, he was buried without fanfare or memorial. The reasons behind this are unknown. His family was in New York and with him at the time of his death, and they did purchase him a plot in the prestigious Green-Wood Cemetery. Yet his grave was underwhelming and no memorial was erected to honor him.

In 2002, when it was discovered that Mr. Beard was an artist of importance, a fund was started in an effort to memorialize him in a more proper fashion. Eventually, Colorado artist Dan Ostermiller agreed to donate the bear sculpture that now stands out among the fields of Green-Wood.

Mix Up

Tom Mix was the first real cowboy hero of the big screen. He starred in literally hundreds of films between 1920 and 1935 and has been credited with redefining the western movie genre with his hard-riding, action-packed performances. In his signature ten-gallon hat, Mix paved the way for men like Tex Ritter, Roy Rogers, and John Wayne.

Yet these days, Mix appears to be more famous for his death. His monument along Highway 79 between Phoenix and Tucson marks the place where, on October 12, 1940, his ride into the sunset ended. Mix was headed to Phoenix on his way west from New Mexico after a night in Tucson. According to reports, he had been up pretty late the previous night drinking in his room with a group of musicians, and left the hotel around noon in his convertible. On the way, Mix stopped at a bar in Oracle Junction for a quick chat with a friend, which turned into rounds of whiskey and a few hands of poker.

As he roared up Highway 79 in his yellow roadster, Mix completely missed detour signs. A flash flood had washed out part of the road, and a crew was working on repairing the damage. According to the men on the scene, Mix never even slowed down. His car flew through the barriers, flipped, and came to rest on its side. Some say Mix was killed in the impact, but at least one witness reported seeing him free himself and begin to stand. At that moment, one of his metal suitcases fell on him and broke his neck. Legend says it was full of silver dollars.

Today, he'd probably just get one of those little roadside crosses with some plastic flowers; but in 1947, fans dedicated a full-fledged monument in Mix's honor. Just north of the ditch that took his life, now known as Tom Mix Wash, the Pinal County Historical Society erected a seven-foot-tall stone obelisk memorializing the onetime king of cowboys. It bears a photo of the actor and two copies of an article about Mix's life and death, maintained to this day by an unknown caretaker. Its apex features a profile of Mix's trusty steed, Tony the Wonder Horse, his saddle empty and his head bowed in grief, marked by a cluster of bullet holes.

There's a whole branch of writing dedicated to epitaphs. Oh, you certainly have to put names and dates on a grave marker, and it doesn't hurt to add a verse from the Bible or other favorite quote. Great wits like Dorothy Parker made a point of crafting humorous epitaphs (our favorite, her own: Excuse my dust). And then there are grave inscriptions like this one—that just leave you scratching your head and saying, "What?!"

HERE LIES OLD JACK CROW IT WAS TOO BAD HE HAD TO GO

WHIL ON THIS EARTH HE WAS HELL-BENT

AND HE KNEW SOME DAY HE WOULD UP AND WENT

Murdered by Human Wolves

The grave of Katherine Cross in the Konawa-Violet cemetery in Konawa, Oklahoma, bears the inscription MURDERED BY HUMAN WOLVES. Not many locals know the story, but she died at the age of eighteen on October 10, 1917, at the hands of a Dr. A. H. Yates and Frederick O'Neal, a local schoolteacher, in what was called by the *Seminole County News*, a "criminal operation."

It is said that when it is quiet, if you stand at her grave long enough, you will hear the growling of wolves. There is also a rumor that several more headstones around the Konawa area bear the same legend. Elise Stone and other girls died at the same hands.

I am sure that this legend stems purely from the headstone's line. I felt I had found a place of peace and rest.—*Colby Weaver*

Anybody Know Sheila Shea?

Concord, Massachusetts, is known for being a very proper upper-class town; but in the famous Sleepy Hollow Cemetery, there is one headstone that blatantly thumbs its nose at propriety. It belongs to Sheila Shea.

When I was in high school, I became friends with Sheila's daughter, Cindi. Her mom was a rarity to a middle school kid: She was cool. She'd get us pizza on Fridays and we'd sit in her kitchen playing cards, backgammon, or other games.

As we got older, Cindi and I drifted in different directions. Years later I heard her mom had died. She had purchased a plot in Sleepy Hollow Cemetery, the final resting place of Emerson, the Alcotts, and Thoreau. Being her true irreverent self, she chose the perfect epitaph to let all who see it know she was a woman of great humor. Much to the town's dismay, it simply says, WHO THE HELL IS SHEILA SHEA.
    —*Dawn Delsie-Pence*

Aurora's Alien Crash Site

Few cemeteries can claim that they are the final resting place of extraterrestrials. In fact, we know of only one: the Aurora Cemetery, just north of Fort Worth, Texas.

In an April 19, 1897, story published by the *Dallas Times Herald,* E. E. Hayden reported that a strange airship had flown over town early that morning and crashed on the property of Judge J. S. Proctor. The unidentified craft "went to pieces with a terrific explosion," destroying Proctor's windmill and, tragically, his flower garden.

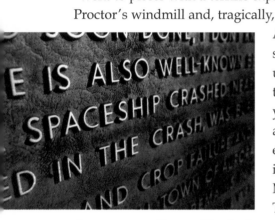

At that time, airship sightings were not uncommon. Starting the fall of the previous year, stories of a strange aircraft had spread eastward from California into Kansas, Nebraska, Missouri, and eventually, Texas. It crashed in Aurora, according to Hayden's article, and a small humanoid body was recovered from the wreckage. The being was reportedly disfigured by the accident, but was clearly "not an inhabitant of this world."

Those who arrived on the scene subsequently buried the creature in the Aurora Cemetery. A small grave marker was erected, carved with an image resembling the visitor's spacecraft. Unfortunately, when the story resurfaced in the 1970s, vandals made off with the gravestone.

These days, the legend has been brushed aside. Most locals refute it as a hoax. They'll tell you Judge Proctor never even had a windmill and that it's very likely he cooked the whole thing up with E .E. Hayden. If it weren't for the historical marker outside the cemetery, which briefly mentions the story, Aurora wouldn't offer any evidence of the event at all.

The Wright Stuff

Phineas Wright was an eccentric who lived in the late 1800s. Lived as a pauper, died rich, and was a notorious atheist. Before he died, he erected this monument to himself. Note the motto GOING, BUT KNOW NOT WHERE.—*Cheryl LeBeau*

Victim of the Beast 666

The grave of Lilly E. Gray stands in the Salt Lake City Cemetery in Utah. It's a simple, plain flat stone that lists birth date and death date (June 6, 1881, and November 14, 1958). It's what's written next to these figures that makes this stone legendary: VICTIM OF THE BEAST 666.

That's all that is carved on Lilly E. Gray's grave, except for a few flowers (primroses, to be exact, which are often referred to as the devil's lantern). According to hospital records, Lilly died of natural causes. Her short obituary listed nothing extraordinary. In other words, there are no records or hints to explain this mysterious message.

Heightening the mystery is the fact that Lilly's husband, Elmer Gray, is buried in the same cemetery but far away from Lilly, in a different section. This has led to much speculation that he was the beast in question in Lilly's life. Was he responsible for her death? Did one of Lilly's friends or relatives intend the inscription to condemn Elmer? Or was this, as some people seem to think, a reference to occultist Aleister Crowley, who liked to call himself the Beast 666? If so, how was he connected to Lilly?

Nobody knows the answers. Only the bare facts remain. Lilly moved to the area in 1950, only eight years before her death, and her grave has grown into a local Salt Lake City legend. And this strange epitaph deserves its prominent place in Utah folklore.

Time Expired in Oklahoma

Here's a unique grave marker that became the subject of literally millions of forwarded e-mails during the summer of 2007. The memorial can now be found on dozens of Web sites, all bearing the original e-mail message text telling the story of the stone:

"This lady had a great sense of humor and always used it to say that when she died she wanted a parking meter on her grave that says "Expired." So her nephew got her one on eBay! She said that her grave is right by the road so everyone can see it and many people have stopped to get a chuckle."

Unfortunately, nobody seems to be able to track down the original source of the e-mail message. All we know for sure is that the grave of Barbara Sue Manire can be found in Highland Cemetery in Okemah, Oklahoma, and that her time has indeed expired.

Home Sweet Stone

Some people call cemeteries the Cities of the Dead. We think that's a good description, especially when you look at some of these grave markers. Because when individual grave markers look like houses or other buildings, you can be sure that taken all together, they will begin to take shape as a city.

Ticonderoga Tombstone

There's only one veteran of the Revolutionary War buried in Minnesota: Stephen Taylor of the First Massachusetts Regiment of the Continental Army. His proud boast was that he was one of the heroes of Ticonderoga who fought alongside Ethan Allen in 1775. Historians doubt that he actually was, but that's what his gravestone says—in no uncertain terms. His grave in the Woodlawn Cemetery in Winona is surrounded by a replica of the fort.

Three Women of the House

Springfield Cemetery on Maple Street in Springfield, Massachusetts, is the final home to several notables, but by far the most notable stone belongs to the Titus family. On the Cedar Street side of the cemetery is a six-foot-tall, two-story house carved from solid white marble. At the base are four East Longmeadow brownstone steps leading up to the carved front door. The epitaph reads IN MANSIONS ABOVE, but the stone itself is a monument to Mr. Titus's three wives: Louise (1834–1921), Mary (1821–1889), and Pamelia (1823–1891).

Elephant Man and the Log Cabin of Elmwood

One of the more curious tombstones in Charlotte, North Carolina's old Elmwood Cemetery is that of John King, a performer and elephant trainer in the great Robinson Circus. King died when his elephant Chief attacked him on September 22, 1880. The *Charlotte Observer* reported that in a rage, the animal turned on King and crushed him, whereupon "King sank to the ground without a groan and the men who were with him fled precipitately. The crowd scattered up Trade Street." Naturally, King's colleagues erected a marker over his grave featuring the animal responsible for his death. The show must go on.

Elmwood includes a number of other peculiar monuments, among them a granite log cabin dedicated to Henry Severs. The cabin is so detailed in so many respects—down to the checks and growth rings in the logs and the proper orientation of flat nails in the faux board sign (across the grain)—that it seems quibbling to point out that the roof should have been made of split shakes or shingles, and that the chimney should have stood outside the "logs" at the end. It suggests that whoever designed it had only dreamed of the simple cabin life without having actually lived it. Better late than never, though.

In a Family Way

When private cemeteries took over from churchyards as the main place to bury people, the idea of a family plot took over. People bought whole neighborhoods of cemetery land and sometimes erected huge monuments to celebrate the whole family. And of course, some of those monuments were a little out of the ordinary....

Davis Memorial

They say love is fleeting, but one resident of Hiawatha, Kansas, set out to prove them wrong. When Sarah Davis died in 1930, her loving husband, John Milburn Davis, began erecting a memorial unlike any other. The Italian marble memorial in Mount Hope Cemetery contains statues depicting Sarah, John, and a few others, and was estimated to cost more than $200,000—and that was at the height of the Great Depression. Many regarded the widowed man as foolish and selfish for spending so much money on a grave during such economically desperate times. But Davis was also a secret benefactor to residents of Hiawatha who had fallen on hard times, though his private donations garnered less attention than his wife's grave. The Davis Memorial still stands today. Hundreds of people travel to Hiawatha to visit it each year.

Woolridges of Mayfield

The Maplewood Cemetery in Mayfield, is home to what is probably the most overstated grave marker in Kentucky—perhaps all the states. It celebrates Henry G. Woolridge—over and over again. Woolridge seemed to be a little obsessive when it came time to pick out a grave marker for his burial plot. First he erected a tall and majestic monument with ornate touches such as a rifle, a horse, and a Masonic emblem. Then, at great expense, he had a statue of himself carved from marble by Italian sculptors. But it still wasn't enough. He added another statue. And another. And another. By the time of his funeral, there were no less than eighteen markers crowded together at his grave site.

Two of the statues depict Woolridge— one at a lectern and one astride a horse—

and others portray various family members such as his mother, sisters, brothers, and nieces. Also in the parade are a fox, a deer, and two dogs. His father is conspicuously absent.

In another section of Maplewood, you'll find the grave of Henry Bascom Hicks, an accused spy who was executed by a firing squad in August 1864. (Legend has it that he refused the traditional blindfold, stating, "I can look you in the eye.") And another grave holds eleven people from the Drew and Lawrence families, who all died in a mysterious house fire in 1921 that some say was deliberately set to destroy the evidence that they had already been killed. The charred remains fit into one coffin and are buried in a single plot, with one stone.

MINERVA NICHOLS
BORN 1820

Suffer the Little Children

There is nothing more poignant than a memorial to a lost child. In the days before antibiotics and advanced medicine, mourning the death of a child was much more common than it is today. And so, even though some of them have us scratching our heads, we respectfully turn our gaze to the sad memorials for minors who were cut off before they even reached their prime.

Little Pillow in Lizzie's Dollhouse

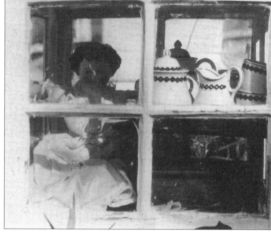

When Lizzie Eckel died at age twelve in 1882, her father, Emmanuel, placed a dollhouse next to her tombstone in the cemetery of the Trinity United Church in Warren, New Jersey. The miniature dwelling had a red gabled roof and chimney and was constructed of panes of wood and glass, through which one could see a child's tea set, a small table, a doll in Victorian dress with a porcelain head, and a children's book entitled *Little Pillow.* The grave was quite a well-known local site in its day, even earning mention in *Ripley's Believe It or Not!*

There is a small obelisk-shaped stone marking Lizzie's grave that bears the inscription: SHE WAS LOVING, SHE WAS FAIR, AND FOR A WHILE SHE WAS GIVEN; THEN AN ANGEL CAME AND CLAIMED HER OWN AND BORE HER HOME TO HEAVEN.

For nearly a century, the dollhouse was lovingly maintained by the church and its congregation, though it was occasionally vandalized. Then in 1973, someone stole the dollhouse and its contents from the cemetery. A few days later, pieces of the dishes it contained were discovered discarded in a field in nearby Martinsville. The church gathered up the broken pieces they could find and decided it would be best to move them indoors. We are told that they remain to this day in the church's attic.

Crenshaw Kids of Magnolia Cemetery

One of the saddest-looking bunches of kids you'll ever see is the Crenshaw children, whose collective grave is marked by a group of life-size marble statues in the middle of Magnolia Cemetery, at North 19th and Main Streets in Baton Rouge, Louisiana. However sad they might have been, their parents were surely even more distraught. In one year, 1858, they lost four children, probably to one of the epidemics that used to sweep the state. Three days after William and Mary Crenshaw's oldest daughter, Fannie Bell, died, their son (and father's namesake) Willie H. died before he would have turned seven. Then four months later, one-year-old Mattie Pike Crenshaw passed away. The tomb also holds the remains of a baby whose life was even shorter, memorialized only as the Nameless One.

Little Nadine's Playhouse

The birthday party didn't have the customary air of celebration. Although cake and ice cream were served, the guests may have felt uncomfortable running and playing—the guest of honor had died four months earlier and guests were celebrating atop her grave.

Little Nadine Earles died of diphtheria a week before Christmas 1933. She was only four years old.

Her father had begun building her a playhouse as a Christmas gift when she fell ill in November. As Christmas approached, Nadine grew weaker. To raise her spirits, her parents gave her early Christmas gifts: a life-size doll and a china tea set. But Little Nadine wanted her playhouse. When her father promised to continue work when she got well, the child said, "Me want it now."

After her death, Nadine's father completed the brick playhouse and installed it atop her grave in Oakwood Cemetery in Lanett, Alabama. Complete with awnings on its windows, a chimney, and a small front porch, the house was the site of Little Nadine's postmortem birthday party in 1934. Inside, a photo of that celebration sits on the mantel, alongside the doll and the china tea set her parents gave her that long-ago December.

Her marker is inscribed with these words:

OUR DARLING LITTLE GIRL

SWEETEST IN THE WORLD

LITTLE NADINE EARLES

"ME WANT IT NOW"

The Earles continued to fill the house with toys and gifts—sometimes placed beneath a decorated Christmas tree—until their deaths. They are buried on the same site as their daughter.—*Kelly Kazek*

Dollhouses of the Dead

It's not uncommon to find graves adorned with toys, stuffed animals, and dolls. But if some of those dolls find their current living conditions getting a bit cramped, they might consider a move to Indiana, where they will have their choice of not one but two cemetery dollhouses to choose from.

The first dollhouse lies within the gates of City Cemetery in Connorsville, Indiana. In 1900, a year after the death of their five-year-old daughter, Vivian, Horace and Carrie Allison placed the fully furnished house over her grave. They lovingly looked after the house until Horace died in 1946, after which Carrie continued to care for it until her death in 1969. A series of caretakers followed, beginning with Vivian's sister, Lovell Allison Beeson, a gentleman named John Powell who lived near City Cemetery, and two local men, retired carpenter Louis Brockman and Connorsville police officer Darrell Maines. Maines and Brockman gave the dollhouse a complete renovation inside and out. They added new furniture to the inside, including a miniature photograph of the *Mona Lisa.* New windows were also added and old, worn wood replaced. They even poured a new concrete foundation, bolted the dollhouse down, and landscaped around the grave.

The second dollhouse is located only a short drive away, at East Hill Cemetery in Arlington. This dollhouse marks the grave of Lova Cline, daughter of George and Mary Cline. Lova was born an invalid in 1902, and the dollhouse was one of her few pleasures. But sadly, she did not enjoy it for long, as she passed away in 1908. Grieving for his daughter, George moved the dollhouse to Lova's grave, where it has remained to this day. He did contemplate destroying the house in 1945 when his wife died, but he changed his mind and later appointed family friend Lova Ward-Wooten the official caretaker of the dollhouse. Several times in the 1970s,

the house was robbed of its valuable furnishings, so Ward-Wooten and her daughter, Sheila Wooten-Hewitt, painstakingly created furnishings for the house that were made entirely out of "worthless" cardboard, touched up with paint and fabric. Ward-Wooten passed away in 1999, but her daughter continues to care for the dollhouse to this day. In 2002, she even erected a laminated paper sign in front of the dollhouse, chronicling its long history. In a macabre final touch, at the bottom of the sign is a faded, almost unrecognizable copy of a monochrome photo showing the young Lova lying in her coffin.

The Little Boy Who Was Afraid of the Dark

Little Merritt Beardsley died of a high fever in Oxford, New York, on December 15, 1865, at the tender age of eight. As he grew steadily weaker, the boy told his father how scared he was, and as William Beardsley held his son's hand, Little Merritt made a final request: "Daddy, can I have a window in my grave so I won't be afraid of the dark?" His father said, "Yes, son," and with that reassuring statement, Little Merritt passed away.

His father was as good as his word: A tomb with a window rests in a long forgotten cemetery near the old Beardsley home in Oxford, hidden behind a fieldstone wall on Joe Hoben Road. It is overgrown with weeds, poison ivy, and tall pine trees.

Little Merritt's father joined his son about twenty-three years later in the small family plot, next to his wife, Sarah, but there is no death date chiseled onto Sarah's gravestone—another mystery long forgotten. Today, although the grave is not often visited, occasionally people leave toys and mementos for the little boy who was afraid of the dark.—*Al Legar*

The Telltale Stone

Young Michael Brown was exactly one month away from turning sixteen when a car struck him down while he was walking his dog. On the back of his headstone in the town cemetery of Springfield, Livingston Parish, Louisiana, is a strange, childlike sketch providing an overview of the scene, sandblasted into the hard granite to leave a perpetual reminder of the day. According to the story we were told, a number of people (named on the stone, along with the accused driver) drove by the dying boy without stopping to help. Below the crude map are the words, "By Dogs Mind," but their exact meaning—or the intended purpose of the whole drawing—is hard to decipher.

A Grave ID

There's this story about a little boy out in Springfield who was knocked off his bike, and ran over by a truck. There were only a few witnesses, but nobody recognized the truck or could give a description of the two men in it.

The morning after the funeral, the parents returned to the grave site. To their astonishment, on the back of the tombstone they found a perfectly engraved scene of what happened at the accident, with stick figures and houses in little squares and triangles, as if drawn by a child. Each stick figure had a name underneath it: the little boy, the three witnesses, and the two men in the truck. The mother recognized the handwriting under each stick figure was that of her dead son.

The engraving is still there to this day. I have personally been to this graveyard before and have seen the tombstone. You get the weird feeling that a little kid is looking up at you or standing right there with you.—*Blake Taylor*

MICHAEL B. BROWN
SEPT. 20, 1967
AUG. 20, 1983

Tombs with Tales to Tell

In olden days, people on the search for a good graveyard story would consult the sexton—the church employee charged with taking care of graves and burials. Nowadays, the graves themselves tell their tales. And what tales they are!

Mary Bibb and the Swinging Kids

In my hometown of Huntsville, Alabama, there is an old cemetery surrounded by a brick wall. It is so old that soldiers from the Civil and Revolutionary Wars are buried there. There is also a woman named Mary Bibb who is in a family vault. It is said if you knock three times on the "O," in, "October," and ask, "Mary Bibb, Mary Bibb, what happened?" you are supposed to hear her moan, "Nothing." It is also said that on some nights, you can hear her rocking in a rocking chair.

Behind the cemetery, there is a park called Dead Children's Playground. It is said that late at night, around 11:00 p.m., you can see swings moving by themselves without wind, and you can hear disembodied laughter.–*Dustin Aurand*

Lightning Striking Again (and Again and Again)

William Cosper of Childersburg, Alabama, disproved the theory that lightning doesn't strike the same place twice. He fell victim to lightning twice in life—and his luck didn't change after his death. The first strike William suffered set fire to the pile of wool he was spinning, but it didn't actually harm anyone. About a month later, William was standing on his front porch watching a rainstorm when a second bolt of lightning struck and killed him.

His family buried him in Childersburg City Cemetery, but soon after, his tombstone was reduced to a pile of rubble by another lightning bolt. His family placed a new monument in its place. Yet again, lightning struck, leaving only pieces of the marble monument.

Unable to purchase yet another expensive monument, William's family placed a stack of bricks to mark his final resting place.–*Kelly Kazek*

One for the Road

William T. Mullen was on the road to ruin, and despite his wife's pleas, he wouldn't give up his long affair with the bottle. In the end, it seemed, whiskey did not love him back. William died before his thirtieth year, on July 18, 1863. His widow chose a plot in the small cemetery beside Clayton Baptist Church in southern Alabama and erected a monument to the thing her husband loved most: the bottle. The granite marker shaped like a whiskey bottle is engraved: IN MEMORY: W. T. MULLEN, SON OF J. AND N. MULLEN.

The Statue That Jack Built

As you enter the Oakland Cemetery in Atlanta, Georgia, you get the impression you're being watched very closely. That impression is helped along by the massive statue of local real estate magnate Jasper Newton Smith that stares down from its enormous pedestal just inside the gates.

Jack, as he was known, acquired a fortune managing plantations and estates in Walton County (some say he embezzled it), and plowed his wealth into two of the largest buildings in Atlanta's postwar boom. He was so famous for financing downtown building after the Civil War that many people think he's the origin of the folk verse about the house that Jack built. He was a bit of an eccentric too. He insisted that the cornerstone of one building should remain, even if the rest of the building was demolished. You can still see it at the entrance of the Peachtree Center MARTA station on Carnegie Way.

And if you look at Jack's statue, you can see he's wearing an open-necked shirt. He apparently had a morbid fear of strangulation by necktie, and refused to pay for the statue until the sculptor chiseled off a natty cravat he'd included.

Soda Fountain King—Green-Wood Cemetery

It would be fair to say that John Matthews, like many of his contemporaries, was obsessed with soda. The bubbly carbonated water that we take for granted today was one of the most highly sought-after developments of the nineteenth century. While bubbling water does naturally occur, it has not always been easy to manufacture. Its popularity in earlier times for both recreational and medicinal purposes made it clear that whoever could master the process of carbonation was going to make a lot of money.

Matthews moved from England to America to follow his dreams of creating soda water. Before Matthews, a few people had filed patents related to the process. Matthews, though, became rich and famous for creating the first soda fountain. His device made it easy to create the proper gas at the proper pressure. People could utilize his fountain to carbonate water and infuse it with flavored syrups. Soon they began popping up all over America, as soda caught on as a craze in Middle America. Matthews continued developing his product, and by the time of his death in 1870, he was known the world over as the Soda Fountain King.

His Brooklyn, New York, memorial is both ornate and indicative of his life's obsession. His tomb is impressive even if you don't know the man or his history—marble and sandstone combine into four columns, with two levels. A statue of Matthews lies on its back, almost as if the grave was built to resemble a four-poster bed that he lies in for eternity. Gargoyles and engravings stare out from the corners of the structure, and the statue of a grieving woman is housed within its canopy.

Those who are aware of Matthews's history, though, know that when visiting his grave it's important to look at things from his perspective—literally. Lying next to the statue of Matthews, one can see that etched into the ceiling above him are a number of scenes. These scenes show off events from Matthews's life in the world of soda, as well as some depictions of his family life. The Soda Fountain King erected his own grave in a way that would allow him to stare, for eternity, at representations of his work and accomplishments within the effervescent world of sparkling water.

Many of us have lifelong obsessions. Not many of us go the extra mile and build our graves around experiencing those obsessions from beyond the grave. John Matthews certainly did, and in doing so reaffirmed why he was and always will be the Soda Fountain King.

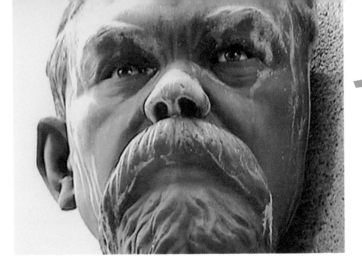

A Glassy-Eyed Gaze

The largest nonprofit private cemetery in the United States, Spring Grove Cemetery, contains a wonderful cross-section of statuary (including a sphinx), several ponds, and even waterfalls. It is also home to one of Ohio's strangest legends—the statue with human eyes. As the story goes, a man wrote in his will that his eyes should be removed and placed into the sockets of the bust on his tombstone. No one is sure why— perhaps he wanted to keep watch over his grave, but local legend also states that those human eyes actually follow you as you walk around the cemetery. No matter where you stand, if you can see the bust, it will appear to be watching you. In certain situations, the statue will even turn its entire head to keep watch. And if you're really lucky, some people say the bust will even speak to you.

So are the stories true? Well . . . sort of. The grave of a man named C. C. Bruer does feature a bust with lifelike eyes, but on closer inspection it's quite easy to tell that they are glass.

But do the bust's eyes seem to follow you wherever you go? They certainly appear to. So if you try to sneak into Spring Grove Cemetery late one night, don't be surprised if you get the feeling that someone is watching your every move. And it might not be cemetery security chasing off trespassers.

The Crypt Keeper Knocks Back!

This is one creepy phenomenon I know to be true, because I heard it. In a cemetery located on Route 8 in New York State between Unadilla and Bridgewater is a crypt belonging to Eunice Welsh. If you knock on the door, you will hear a rustling sound from inside, and you will have your knock returned! I have done it and I have heard it! I have tried this phenomenon twice, once alone and again six months later with a girlfriend, who swears she heard a voice hiss, "Leave me, leave me, go!" I didn't hear that, but I did hear the two knocks returned. Eunice is buried in the last row of graves on the hill behind the crypt, a holding crypt for the deceased during the winter when the ground was too frozen to dig. The cemetery has no name, but is visible on the left-hand side going north on Route 8 on a slow curve of road followed by a large cornfield.—*Red*

Unique Interments

Not every burial takes place in a graveyard. Instead of celebrating the life that's passed or mourning the loss of the surviving family, the usual reasons for burying the dead, some dead bodies are placed in car trunks in fields and even stuck in freezers for the advancement of science. Welcome to the world of unusual interment—and what a weird place it is.

Grisly Crop of the Body Farm

The University of Tennessee is home to a certain field that looks like the stamping grounds of a serial killer. Surrounded by a wooden fence and razor wire, these few acres contain more than forty bodies. Some are stuffed into the trunks of cars, some buried in shallow graves, some simply left to rot directly in the sun.

This is the Body Farm, and it is not the result of murder, but of science. Officially known as the University of Tennessee Forensic Anthropology Facility, the Body Farm is used to study the process of decomposition. By taking into account the effects of the elements and insects on the process, scientists have been able to determine times of death more accurately—and help solve murder cases.

The Body Farm is the brainchild of Dr. William Bass, who started it in 1971 with just one body. Before becoming a professor here, Bass had worked in the field of forensic science in Kansas, which led to his quest to study decomposition. Nowadays, Bass leads a team of scientists and students in studying dozens of bodies at a time.

In 1993, scientists at the farm offered up information that helped lead to the conviction of a Mississippi resident who murdered an entire family. And each year, the Federal Bureau of Investigation sends agents to the farm to explore simulated crime scenes that the Body Farm has constructed using actual human bodies.

For more than thirty years, fresh batches of bodies have made their way to the Body Farm, donated either by the deceased themselves or by medical examiners when the bodies were unclaimed. Each year, a memorial service is held honoring those who have given their bodies to the cause.

Alcor's Frozen Fraternity

Tucked away in an office park next to Scottsdale Airport in Arizona, Alcor looks like your average nonspecific tech company, with its windowless facade and manicured shrubbery. Inside, it's a different story. In the back, you'll find a concrete vault containing, at last count, about seventy human icicles. That's right, frozen folks. Mostly heads.

You could call it a tomb, but Alcor doesn't see their iced-down residents as dead. They're just at the end of their "first life cycle." Alcor is in the longevity business: The company's full name is the Alcor Life Extension Foundation. (See page 61, "Ted Williams—A Hero on Ice.")

This frosty fraternity refers to its customers as "members" and requires a months-long legal procedure to join. Essentially, it's just one long drawn-out scientific experiment to show that dead isn't necessarily dead. In the case of a terminally ill patient, a standby team waits until the patient is pronounced legally dead, then jumps in to administer cardiopulmonary support. The goal is not to resuscitate the patient, only to keep the tissue alive until the body can be prepared for freezing. The formation of ice would completely destroy a body's cells. So first, members' fluids are replaced with ice-inhibiting compounds, then submerged in liquid nitrogen and kept at a constant temperature of -196° until the day when medical criteria no longer define them as legally dead, at which point they can be resuscitated and cured.

We're not saying the whole thing isn't still way up there on the freaky meter (one fellow legally changed his name to FM-2030 before entering stasis), but once you understand what it is they're doing, it isn't quite as lunatic as it sounds. Still, the fact that most members have selected the noggin-only option over the full-body package keeps this place filed on the trippy shelf. True, head-only storage may be significantly cheaper, but you'd think

growing a new torso from scratch or purchasing a robot chassis would offset those savings in the future.

The really great thing about Alcor, though, is that they give tours. Anyone interested in cryonic preservation, or who just suffers from insatiable curiosity, can go to their Web site at www.alcor.org and request a walk-through. Just don't expect a lot of sci-fi light panels and bio-monitor displays. It's closer to garage medicine than anything, with members stored in what are essentially ten-foot-tall custom-built thermos flasks.

Of course, it all comes down to one question in the end: Is it possible to thaw people out and revive them? Well, nobody knows. Members are just placing a sort of Pascal's wager (that it's better to believe than not). If you're frozen and they can't revive you, *c'est la vie*. But if you're not frozen and they can, it's tough because you're already dead.

Coon Dog Memorial Graveyard

L. O. Bishop likes to tell of the time during a funeral when the pallbearers got distracted by a rabbit, dropped the casket, and set off in hot pursuit. It's a tall tale, of course, but what do you expect at a festival held in the Key Underwood Coon Dog Memorial Graveyard? Each Labor Day, the cemetery hosts a celebration that includes music, dancing, food, and a liar's contest.

When there are pallbearers at this dog cemetery, maintained by the Tennessee Valley Coon Hunters Association and located twenty miles south of Tuscumbia in Colbert County, Alabama, they are of the human variety. But only canines certified as coon-hunting dogs may be buried there. The cemetery Web site at coondogcemetery. com includes eulogies and descriptions from mourners,

including father and son William and Bradley Ramsey, whose Ole Red was buried in a full service:

> A group of solemn men, dressed in black mourning coats and hip boots, wearing carbide lamps on their heads, stood beside a mound of soil and a freshly dug hole. A hunting horn sounded and the bay of hounds filled the air. Four similarly dressed men walked slowly toward the gathered crowd, a small wooden box carried between them.

The last lines of William's eulogy memorialize the relationship between hunter and dog:

> He knows in coon dog heaven he can hunt again when the sun goes down and the tree frogs holler. May the bones of Ole Red rest in peace, through the mercy of God, and may the coon hunters light perpetually shine upon him.

The cemetery has been featured in newspapers and magazines such as *Southern Living, Field & Stream,* and *Bassmaster,* as well as on television shows such as Charles Kuralt's *On the Road.* People walk into the Colbert County Tourism and Convention Bureau daily asking for directions, bureau executive director Susann Hamlin said. The cemetery has become so popular, she told us, that the bureau now sells the world's only Official Coon Dog Memorial Cemetery T-shirts and camouflage baseball caps.

The cemetery is named for Key Underwood, who buried his dog, Troop, in the woods where they hunted together in 1937. In a 1985 interview, Underwood said he never intended the site to become a cemetery. But as other hunters needed a place to honor their loyal hunting dogs, the secluded site became a popular burial ground.

About 185 dogs have been buried at the site, with names such as Straight Talkin' Tex, Doctor Doom, Beanblossom Bommer, Hardtime Wrangler, and High Pocket. It's a tremendously popular place. Groups of twenty or more can order a tour with watermelon and lemonade by calling the Tourism and Convention Center. No admission is charged for viewing the cemetery.

L. O. Bishop, a longtime supporter, said as many as 400 people may visit the cemetery during the Labor Day celebration. On other days, visitors come whenever the urge strikes. But whatever you do, don't ask if you can bury your cat there. It's dogs only, and only coon dogs. In fact, a member of the local coon hunters' organization must be allowed to view the coonhound to ensure it's the genuine article.

"We have people call and ask us if they can bury their pets there and we say, 'No, this is not a pet cemetery,'" Hamlin said.–*Kelly Kazek*

Toothy Tomb for a Terrier

Founded in 1902, the Arkansas Alligator Farm in Hot Springs boasts more than a century of toothy history. From its unbelievable eighteen-foot ten-inch *Guinness*-record-winning gator to the more unbelievable "merman" allegedly captured off the coast of China, the reptile sanctuary offers plenty of past to peruse.

One of its more interesting—and morbidly amusing—features, though, is often overlooked. Amid the central pond holding the largest of the farm's two hundred-plus alligators stands a small memorial to the attraction's one and only casualty, a fatally curious pet dog, swallowed in 1906.

Some people think the headstone is just a sick gag, but Jack Bridges, who's owned the farm for more than half its run, says it's no joke. The dog's owner, likely one of thousands who had come to enjoy the local thermal baths at the time, was standing at the edge of the gator pit when her little friend got a bit too excited and jumped out of her arms and into the water.

"It was a little terrier, a little black-and-white terrier," Jack says. "Those little ones that make good squirrel dogs, you know? About that size." For one lucky alligator, it probably took only one bite. "They feed on nutria, beaver, and muskrat, so to them that's a strawberry shortcake."

As the rest of the story goes, the grieving owner later sent the tombstone and asked the farm's owner to place it in the pit, where it's stood ever since. "Now, this is years ago she done this," says Jack, "'cause if it happened today, we'd be sued."

INDEX
Page numbers in **bold** refer to photos and illustrations.

A

Abandoned places
Glenn Dale Hospital (MD), 281–284, **281, 282, 283, 284**
Hotel Hell (WI), 285, **285**
Abita Mystery House and UCM Museum (LA), 198, **198, 199**
Abraham's Oak (TN), 320–321, **320**
Adefunmi, King, 186, **186**
African village (SC), 186, **186**
Akhenaton, Pharaoh, 173
Albany Bulb (CA), 90–91, **90, 91**
Albino animals (OH, WI), 216, **216**, 222, **222**
Alcor Life Extension Foundation (AZ), 61, **61,** 341, **341**
Aliens and UFOs
abductions (AR), 53–55, **53,** 54, 55
grave of (TX), 324, **324**
Space Brothers of Unarius (CA), 184–185, **185**
Toynbee tiles (DC, MD, NY, OH, PA), 308–309, **308–309**
UFO car (MN), 310–311, **310**
Allen County Museum (OH), 216, **216–217**
Alligator Farm tombstone (AR), 343, **343**
Allison, Vivian, 332
Aluminum Tree & Aesthetically Challenged Seasonal Ornament Museum and Research Center (NC), 223
Amargosa Opera House (CA), 60
Americana collection (NC), 218, **218**
AMORC (Ancient and Mystical Order Rosae Crucis; a.k.a. Rosicrucian Order) (CA, PA), 172–174
Angola Horror (NY), 270
Armstrong, Peter, 193
Arpaio, Joe, 49–51, **50**
Art. *See also* Sculpture and statues
cars (TX), 246, **246, 247**
murals (NJ, PA), 69–71, **69, 70, 71,** 77–79, **77, 78–79**
parks (CA, GA), 90–91, **90, 91,** 142–143, **142–143**

religious theme (LA, VA), 144–145, **144, 145**
Art Car Weekend (TX), 246, **246, 247**
Aurora Cemetery (TX), 324
The Awakening (DC, MD), 102, **102**
Ax Murder House (IA), 34–35, **34–35**

B

Bach, Carl and Mary, 214
Bald Is Beautiful convention (NC), 261
Barrow, Clyde, 249–250, **249, 250**
Bass, Dr. William, 340
Beard, Dr., 181–182, **181**
Beard, William Holbrook, 321
Beardsley, Merritt, 334
Bear tombstone (NY), 321, **321**
Becket, Marta, 60
Behringer-Crawford Museum (KY), 205, **205**
Bethel, Brian, 30
Bibb, Mary, 336
Biblical statuary, huge (AR, FL, IA, IL, KY, MA, MI, MO, MT, NC, OH, TN, TX), 149–155, **149, 150, 151, 152, 153, 154, 155**
Big Mike's Mystery House (KY), 128, **128**
Bird, Larry, 119
Bird Cage Theatre (AZ), 215
Bishop, Darlene and Lawrence, 153
Bishop Castle (CO), 66–67, **67**
Blackbeard Festival (VA), 252–253, **252, 253**
Black-eyed Kids (TX), 30, **31**
Blob Fest (PA), 254, **254**
Blue Mound Wayside Chapel (MI), 158
Blue Whale (OK), 107, **108**
Boat Stone (MA), 299
Body Farm (TN), 340, **340**
Boll weevil monument (AL), 106, **106**
Bone Zone (NM), 88–89, **88, 89**
Bonnie and Clyde Festival (LA), 249–250, **249, 250**
Brady, "Diamond Jim," 233
Brethauer, Gus, 81
Brown, Michael, 335

Bruer, C. C., 339
Brunrichter, Adolph C., 33
Buckeridge, Byron, 223, **223**
Buford Pusser Home and Museum (TN), 220, **220**
Builders of the Adytum (B.O.T.A.) (CA), 187, **187**
Bun museum (OH), 219, **219**
Burning Man Festival (NV), 258, **258**

C

Cadillac Ranch (TX), 112, **112**
Calico Town (CA), 131, **131**
Can Can Merman (AZ), 215, **215**
Cannibal (CO), 13–16, **13, 15**
Capone, Al, 280, 285
Captain Jackson (MI), 46–48, **47, 48**
Cars
art (TX), 246, **246, 247**
Cadillac Ranch (TX), 112, **112**
Carhenge (NB), 113, **113**
UFO (MN), 310, **310**
Carson, Johnny, 225, **225**
Case, Paul Foster, 187
Cathedral Canyon (NV), 27
Cattle
freak collection (OH), 213, **213**
Testicle Festival (MT), 256, **256**
Cave exploration (KY), 17–18, **17, 18**
Celesta (Celestia) (PA), 193, **193**
Cemeteries and graves, 19, 266–267, 314–343
Center of the Universe (OK), 303, **303**
Chain gangs (AZ), 49–51, **49, 51**
Chapel of Memories (IA), 158
Chapels, tiny (GA, IA, IL, KA, KY, LA, MI, MN, NJ, NY, OK, PA, SD), 156–158, **156, 157**
Charlie No-Face. *See* Green Man
Cheesman Park (CO), 266–269, **266–267, 268**
Cherry, Ben, 253, **253**
Chicken, headless (CO), 248, **248**

Child, Thomas Battersby Jr., 136–137

Childersburg City Cemetery (AL), 336, **336**

Christ Church. *See* Little Church

Church of God of Prophecy (NC), 149–150

City Cemetery (IN), 332, **332**

Cline, Lova, 332–333

Cline, Marc, 116–117, **117**

Clothespin tombstone (VT), 318, **318**

Coffin races (CO), 263, **263**

Colby, George, 176

Coleman, Loren, 231, **231**

Collins, William Floyd, 17–18, **17**

Colorado University, 15, **15**

Conch Republic Festival (FL), 245

Concretion Museum (WI), 223, **223**

Confusion Hill (CA), 130, **130**

Congolier Mansion (PA), 32–33, **32**

Conspiracy house (OK), 52, **52**

Constan, Randy, 42–44, **42, 43, 44**

Conway, Helen, 306–307, **307**

Coon dog cemetery (TN), 342–343, **342**

Cosmos Mystery Area (SD), 129, **129**

Coso Geode (CA), 300–301, **300**

Country Doctor Museum (NC), 235

Courthouse window face (AL), 36, **36**

Cowan, Henry C., 48

Crenshaw Children tomb (LA), 330, **330**

Crimefighter Corps (MI), 46–48, **47**

Cronkite, Walter, 15

Crosby, Bing, 214

Cross, Katherine, 323

Crosses

    Cross-Carrier Chuck, 56–57, **57**

    giant (FL, IL, KY, MI, TX), 150–151, **150, 151,** 154

    House of Crosses (IL), 147, **147**

    Kay's (UT), 286–287, **287**

    Miracle Cross Garden (AL), 148, **148**

Cross Island Chapel (NY), 157, **157**

Crowley, Aleister, 187, 324

Cryogenics (AZ), 61, **61,** 241, 341, **341**

Crypt of Civilization (GA), 204, **204**

Cryptozoology, museum of (ME), 231, **231**

Crystal Cave (KY), 17–18, **18**

Crystal Shrine Grotto (TN), 320–321, **320, 321**

Cult of the Hellion, 308–309

Cults, 194–195, 308–309

Curious Collections, 196–239

    fiberglass statues (WV), 104–105, **104, 105**

    Somewhere Over the Rainbow (AZ), **80,** 81, **81**

D

Davis, Andrew Jackson, 177

Davis, Hugh and Zelta, 107

Davis Memorial (KS), 328, **328**

Dawson, Jack, 154

Dead Children's Playground (AL), 336

De Antonis, Jason, 90

Death Dealers (NJ), 59

Death- and funeral-related collections (IN, OH, TX, VT), 236–239, **236, 237, 238, 239**

Death masks (AL, VA), 237, **237, 318,** 319, **319**

Deeble, Florence, 76

Desert Christ Park (CA), 140–141, **140, 141**

Didusch, William, 233

Divine Madness (CO), 194–195

Dobberstein, Paul, 161

Dollhouse tombstones (IN, LA, NJ), 330, **330,** 332–333, **332, 333**

Doohan, James, 238, **238**

Drive-in Christian Church (FL), **158,** 159

Ducking (VA), 12, **12**

E

Earles, Nadine, 331

Eastern State Penitentiary (PA), 276–280, **276, 277, 278, 279, 280**

East Hill Cemetery (IN), 332–333, **333**

Eckel, Lizzie, 330

Edison, Thomas, 33

Ed's Museum (MN), 221, **221**

Electric chair (TX), 210–211, **211**

Elephant Man (DC), 200, **200**

Eliphante (AL), 64, **64–65**

Elmwood Cemetery (NC), 327, **327**

Emma Crawford Coffin Races and Festival (CO), 263, **263**

Epitaphs, unusual (MA, OK, TX, UT), 323–325, **323, 324, 325**

Eugene (corpse) (OR), 24

Evans, Dixie Lee, 230

Ewegen, Bob, 15

Exotic World (CA), 230, **230**

Eye of the World Museum (TX), 228, **228**

F

Famous Endings collection (OH), 238–239, **238, 239**

Fantastico, 46

Fantasy Farm (WV), 104, **104, 105**

Farmica, Cancetto, 25, **25**

Farnham, Pam and George, 104

Fence, shoe (NE), 125, **125**

Festivals, far-out, 240–263

Fine, Ira, 219, **219**

Finster, Howard, 142–143

Foamhenge (VA), 116–117, **116–117**

Forbidden Gardens (TX), 108, **108–109**

Forensic Anthropology Facility, University of Tennessee, 340, **340**

Fort Ticonderoga gravestone (MN), 326, **326**

Freemasons (VA), 170–171, **170, 171**

Freville, Denise, 103

Frog Festival (LA), 259, **259**

Frozen Dead Guy Days (CO), 242, **242**

Funeral History, National Museum of (TX), 236, **236**

G

Galuszka, Greta, 279

Gavrelos, "Poppa" John, 228

Geographical Center Chapel (KS), 158

George Washington Masonic National Memorial (VA), **170,** 171, **171**

Ghosts and haunted places, 11, 32–33, **32,** 264–289

Gilgal Gardens (UT), 136–137, **136, 137**

Gilmore, Lyman, 85

Glenn Dale Hospital (MD), 281–284, **281, 282, 283, 284**

Glore Psychiatric Museum (MO), 235, **235**

Goat Man (GA), 21–22, **21**

Gourd collection (NC), 223

Grace, Bill, 180

Graves. *See* Cemeteries and graves

Gravity House (CA), 130, **130**

Gravity spots. *See* Mystery spots

Gray, Elmer and Lilly E., 324

Greco, John Baptist, 138

Green Man (Charlie No-Face) (PA), 10–11, **10**

Green-Wood Cemetery (NY), 321, **321,** 338, **338**

Grotto for the Blessed Mother (WI), 162, **162**

Grotto of the Redemption (IA), 160–161, **160, 161**

Groundhog Day (PA), 241, **241**

Guerin, Mother Theodore, 163

Gullo, Anthony, 157

Gunn, James, 299

H

Harper, Agnes, 156

Heavener Runestone (OK), 293–294, **294**

Heinemann, Mark, 195

Heinz, Pat and Ed, 152

Hemingway look-a-like competition (FL), 255, **255**

Henry's heroes (NC), 48, **48**

Heroes and villains, 40–61

Herzig, John, 238–239, **239**

Hicks, Henry Bascom, 329

Highland Cemetery (OK), 325, **325**

Hill, Doug, 115

Hobo Convention (IA), 256, **256**

Hoffman, Nancy, 3, 220, **220**

Hollow Earthers (FL, OH, NJ), 178–182, **178, 179, 180, 181, 182**

Hollywood Forever Cemetery (CA), 316–317, **316, 317**

Holton, Harriet, 188–189, **189**

Holy Land U.S.A. (CT, VA), 138–139, **138, 139**

Hotel Hell (WI), 285, **285**

House of Blue Lights (IN), 29, **29**

House of Crosses (IL), 147, **147**

House tombstone (MA), 326, **326**

Hum, mysterious (NM), 312–313

Hyman, Ray, 133

Hyslin, Richard, 152

I–K

Igneri, David, 37–39

Illuminati, 170, 171

Ink tube collection (NJ), 225

International Museum of Cryptozoology (ME), 231, **231**

Irving, Dr. John, 306

Israelite House of David (MI), 183, **183**

Jackson, Stephen, 223

Jacobs, Dr. Thornwell, 204, **204**

Jefcoat, Brady C., 218

Jesus

Desert Christ Park (CA), 140–141, **140, 141**

giant statues of (AR, OH), 153, **153,** 154

in a light beam (AZ, TX), 311, **311**

Johnson, Anderson, 144, **144–145**

Johnson, Chuck, 56–57, **57**

Johnson, Francis, 111

Johnson, Gary, 279

Johnson, J. Seward, 102

Johnson, Marvin, 223

Johnson, Val, 310–311

Jurassic Technology, Museum of (CA), 201, **201**

Kahn, Michael, 64

Kay's Cross (UT), 286–287, **287**

Kennedy, Kevin and Tracy, 184–185

Kensington Runestone (MN), **295,** 295–296, **296**

Key Underwood Coon Dog Memorial Graveyard (TN), 342–343, **342**

Kinetic Sculpture Race (CA), 251, **251**

King, John, 327, **327**

King, Walter Eugene, 186, **186**

Koreshans (FL), 179–180

Krueger, Ed, 221

L

Lady, The (IN), 103, **103**

Lady of the Lake (NY), 37–39, **38–39**

Larimer, William, 266

Laurinburg Mummy (NC), 25, **25**

Lava Beds National Monument (CA), 297, **297**

Lee, "Deaf Bill," 24, **24**

Lemuria, 297

L'Enfant, Pierre Charles, 171

LeQuire, Alan, 101

Levin, Fred and Pam, 114

Lewis, Harve Spencer, 173, 297

Liggett, M. T., 86–87

Lilley, John, 146, **146**

Little Church (Christ Church) (GA), 156, **156**

Livant, Leda, 64

M

Mabe, Joni, 229, **229**

Mad Mark, 91

Madonna Chapel (LA), 157, **157**

Madonnas, giant (MA, MO, OH), 152, **152,** 154

Magic Garden (PA), 77, **78–79,** 79

Magnolia Cemetery (LA), 330, **330**

Manuse, George. *See* Parrot, Big Nose George

Maplewood Cemetery (KY), 329, **329**

Maribel Caves Hotel (WI), 285, **285**

Martin, Frank Antoine, 140–141

Martin, Riley, 53–55, **53**

Matthews, John, 338, **338**

Maxwell, Lucien Bonaparte, 22, **22**

Mayes, Henry Harrison, 167

McCartney, Charles "Ches," 21–22, **21**

McCoy, Bob, 232

McCurdy, Elmer, 23, **23**
McLean, Clair, 227
Medical collections (MD, MN, MO, WI),
    232–235, **232, 233, 234, 235**
Medical Progress, Museum of (WI), 234, **234**
Memorial Park Cemetery (TN), 320–321,
    320, 321
Memory Park Christ Chapel (GA), 158
Merrick, Joseph, 200, **200**
Mike the Headless Chicken (CO), 248, **248**
Millennium Manor (TN), 67–68, **67, 68**
Millerites, 193
Mindfield (TN), **96,** 97, **97**
Miracle Cross Garden (AL), 148, **148**
Missile silo house (KS), 92–93, **92, 93**
Mix, Tom, 322, **322**
Momen, Karl, 110
Monte Casino Chapel (KY), 158
Monuments. *See* Sculpture and statues
Moore, Josiah B., 34
Mormon sites
    Gilgal Gardens (UT), 136–137, **136, 137**
    Kay's Cross (UT), 286–287, **287**
    Voree (MI), 190, **191**
Morning Star Chapel (IA), 158
Morstoel, Bredo, 241
Mothman Festival (WV), 260, **260, 261**
Mt. Hope Cemetery (KS), 328, **328**
Mt. Nebo Cemetery (AL), **318,** 319, **319**
Mullen, William T., 336
Mummies (CA, IL, IN, OR, NC, NV, WA),
    23–27, **23, 24, 25, 26,** 202–203,
    202
Mural Arts Project (PA), 77, **78–79,** 79
Mural house (NJ), 69, 71, **69, 70, 71**
Museums. *See* Collections
Musica (TN), **100,** 101
Myers, Larry, 103
Mystery Shack (CA), 131, **131**
Mystery spots (CA, KY, MI, OH, OR, SD,
    WV, WY), 126–133, **127, 128, 129,**
    130, 131, 132–133
Mystery Stone (NM), 292–293, **292**

N

Native Americans
    Dark Place (PA), 33
    Lady of the Lake (NY), 37–39,
        38–39
    mystery spot (NC), 131
    petroglyphs (CA), 297, **297**
    Queho (NV), 26–27, **26**
    slayer of (PA), 20, **20**
    Thunder Mountain Monument (NV), 82–85,
        82, 83, 84, 85
Nemechek, David, 52
Nettles, Isaac Sr., 319
Neumann, Osha, 90
Nicholson, William Andrew and Fair,
    67–68, **67**
Nixon, Richard, 225
Norman, Ruth and Ernest, 184–185, **185**
Norse runes (MN, OK), 293–296, **294,**
    295, 296
Noyes, John Humphrey, 188–189, **188**

O

Oak Hill Cemetery (MO), 318
Oakland Cemetery (GA), 337, **337**
Oakwood Cemetery (AL), 331, **331**
Ohman, Olof, 295–296
Oneida community (NY), 188–189, **188,**
    189
Osborne, Dr. J. E., 212
Ottavi, Father Philip, 159
Our Lady of Mount Carmel Monastery (IN),
    164–165, **164, 165**
Oyotunji (SC), 186, **186**

P

Packer, Alferd, 13–16, **16**
Palace of Wonders (DC), 200, **200**
Paradise Gardens (GA), 142–143, **142, 143**
Parker, Bonnie, 249–250, **249, 250**
Parker, Trey, 15
Parking meter tombstone (OK), 325, **325**
Parrot, Big Nose George (George Manuse),
    212, **212**

Peaceville Valley (NC), 146, **146**
Peden, Edward, 92–93
People and places, legendary, 8–39
Peter Pan, 42–44, **42, 43, 44**
Petroglyphs (CA), 297, **297**
Piano tombstone (TX), 317, **317**
Pigman Road (NY), 270–272, **270, 271, 273**
Place of Prayer (NC), 149–150
Place Where the Rocks Move (NV), 301–302,
    301, 302
Poe, Edgar Allan, 28
Poe Toaster (MD), 28, **28**
Poon, Ira P. H., 108
Porter, Dick, 224, **224**
Porter, Wayne, 98–99
Porter Sculpture Park (SD), 98–99, **98, 99**
Praying hands (MO), 154
Presidential Pet Museum (MD), 227, **227**
Presidents Hall of Fame (FL), 226, **226**
Presley, Elvis, museum (GA), 229, **229,** 238,
    257, **257**
Prince, Thomas Binkley, 209
Prisons
    Eastern State Penitentiary (PA), 276–280, **276,**
        277, 278, 279, 280
    museum of (TX), 210–211, **210–211**
Providence Home Geode Grotto (IN), 159, **159**
Purnell, Benjamin Franklin and Mary, 183
Pusser, Buford, 220
Puzzles, past and present, 290–313
Pyramids (PA), 174, **174**

Q–R

Queen of Hearts, 47, **47**
Queho (NV), 26–27, **26**
Questionable Medical Devices, Museum of (MN),
    232, **232**
Quick, Tom, 20, **20**
Raisin box collection (NJ), 219, **219**
Rattlesnake Roundup (TX), 243, **243**
Reeser, Mary, 305–306
Reinders, Jim, 113
Religious sites and people, 134–167
Rice, Frank H., 16

Rice, William C., 148
Riugra, Angel, 279
Roadkill
    cook-off (WV), 262, **262**
    stuffed (WI), 222, **222**
Roadside distractions, 94–133
Robertson, Royal, 144, **144**
Robinson, Raymond, 10–11, **10**
Rocks. *See* Stones and rocks
Rodriguez, Dionicio, 320–321
Roman artifacts (KY), 298, **298**
Rose Hill Cemetery (TX), 317, **317**
Rosicrucians. *See* AMORC
Runestones (MN, OK), 293–296, **294, 295, 296**
Runners' society (CO), 194–195

S

Saint Mary-of-the-Woods (IN), 163, **163**
Saint Stupid's Day Parade (CA), 243, **243**
Salt Lake City Cemetery (UT), 324
Sandwiches, collection of partially eaten (IL), 225, **225**
Sanfillippo, Sam, 222
Satanists (UT), 286–287
Scarberry, Linda, 260
Sculpture and statues
    Abraham's Oak (TN), 320–321, **320**
    Albany Bulb (CA), 90–91, **90, 91**
    Awakening, The (DC, MD), 102, **102**
    boll weevil (AL), 106, **106**
    death masks (VA), 237, **237**
    Eliphante (AZ), 64, **64–65**
    Fantasy Farm (WV), 104, **104–105**
    Gilgal Gardens (UT), 136–137, **136, 137**
    Henry's heroes (NC), 48, **48**
    Jesus (AR, CA, OH), 140–141, **140, 141**
    of Lucien Maxwell (NM), 22, **22**
    by M. T. Liggett (KS), 86–87, **86, 87**
    Madonna (MA, MO, OH), 152, **152**, 154
    Mindfield (TN), **96**, 97, **97**
    Musica (TN), **100**, 101
    Porter Sculpture Park (SD), 98–99, **98, 99**

Stonehenge reproductions (MI, NB, TX, VA), 113–117, **113, 114, 115, 116–117**
Terra-cotta army (TX), 108, **108–109**
Tree of Utah, The, 110, **110**
Weeping Woman (WV), **288–289**, 289
by Wickham (TN), 72–73, **72–73**
Winds of Change, The (IN), 103, **103**
Sensabaugh Tunnel (TN), 274–275, **274, 275**
Servants of Mary Center of Peace (OH), 152, **152**
Severs, Henry, 327, **327**
Sharkey, Jonathan "The Impaler," 58–59, **58**
Shea, Sheila, 323
Shealy, David, 252
Shepperd, Al, 115
Sherwood, Grace, 11–13
Shoes
    fence (NE), 125, **125**
    of human skin (WY), 212, **212**
    trees (AR, AZ, CA, ID, IN, MI, NY, OR), 118–124, **118, 119, 120, 121, 123, 124**
Shrunken heads (KY), 205, **205**
Signs
    conspiracy house (OK), 52, **52**
    Get Right with God (KY), **166**, 167, **167**
    by M. T. Liggett (KS), 86–87, **86, 87**
Simpson Mortuary Museum (IN), 237, **237**
Sinclair, Henry, 299
Skiles Test Nature Park (IN), 29
Skunk Ape Festival (FL), 252, **252**
Sleepy Hollow Cemetery (MA), 323
Smith, Jasper Newton, 337, **337**
Smothers, Tommy, 255
Sneaker Trees (NY), 124, **124**
Societies, strange, 168–195
Soda Fountain King grave (NY), 338, **338**
Somewhere Over the Rainbow park (AZ), **80**, 81, **81**
Southcott, Joanna, 183
Space Brothers (CA), 184–185, **185**
Spamarama (TX), 244, **244**
Spark plug, in stone (CA), 300–301, **300**
Spelunkers (KY), 17–18, **17, 18**

Spiritualists (FL, NY, WI), 175–177, **175, 176, 177**
Spitler House Museum (OH), 213, **213**
Spontaneous human combustion (FL, PA), **304**, 305–307, **305, 307**
Spook Hill (WI), 177
Springer, Curtis Howe, 192
Springfield Cemetery (MA), 326, **326**
Spring Grove Cemetery (OH), 339, **339**
Squirrel and Chipmunk Museum (WI), 222, **222**
Standley, Joseph Edward, 202
Statue of Liberation Through Christ (TN), 155, **155**
Statues. *See* Sculpture and statues
Stevenson, Rus and Fredda, 122
Stoeber, Frank, 111
Stone, Matt, 15
Stonehenge reproductions (MI, NB, TX, VA), 113–117, **113, 114, 115, 116–117**
Stone Man (IN), 27
Stones and rocks
    moving (NV), 301–302, **301, 302**
    Mystery Stone (NM), 292–293, **292**
    petroglyphs (CA), 297, **297**
    rock gardens (AZ, KS), 74–76, **74, 75, 76**
    runestones (MN, OK), 293–296, **294, 295, 296**
    Stonehenge reproductions (MI, NB, TX, VA), 113–117, **113, 114, 115, 116–117**
Strang, James Jesse, 190
Sunnyslope Rock Garden (AZ), 74–75, **74, 75**
Superheroes (MI, NY), 45–48, **45, 47, 48**
Swallowed objects collections (MO, OH), 216, **216–217**, 235, **235**
Swan, Israel, 13, 14
Sylvester, Wilberforce, 69, 71, **71**
Symmes, John Cleves, 178
Synagogue, smallest (PA), 158
Szewczyk, Mitch, 147

T

Taos Hum (NM), 312–313
Tattoo Tammy, 88–89, **88**
Taylor, Stephen, 326

Teed, Cyrus, 179–180, **179**
Tennis ball tree (UT), 110, **110**
Tent City jail (AZ), 49, **49,** 51
Terrifica, 45–46, **45**
Test, Skiles, 29
Testicle Festival (MT), 256, **256**
Teton Mystery Spot (WY), 131
Texas Prison Museum, 210–211, **210, 211**
Thermometer museum (MA), 224, **224**
Thing, The (AZ), 208–209, **209**
Thompson, Grover Cleveland, 74–75
Thompson, Hunter S., 239
Thunder Mountain Monument (NV), 82–86,
    82, 83, 84, 85
Tick Collection, U.S. National (GA), 212
Tiles, Toynbee (DC, MD, NY, OH, PA),
    308–309, **308–309**
Time capsule (GA), 204, **204**
Tinkertown museum (NM), 206–207,
    206, 207
Tiny Town (NM), 88–89, **88, 89**
Tizer, Marc "Yo," 194–195
Toland-Herzig Funeral Homes (OH),
    238–239, **238, 239**
Tomlinson, Ambrose Jessup, 149–150
Tony Packo's (OH), 219, **219**
Toynbee Idea (DC, MD, NY, OH, PA),
    308–309
Trains
    ghost (NY, PA), 11, 270
    wreck (NY), 270, 272
Traveler's Chapel (IL), 158
Tree of Utah, The, 110, **110**

Trees
    shoe (AR, AZ, CA, ID, IN, MI, NY, OR),
        118–124, **118, 119, 120, 121, 123,**
        124
    tennis ball (UT), 110, **110**
Tripp, Billy, 97, **97**
Tuxedo, denim (NV), 214, **214**
Twine balls, world's largest (KS, MN), 111, **111**

U

UCM Museum (LA), 198, **198, 199**
UFO Car (MN), 310–311, **310**
UFOs. *See* Aliens and UFOs
Umbrella Cover Museum (ME), 220, **220**
Unarius (CA), 184–185, **185**
Underwood, Key, 343
University of Tennessee Forensic Anthropology
Facility, 340, **340**
Urological museum (MD), 233, **233**
Utopians (CA, FL, MI, NJ, OH), 178–182, **179,**
    181, 182, 183, 192

V

Valentine, Edward, 237
Vampires (NJ), 58–59, **58**
Van Zant, Frank, 82–86, **82**
Ventriloquist convention (NV), 254–255, **255**
Viking carvings (MN, OK), 293–296, **293,**
    294, 295, 296
Voree, plates of (WI), 190, **191**
Vortices (CA, KY, MI, NC, OH, OR, SD, WV, WY),
    126–133, **126, 127, 128, 129, 130,**
    132–133
Vox, Valentine, 254–255

W

Ward, Madge, gravestone of, 317, **317**
Ward, Ross, 206
Wardlow, Dennis, 245
Washington, George, 171
Wayne, Major General Anthony, 19, **19**
Wayside Chapel (MI, SD, WA), 158, 159,
    159
Weeping Woman statue (WV), **288–289,**
    289
Wells, Henry, 36
Welsh, Eunice, 339
Wernerus, Father Mathias, 162
Westford Knight (MA), 299
Wickham, Enoch Tanner, 72–73, **72**
William P. Didusch Center for Urological
History (MD), 233, **233**
Williams, Alton R., 155
Williams, Ted, 61, **61**
Winds of Change, The (IN), 103, **103**
Witches (VA, WI), 11–13, 285
Wonewoc Spiritualist Camp (WI), 177
Woodlawn Cemetery (MN), 326, **326**
Woolridge Memorial (KY), 329, **329**
Worlds of their own, 62–93
Wright, Phineas, 324

X–Z

X-Files Ranch (OK), 52, **52**
Ye Olde Curiosity Shop (WA), 202–203,
    202, 203
Yingling, Drs. Walter and Estey, 216
Zagar, Isaiah, 77, **77,** 79
Zweifel, John, 226
Zzyzx (CA), 192

PICTURE CREDITS

All photos and illustrations by the authors or public domain except as noted below:

EDITORIAL CREDITS

In addition to the *Weird U.S.* writers credited on page 352, the following authors either wrote or contributed information to the following articles:

Jeff Bahr: p. 139, Holy Land USA; 237, Death Masks. **Jeff Belanger:** 61, Ted Williams–A Hero on Ice; 299, The Westford Knight; 326, Three Women of the House. **Greg Bishop:** 140, Desert Christ Park; 187, Builders of Adytum; 192, A Utopia Spelled Z-Z-Y-Z-X; 230, Dixie Lee's Exotic World; 300, Coso Spark Plug; 301–302, World's Slowest Racetrack; 316–317, Deathstyles of the Rich and Famous. **Charlie Carlson:** 179–180, Journey to the Center of the Earth; 252, Skunk Ape Festival. **Joseph Citro:** 138, Holy Land; 220, Where to Go When It Rains. **Tim Cridland:** 26–27, Queho's Quorpse; 82–83, Chief Rolling Mountain Thunder; 123, Nevada Shoe Trees. **Eric Dregni:** 221, Ed's Museum; 232, Museum of Questionable Medical Devices; 295–296, Mystery of the Kensington Runestone; 326, Ticonderoga Tombstone. **Charmaine Ortega Getz:** 13–16 Alferd Packer, Man-Eater; 242, Frozen Dead Guy Festival; 248, A Fowl Fest in Fruita. **Linda Godfrey:** 46–48, Looking for Action with Captain Jackson; 114, Stonehenge, Mysterious Ruins of . . . Michigan; 177, Spiritualists of Spook Hill; 183, Israelite House of David; 190, James Strang and the Plates of Voree; 222, Rodent Resurrection; 223, Concretion Museum; 234, Fort Crawford Museum. **Jeffrey Scott Holland:** 298, Roman Artifacts in Kentucky; 329, Woolridges of Mayfield. **Kelly Kazek:** 36, Face in the Courthouse Window; 319, Frozen Faces of Mt. Nebo Cemetery; 331, Little Nadine's Playhouse; 336, One for the Road, Lightning Strikes Again; 342–343, Coon Dog Memorial Graveyard. **Roger Manley:** 25, Spaghetti, the Mummy of Laurinburg; 48, Henry's Heroes; 144, Prophet Royal Robertson; 145, Anderson Johnson; 146, Peaceville Valley; 157, World's Smallest Real Church; 186, African Village of Oyotunji; 198, Albita Mystery House; 327, Elephant Man and the Log Cabin of Elmwood; 330, Crenshaw Kids of Magnolia Cemetery; 335, The Telltale Stone. **Mike Marinacci:** 297, Pecked Pictures of Petroglyph Point; 300, Coso Spark Plug. **Jim Miles:** 142–143, Howard Finster's Paradise Garden; 156, For Ye of Little Faith; 229, Elvis Is in the House; 230, Cryptozoological Museum; 337, The Statue That Jack Built. **Janice Oberding:** 214, Bing Crosby's Denim Tuxedo. **Joe Oesterle:** 60, Marta Becket–Death Valley Diva; 173, Rosicrucian Park; 201, Museum of Jurassic Technology; 316–317, Deathstyles of the Rich and Famous. **David Pike:** 22, This Land Was His Land; 292–293, Mystery Stone; 312–313, A Haunted Hum. **Jim Strait:** 235, Glore Psychiatric Museum; 318, World's Smallest Tombstone. **Troy Taylor:** 24, Skeleton in the Funeral Home Closet; 147, Mitch's Cross House; 266–268, Unrest in Cheeseman Park; 276–279, The Haunted "Big House." **Wesley Treat:** 17–18, Floyd Collins; 64, Eliphante; 81, Somewhere Over the Rainbow; 97, The Mindfield; 101, Musica: Busts of Bronze; 103, Monument to Strong Women; 108, Forbidden Gardens; 112, Cadillac Ranch; 115, Stonehenge II; 121, Arizona Shoe Trees; 151, Cruci-fixation; 155, Statue of Liberation Through Christ; 208–209, The Thing; 125, Can Can Merman; 228, Eye of the World Museum; 236, National Museum of Funeral History; 311, Jesus in a Light Beam; 317, The Granite Grand; 322, Mix Up; 324, Aurora's Alien Crash Site; 341, Alcor's Frozen Fraternity; 343, Toothy Tomb for a Terrier. **Clint Wardlow:** 136–137, Gilgal Gardens; 286–287, The Many Mysteries of Kay's Cross. **Jim Willis:** 29, House of Blue Lights; 119, Flying Footwear; 152, Giant Madonna; 153, Giant Jesus; 163, Sanctuary by the Sea; 164–165, Ultraviolet Apocalypse; 213, Creepy Cattle on Display; 214, Three Fingers of Mary Bach; 216–217, Albino Animals and Swallowed Objects; 238–239, Keeping the Fun in Funeral; 332–333, Dollhouses of the Dead; 339, A Glassy-eyed Gaze.

AKNOWLEDGMENTS

As with all of the books in our *Weird* series, the creation of *Weird U.S. The ODDyssey Continues* was very much a team effort. This book would not have been possible without contributions of an extremely talented group of authors from around the country with whom we have had the pleasure of collaborating over the past half-dozen years. (A full listing of their credits can be found on page 351.)

In addition to our far-flung stable of field reporters, we must acknowledge the great contributions made to this work by our in-house *Weird* staff of writers, artists, and researchers, including Chris Gethard, Joanne Austin, Ryan Doan, Heather Wendt-Kemp, and Abby Stillman-Grayson. We'd also like to thank our associates at Sterling, Emily Seese and Gina Graham, for their editorial expertise; Alexandra Koppen and Dave Hall for their sharp eyes; and our art director, Richard Berenson, who makes us all look so good.

Matt would like to thank various members of the Tunstall, Craig, and Lake clans for hundreds of different reasons. . . and the Tillmans and Galeanos for just one.

And last but not least, we owe a tremendous debt of gratitude to all those folks across this vast land who have sent us letters over the years offering stories, photos, or simply cryptic tips that have led us off into parts unknown. It's been a very weird ride, and we thank you all for that!

—Mark, Mark, and Matt

SHOW US YOUR WEIRD!

Do you know of a weird site found somewhere in the United States, or can you tell us about a strange experience you've had? If so, we'd like to hear about it! We believe that every town has at least one great tale to tell, and we're listening. It could be a cursed road, haunted abandoned site, odd local character, or bizarre historic event. In most cases these tales are told only in the towns in which they originated. But why keep them to yourself when you could share them with all of America? So come on and fill us in on all the weirdness that's lurking in your backyard!

You can e-mail us at: Editor@WeirdUS.com,
or write to us at:
Weird U.S., P.O. Box 1346, Bloomfield, NJ 07003.

www.weirdus.com